The Fragmenting Family

Brenda Almond throws down a timely challenge to liberal consensus about personal relationships. She sees the source of many of Western society's problems in the fragmentation of the natural family and in attempts to reinterpret it as no more than a set of legal and social relationships. She urges that we reconsider our attitudes to sex and reproduction in order to strengthen our most important social institution, the family, which is the key to ensuring healthy relationships between parents and children and a secure upbringing for the citizens of the future.

Anyone who is concerned about how the framework of society is changing, anyone who has to face difficult personal decisions about parenthood or family relationships, will find this book compelling. It may disturb deep convictions, or offer an unwelcome message, but it is compassionate as well as controversial.

Brenda Almond is Emeritus Professor of Moral and Social Philosophy at the University of Hull. She studied philosophy under A. J. Ayer and has taught philosophy at various universities in the UK and worldwide. She holds an honorary doctorate for her work in philosophy from Utrecht University and is an elected foreign member of the Austrian Academy of Sciences.

She has served on the UK's Human Fertilisation and Embryology Authority and on the Human Genetics Commission. Her books include *Exploring Ethics: A Traveller's Tale* (1998), *Exploring Philosophy: the Philosophical Quest* (1995), and (ed. with Michael Parker) *Ethical Issues in the New Genetics* (2003).

The Fragmenting Family

Brenda Almond

CLARENDON PRESS · OXFORD

OXFORD

UNIVERSITY PRESS

Great Clarendon Street, Oxford OX2 6DP

Oxford University Press is a department of the University of Oxford.
It furthers the University's objective of excellence in research, scholarship,
and education by publishing worldwide in

Oxford New York

Auckland Cape Town Dar es Salaam Hong Kong Karachi
Kuala Lumpur Madrid Melbourne Mexico City Nairobi
New Delhi Shanghai Taipei Toronto

With offices in

Argentina Austria Brazil Chile Czech Republic France Greece
Guatemala Hungary Italy Japan Poland Portugal Singapore
South Korea Switzerland Thailand Turkey Ukraine Vietnam

Oxford is a registered trade mark of Oxford University Press
in the UK and in certain other countries

Published in the United States
by Oxford University Press Inc., New York

© Brenda Almond 2006

The moral rights of the author have been asserted
Database right Oxford University Press (maker)

First published 2006
First published in paperback 2008

British Library Cataloguing in Publication Data

Data available

Library of Congress Cataloging in Publication Data

Data available

Typeset by Laserwords Private Limited, Chennai, India
Printed in Great Britain
on acid-free paper by
Clays Ltd, St. Ives plc.

ISBN 978-0-19-926795-8 (Hbk.)
ISBN 978-0-19-954870-5 (Pbk.)

1

For Ella, Toby, Jamie, and Joe

Contents

To forget one's ancestors is to be a brook without a source, a tree without a root.

(Chinese proverb)

Introduction

What is the family? There are many ways of answering this question, but I take as my starting point here G. K. Chesterton's striking metaphor of family as 'this frail cord, flung from the forgotten hills of yesterday to the invisible mountains of tomorrow'.[1] In more prosaic terms, it is the chain of personal connections that gives meaning to our human notions of past, present and future—a mysterious genetic entity that binds us in our short span of individual existence to our ancestors and to our successors. But for many people, these familiar domestic foundations, taken for granted by previous generations, have begun to crumble. The signs are there in personal lives diminished by unstable relationships, broken commitments, and loss of contact with a whole range of peripheral but important relationships, from grandparents and in-laws to distant cousins and aunts. But, while the family is not indestructible, it is resilient. The family is, and always has been, the foundation of communities in which the cherishing of each individual person can flourish, and perhaps the only one that can survive social change, preserving the shape and structure of civil society through the vicissitudes of history: war and peace, the rise and decline of nation states, demographic fluctuations and economic change. The original architects of a liberal and individualist social philosophy are often taken to have propounded a message of self-interest and egotism. But, even for these earlier thinkers, the 'atomic individual' of modern political thought was an alien concept, unless perhaps as hermit, recluse, or solitary mystic. Even for them, as for their contemporary successors, the 'individual' whose self-determination sometimes needs protection from an over-zealous state can be seen, not as a rival concept, but as one that is itself deeply embedded in the broader concept of family.

The assumption of the foundational importance of the family is so solid that its significance in the life of human communities can easily be missed. But now the family is fragmenting. Just as the trembling of the earth in an earthquake zone brings an uneasy awareness of a city's vulnerability, so the rapidly increasing instability of the family in contemporary Western societies strikes as a warning of possible wider social disintegration. As more people begin to recognize this, self-congratulation at the passing of 'Victorian values'—the values of prudish and intolerant previous generations—is giving way to a more cautious appreciation of the interconnectedness of social values, political organization, and personal well-being, and a greater readiness to regret the loss of constancy, continuity, and reliability in personal relationships.

Even if this growing structural instability is acknowledged, tracing its causes is a more complex task. Nevertheless, my purpose here is to take at least a step in this direction by identifying some of the very diverse sources that have combined to bring it about. To begin with, I believe that many of those who together represent Western wisdom and technological expertise have played a primary part. Amongst these are legislators who head too eagerly into 'reform' of an area where rights, duties, and obligations have held interlocking sway for most of recorded history; and 'modernizing' policy-makers who, often carelessly or unintentionally, mould and reshape family structure, unilaterally and without fanfare rewriting family law to reflect new constructivist conceptions of family, partnering, and parenthood. This has been taken to unprecedented lengths recently in a 'postmodernist' legal deconstruction of the family which seeks to banish mention of its principal components from the statute-books—a policy that has been taken furthest perhaps in North America, where a 2002 report of the American Law Institute recommends two far-reaching changes: the first, 'de-privileging' marriage; the second, replacing the focus on biological parenthood with one on *functional* parenthood.[2] A Canadian report, *Beyond Conjugality*, follows the same path in recommending making 'close relationships' the new focus of family law to replace the institutional relationship of marriage.[3] As a Canadian commentator points out: 'Both of these reports push family law in profoundly new directions whose purposes and aims are sometimes far removed from (and often contrary to) family law's former public purposes that included protecting marriage and the best interests of children.'[4]

In both Canada and part of the United States, these aims are being turned from aspiration to reality as, for example, in some 'consequential amendments' to the Canadian Civil Marriage Act of 2005, which remove gendered wording from references to spouses and replace 'natural parent or 'biological parent' as well as 'blood relationship' with the term 'legal parent'.[5] In the interest of degendering family structures and removing any necessary link with procreation, the biological or genetic father or mother has become simply unmentionable. The speed of these developments—the unravelling of basic assumptions about family structure—is astonishing. From its origins as radical thinking in the 1980s, the social construction of family relationships has become a dominant thesis in a network of related academic disciplines and a central influence on law-making in Europe, Australasia, and the North American continent. At the same time, in another more immediate and practical family area, changes in taxation and welfare provision for parents and families have cut across other well-established conceptions of relationships and responsibilities.

Theory will, of course, continue to be debated, but practice has its own momentum, and it is impossible to ignore the advances in scientific research in the reproductive field that have created a further gulf between biological and social reality by making it physically possible to separate genetic connectedness from parenthood. In this broader world of practice, the impact of reproductive medicine cannot be ignored. While science and medicine hold out golden promises of ways to overcome the limitations and infirmities of the human condition, helping the infertile and facilitating personal choice, there is the constant risk of focusing too narrowly on expanding technological possibilities, neglecting questions about what is desirable or socially beneficial, and ignoring the way in which innovatory practices in this area may neglect the interests and rights of the children who result. For this reason if no other, the area of reproductive medicine must be a central element in today's debate about the family.

While it is not difficult to see how law, the social sciences, and medicine may have had an impact on the family, there are also other contributory influences of a less obvious kind. In particular, there are many ways in which philosophical thinking has influenced the family debate—through feminist theory, through Marxist political analysis, through postmodernist techniques of deconstruction. But mainstream philosophy, too, has played a role. Until very recently, moral philosophy has had little to say about the special ties and responsibilities of family or friendship, reducing the analysis of human nature, and consequent options for moral choice, to two: selfish egotism or an impartial universalism that makes it difficult to justify partiality to particular others. A philosophical defence of the family needs to find a way of escape between the horns of the dilemmas this narrow view presents.[6] But this means facing another awkward challenge, this time in relation to political philosophy. Increasingly, this offers the contemporary world only a choice between, on the one hand, a form of libertarianism in which liberty shades into licence and, on the other, acceptance of a dominating and intrusive state, in which secularism is as oppressive as religion, and where public agencies have intruded into the heart of the family. As for the dispassionate analysis of words and concepts that has often been seen as a defining feature of philosophy—something that was a strong characteristic of twentieth-century analytic philosophy—an Orwellian approach to meaning in the twenty-first has led to the promotion of some novel and counter-intuitive interpretations of 'family' in which it may have no reference to either biological relatedness or personal commitment.

Finally, it seems that the world of education has fallen victim to some extraordinarily deterministic assumptions. While teachers and others who work with the young are happy to take a proactive role in warning young people against smoking and overeating, in the important area of sex and human relationships they tend to concede to new social fashions immediately, insisting that adult guidance is bound to be ineffective so should not even be offered. In its place they provide education in 'damage limitation' and 'values clarification'. For a brief moment in the 1980s, AIDS pulled these purveyors of bad advice up with a jolt, but since then an epidemic of other conditions affecting fertility and reproductive capacity has been largely ignored. Instead, the focus is overwhelmingly on the minimal aim of cutting teenage pregnancies by any means available. In practice, of course, young people receive their education from other sources as well, especially the role models provided by the media, by popular public figures, and by the creators of much contemporary art, literature, and entertainment. In many ways their influence is more insidious, since it is hard to challenge messages about normal or common behaviour that are put forward not as claims, but simply as a valid portrayal of what life is like.

In what follows I will try to substantiate these admittedly controversial claims. Inevitably they involve some appeal to what can be established by empirical research and observation. Some empirical evidence, then, will provide part of the background to my argument. They are, however, no more than a substratum to what is in fact a much more general philosophical and ethical thesis. What I hope to show is how largely independent projects in many areas of human knowledge and creativity have combined in what is in effect an onslaught on the increasingly fragile institution of the family. In a reversal of Adam Smith's 'hidden-hand' metaphor—the idea that in the economic sphere individuals pursuing their own good unintentionally produce the good of all—I will argue that, in the social sphere, the pursuit of individual best options, narrowly construed, has led to disharmony and brought a worse, rather than a better, outcome for society as a whole. It is an outcome that, on the one hand, leaves individuals exposed and alone in their personal lives and, on the other, makes them more and more subject to the control of government in critical areas of life that, traditionally, were primarily family concerns: birth and death, health and education, care at the beginning and end of life.

PART I

Understanding family: Philosophy's contribution

ℰ 1

Family

It would be difficult to understand the decline and fragmentation of the family without first taking a broad look at the way conceptions of the family have changed. Experts on the family have recently come to regard the definition of 'family' as a serious problem and to propose a surprising variety of possibilities. There are, of course, valid sociological distinctions to be made, for example, between the extended and the nuclear family, as well as legal distinctions, for example, between the adoptive and the natural family, but the process of drawing distinctions in these areas appears to have moved from recognizing straightforward differences based on matters of fact to legitimizing more controversial categories, including wholly unrelated groups, simply by choosing to call them families. Indeed many commentators appear to have adopted the Humpty Dumpty view that words can mean whatever we want them to mean. But it is no more helpful to accept a multiple variety of meanings for 'family' and then to move on from that to structure social policy than it would be to do this in the case of 'environment' or 'terrorism'.

For many people, the most plausible starting point for any analysis is biological. This is not to claim biology as the ethical foundation of the family. Biology makes a reasonable starting point for understanding the concept of a family simply because the family is a ubiquitous social institution, not only in human life, but in that of other mammals and species as well. Whether the consanguineal ('blood') family that is a person's family of origin, or the conjugal family—the one a person creates in sexual partnership and having children—'family' is, in strictly biological terms, a concept that centres on the physical coming-together of male and female and on the cluster of offspring that results from that relationship. In many species, though not all, a pair, once established, continues its relationship while fostering the young to independence. These are such trite and obvious facts that the only reason it is necessary to set them out is that they are currently considered by many people irrelevant to the lives of humans. It is tempting to speculate as to why this should be so. One plausible explanation is that it is, at least in part, a result of the dominance in much public discussion and academic debate of a socio-legal conception of family that conflicts with the biological one. A common analysis of this kind is summed up by one writer in these terms: 'Parenthood is an amorphous concept with roots in biology but the social construction of which changes with time, culture and the status of the observer.'[1]

It is, of course, true that, while most societies have sought to regulate arrangements by setting people's choices in a framework of law and permitted practice, history and culture have provided many variations in basic arrangements. So, for example, while much the most common family pattern is based on following the male line, there have been examples of civilizations, like that of ancient Egypt, based on a matriarchal pattern. More typically, the traditional Chinese family was patriarchal and based on deference; while in the family of the ancient Romans, the *patria potestas* of the father was unchallengeable, giving him the right of life and death over even adult children. Some anthropologists have suggested that, even earlier, before these relatively structured developments, women in some primitive societies may simply have been held in common.[2] Cultural variations can be found right up to modern times, with polygamy or, in a very few cases, polyandry institutionalized as practices. In some societies children may be cared for by the wider family group, or by a woman and her relatives without the father, who has no assigned responsibilities. In others, as in ancient Sparta, women's role may be limited to the early years and male children may be raised in all-male groups. But these are the exceptions rather than the rule, and by far the most common social structure has involved the recognition of kinship groupings centred on a couple and their offspring. Households have often consisted of these, together with an extended family: grandparents, aunts, uncles, and, in the past, depending on wealth, servants and retainers. 'Family', then, has often come to refer to all who share a common roof or, as a Greek poet cited by Aristotle put it, those who share a common bread bin or a common 'manger'.[3]

Of course, to claim the traditional unit as the basic family structure is not to see it as an idyll. According to one historian of the family, Lawrence Stone, family life in England during the period from the sixteenth to the beginning of the nineteenth centuries provided a setting in which people were not respected as individuals, children were not valued as children, and privacy and sexual fulfilment counted for less than the practical and economic aspects of marriage, of which men were the main beneficiaries.[4] What applied to England would have been generally true for other European countries and no doubt for many other parts of the world. Nevertheless, it is a picture that needs some qualification — not least the recognition that, in the circumstances of the time, whatever the failings of family life, the security it provided was in most cases preferable to available alternatives.

Today, though, because of the burgeoning varieties of living arrangements in modern industrialized societies, the overlap between 'family' and 'household' cannot be taken for granted. Some living arrangements may involve a sexual relationship, some ordinary sanguinity (for examples, two sisters, mother and son or daughter, grandmother and grandchildren, etc.) and some just temporary convenience (for examples, an invalid and a carer, co-workers or friends, or people who choose to share a mortgage and a flat in an expensive housing area). For this reason, it may be better to maintain the distinction between the terms 'family' and 'household' and to separate thinking and policy-making about families from thinking and policy-making about households.[5] Indeed, failure to do this can lead contemporary lawmakers to privilege relationships simply because they are sexual, to the disadvantage of other household structures that may be equally deserving of recognition and support.

What is 'natural'?

But, setting aside for the moment what might be described as pragmatic house-sharing, at the root of these historically varied familial arrangements, and also of contemporary alternatives claiming family status, lies the issue of sexual relationships. At some times and in some places, practices or relationships may be validated that at other times or in other places may be regarded as taboo. In some parts of the world, people find themselves liable to extreme punishment, or even a death penalty, for sex outside legally and ethically sanctioned norms. In the West, in contrast, the pendulum has swung in the opposite direction, and much public opinion, as well as some philosophical opinion, holds that sex has no moral implications at all. Igor Primoratz, for example, writes in his book *Ethics and Sex*: 'Sex has no special moral significance; it is morally neutral',[6] while Peter Singer began the first edition of his book *Practical Ethics* with the assertion that: 'Sex raises no unique moral issues at all ... Accordingly, this book contains no discussion of sexual morality.' In the second edition, however, he offers some qualification of his original statement. While admitting that sex can involve considerations of honesty, prudence, or concern for others, he says that the same could be said of decisions about driving a car, adding that, in fact, he considers that this raises much more serious questions than those raised by sex.[7] Influenced by these widely current views, which are supported by an influential liberal elite, or perhaps simply because it is the spirit of the age, politicians in a number of Western countries have pursued that assumption and promoted changes in law and taxation that are aimed at uncoupling the economic and legal links between sex, mutual commitment, and the bearing and raising of offspring.

But, while it is true that morality is not just about sex, it does not follow that sex is in fact a no-go area for morality. In other words, there is no reason to assume that, without a religious or faith foundation, there can be no ethical basis for sexual relationships. It is understandable that people should make that assumption, given that some religious groups—the Roman Catholic Church with its 900 million members, Islam with its worldwide following of one and a quarter billion, and the members of many other world religions—offer their followers strong rules and guidance on sexual ethics. To consider just the Catholic perspective, while it is true that there are important and influential dissenting voices within the Church itself, the Catholic position is, in the contemporary period, very much identified with views that carry, for most believers, the weight of the doctrine of papal infallibility. The Encyclicals *Humanae Vitae* (1968) and *Veritatis Splendor* (1993) spell out in unambiguous terms the Church's opposition to divorce, contraception, and abortion, and the Catholic Church continues to endorse the tradition of celibacy for priests.

But it is not necessary to resolve these large issues of faith and religious belief in order to reach conclusions about personal life and conduct. Indeed, the opposite may be true, for, once the radical question is raised of whether a religious perspective is really essential for a sexual ethic, it is easy to see the *practical* advantages of a broader and more inclusive position as a working basis for personal relationships. However, this is not only a matter of practical utility. The Catholic Church itself owes a considerable debt, not only to early Christian and Judaic sources, but also to sources that pre-date Christianity and lie outside these religious traditions. In particular, the natural-law tradition at the root of much religious thinking was originally the inspiration of people—philosophers, lawyers, law-makers, and poets—who lived in ancient Greece five centuries before the birth of Christ. Perhaps the clearest depiction of the revolutionary concept of a moral law with overriding authority was provided, not by a philosopher, but by a dramatist, Sophocles, whose heroine Antigone had been forbidden to carry out her duty to bury the body of her slain brother. She disobeys, asserting the superior claim of the moral law over a command that conflicted with what she believed to be a higher duty. Addressing the ruler, her uncle, she says:

> Nor did I deem
> Your ordinance of so much binding force
> As that a mortal man could overbear
> The unchangeable unwritten code of Heaven;
> This is not of today and yesterday,
> But lives forever having origin
> Whence no man knows.[8]

Antigone was expressing a view that was already current, if controversial, in the ancient world—not, in this case, a scientific theory about the laws governing natural events, but an ethical claim that recognized a moral law or natural order over and above the laws of convention that were decided by human rulers and rooted in particular localities.

Aristotle set out the distinction more formally in terms of political justice: 'There are two sorts of political justice, one natural and the other legal. The natural is that which has the same validity everywhere and does not depend upon acceptance; the legal is that which in the first place can take one form or another indifferently, but which, once laid down, is decisive.'[9] This idea was an important element in Stoic thought and was reflected in Roman law and in the Christian tradition. Its influence extended into modern times, leading in due course to the contemporary notion of universal human rights. The sources the early defenders of this notion drew on to give it shape and coherence were human reason and a strong conception of human nature and its needs. Together these provided a foundation for an understanding of the end and purpose of human life. The focus on ends and purposes—the quest for meaning in life—provided the psychological underpinning of the philosophy of both Plato and Aristotle, and these ideas permeated the modern world through the influence of Aristotle, who saw purpose and point in largely biological terms. Aristotle's account eventually provided a direction for Catholic thinking in these areas through its influence on the thought and teaching of Augustine (354–430) in the fourth century and Aquinas (1224–74) in the thirteenth.

A gateway between this and a modern secularized notion was provided by Hugo Grotius in the seventeenth century, when he described the law of nature as a dictate of right reason. While Grotius himself sought to unite natural law and biblical authority, he argued that it does not depend on God, but would apply even if God did not exist. Locke later gave the modern notion expression in the claim that natural law is a test of the justice of positive law. While modern formulations may appear to mark a different direction from the classical notion, there is continuity in the role they give to reason. The underlying conception is that, through reflection on the nature and ideal destination of a human life, reason provides a gateway to the moral law. The emphasis must be on the word 'ideal', for many things that are natural are not necessarily good or desirable. This is not, then, to try to derive values from facts—to reason from what *is* to what ought to be. It is rather to look to the facts of nature for an accurate and convincing picture of what human life at its best could be and to take that as a guide to what is to be judged good or right. So the conception of ideal fulfilment and flourishing that was fundamental to the classical theory, and is intrinsically action-guiding, must still lie at the heart of any moves to offer this kind of grounding for morality for modern times. Understood in this way, and with this qualification, the idea of natural law holds out, in the specific area of intimate human relationships, the possibility of a foundation for sexual morality that looks to the facts of human nature rather than to doctrinal teaching or authority for its shape and direction.[10]

During its long historical evolution, the idea of natural law became intertwined with religious doctrine. Even in these terms, however, it need not be interpreted as narrowly as it sometimes is. For example, if a narrow interpretation of what counts as natural may seem to limit the point and purpose of sex to procreation, a broader one may recognize that the interests of procreation are also served by sexuality that maintains and reinforces the bond between parents while they are bringing up their children. Nor would a more generous interpretation of this ethical requirement need to be confined to considering the immediate interests and preferences of adults. On the contrary, it could and should take into account, as well, the social and emotional consequences for children and for the wider community of sexual encounters stripped of any long-term significance. If it is possible to interpret the natural-law tradition in a way that avoids the need to appeal to religious doctrines that can be accepted as a guide only by adherents, this opens up the possibility of an ethical position with much wider appeal: an understanding of sexual morality that is based on serious reflection about what is most fulfilling for human beings at successive ages and stages of life, taking into account their emotional needs and lifetime goals.

An important implication of this is that those who reject the authority of religious leaders as a basis for personal life can still benefit from the combination of psychological understanding and moral commitment represented by the notion of natural law. A non-religious ethical viewpoint that starts from the same ethical and philosophical underpinning as some of the world's faiths can also recognize that linking together sex, commitment, and loyalty is a more reliable way of fulfilling the human quest for happiness than most alternatives. The non-religious thinker must also acknowledge the biological fact that for humans, as for other animals, reproduction represents the only natural function in which a solitary member of the human species is not fully functional and independent. For this alone, apart from some recent but speculative developments in reproductive medicine, the cooperation of male and female is needed. It is this biological truism that gives a unique status to the physical sexual connection of two persons of opposite sex, and it is that unique status that has traditionally been recognized in the idea of marriage as a publicly declared union for the bearing and raising of children.

Law, marriage, and cohabitation

Today, this is not the end of the matter, but rather the place where controversy starts. To begin with, the need for the formal institution of marriage is widely challenged, and living together outside marriage is increasingly the option of choice. In Britain, for example, there is a well-founded expectation that, for the first time since records began in 1801, the unmarried will outnumber the unmarried. This point has been officially estimated as 2011.[11] It is a trend that has led many to ask: is legal marriage really necessary?[12]

There are a number of ways to interpret this question—philosophical, ethical, emotional, analytic. But, initially, at least, there is good reason to adopt a fairly pedestrian interpretation, for in the end it is purely pragmatic considerations that are likely to determine public policy. Government actuaries and accountants are more at ease with the calculation of costs and benefits than with appeals to citizens' higher instincts, and, as it happens, there is a good deal of empirical evidence available on this subject. To give at this point no more than a flavour of how the factual comparison works out, it is possible to say that, while undoubtedly some unmarried couples do remain together for many years, cohabitation is on the whole more unstable than marriage—often intentionally so, since some prefer to avoid the degree of commitment that marriage involves. In Europe, for example, while more than two-thirds of legally constituted marriages last ten years or more, the same is true of only a tiny number of cohabiting or 'living-together' relationships. In other words, couples who are living together without a formal tie are four to five times more likely than married couples to split up. Surprisingly, too, living-together arrangements that include children are even more short-lived than those without children, though neither has the longevity of formal marriage.[13] For children, the implications of this are serious, not least because the break-up of their parents' relationship often means that they themselves will lose touch with one or other parent, with the accompanying loss that that will involve. Policy in all Western countries, however, has been in the direction of changing the legal implications of marriage to something more like those of cohabitation than making the legal implications of cohabitation more like those of marriage. These points will be discussed in more detail later, but, as these statistics demonstrate, the evidence is that the legal tie does bind. Meanwhile, there are two other areas that have played a significant part in the ongoing controversy about the family, and these will form a central focus in the later part of this book. These are, first, the role played by science and the new reproductive technologies, and, second, the issue of same-sex unions and gender equality.

Reproductive choice

For both heterosexual couples and for others, not only the options of fertility or infertility, but many other choices in the generation and bearing of children, have become available through the new reproductive technologies. Primary amongst these are, for those who want to control their fertility, the possibility of avoiding pregnancy through efficient means of contraception and the availability of abortion. The choices of those seeking fertility, though, are at least equally striking in the options that have been opened up to them by the ability to manipulate and exchange generational material—eggs, sperm, and embryos—in the laboratory. The remarkable degree of reproductive control that this provides has led to a focus on the choice, autonomy, and rights of adults seeking parenthood.

In this situation, while children rank high in most individuals' moral consciousness and also in the verbal commitments of politicians and national leaders, the rights and welfare of children born with the help of the new technologies can easily be overlooked. In particular, in the case of those born by assisted reproduction using donated gametes, a new and unfamiliar gulf has opened up between genetic or biological relatedness and social relatedness. For them, questions of rights opened up in the fertility clinic when decisions were taken about them that would crucially affect their future lives.

As a result, reproductive medicine forms another dramatic influence on family change. From one point of view, the influence can be regarded as benign, in that it offers support to family life and a halt to its decline. Certainly it means that children are born to those who strongly want to have children and would otherwise be unable to do so. However, in some ways, which will be discussed later, the possibilities it creates risk contributing to fragmentation of a different kind. This is because those who see the area of assisted reproduction primarily in terms of adult choice seek to push forward moves for less regulation, or indeed none at all, aiming in the end for legal changes that would, if they came about, abolish the root conception of the family. A weakened and diluted conception of family like that favoured by the red-Green coalition in Germany—'family is where children are'—deprives children of many of the rights hitherto taken for granted by human beings, denying them, not only their particular parentage, their own mother or father, but perhaps, too, their self-concept and sense of contextual identity.

Same-sex unions

These aspects feature prominently in discussion of same-sex marriage. While the debate about formal marriage is hardly new, and while the terms in which it is conducted are, on the whole, familiar and traditional, same-sex unions pose a more radical challenge to the concepts of marriage and family. This new challenge focuses on the issue of gender. By a strange irony, while informal arrangements such as cohabitation, or simply 'relationships', are being promoted by some as the arrangements of choice for heterosexual couples, with the freedom from commitment that that involves, legally recognized marriage has become a campaigning goal for same-sex couples, and by 2006 it had already been achieved in a number of countries, including Belgium, the Netherlands, Spain, Canada, and parts of the USA. Not only gay and lesbian people, but liberal politicians and civil libertarians as well, are ready to challenge the earlier, near-universal assumption that marriage is a union of male and female in a permanent and exclusive relationship primarily for the bearing and raising of children. The European Union, pursuing a broad programme of gender equality in this and other areas, has resisted efforts to embody such a definition in law. But, while a tacit consensus seems to rule in European countries, battle lines are drawn up in the USA for a long-drawn-out contest between those, on the one hand, who seek to have written into the Constitution a definition of marriage that specifically defines it as a union of male and female and, on the other, advocates of same-sex marriage. A Massachusetts high court ruling of November 2003 that endorsed same-sex marriage by a majority of 4 to 3 did so using an alternative definition of civil marriage as 'the voluntary union of two persons as spouses to the exclusion of all others'.[14] The notion of marriage as a voluntary and exclusive union of two persons is also reflected in Canadian law, although in that case the reference to *persons* (as opposed to man and woman) pre-dated the controversy about same-sex marriage.

The emphasis on same-sex marriage, however, is the more surprising given that same-sex couples are already offered a civil union or legally recognized partnership in most Western countries. The reasons for this pressure are various and need to be separated from the issue of the moral and legal status of homosexuality itself. Oscar Wilde's trial at the Old Bailey in London for offences of gross indecency is now more than a century distant, and in Britain the decriminalization of homosexuality took place in 1967 with the introduction of the Sexual Offences Act. This institutionalized the view that what consenting adults do in private is 'not the law's business'.[15] So the pressure for same-sex marriage may be based less on a need felt by some individuals to live an openly gay life than on other factors: the attraction of the ceremony itself and the recognition it gives; the wish for parity with heterosexual couples in legal and financial arrangements such as inheritance-tax, and insurance; or a desire to have the opportunity, either through adoption or through the use of reproductive technology, to form a union that includes children. Recognition of these different aspirations is the first step in considering whether and how they can or ought to be satisfied. But, where the desire is the more fundamental one of founding a family in the sense of producing progeny, the picture becomes more complex.[16]

Progress or decline? Evaluating change

In what follows, these themes will be taken up and explored in more detail. The case to be made here is that these diverse areas of dramatic and very speedy change, taken together, have helped to initiate the current decline and fragmentation of the family. This causal explanation forms part of a broader argument that the institution of the family in the Western democracies is at serious risk of internal, self-engineered, collapse through the very success of, on the one hand, scientific and medical progress and, on the other, social policies—legal reforms and tax and benefits programmes. These include not only easy divorce, but also the removal in some countries of tax concessions that used to benefit single-earner, two-parent families. Taken together, the combination of scientific, social, and legal innovation has been destructive of family structures in ways that are often unforeseen and unintended. Sometimes, however, these changes have been advanced for reasons that are more political than social and have been aimed at tipping the balance of priority between state and family, in favour of the state.

Amongst these sociological and political considerations, demographic factors may be overlooked. But, in a world where some countries strictly separate the roles of women and men, confining women to the role of mothers of large families, the decline of the family in the Western democracies is part and parcel of changes that may appear beneficial in themselves and in the short term but that, taken together, threaten the continuity and existence of their communities. The most striking of these may well turn out to be relative changes in population numbers and an ensuing shift in cultural influence and power.[17]

The fragmentation of the family in Western societies, then, is gathering a largely unplanned momentum. Some welcome this trend. One influential commentator, the sociologist Anthony Giddens, writes: 'The persistence of the traditional family—or aspects of it—in many parts of the world is more worrisome than its decline.'[18] But, before an ethical judgement can be passed, other more practical questions must be answered. What are the consequences of family fragmentation? And can they be avoided? The answer must be that, while some of these factors may be beyond human intervention, others are not. In particular, what law can create in a short period, it can also reverse.

However, there is every indication that, as things stand, legislators are determined to make changes that are neither in harmony with their own cultural and ethical traditions nor in the long-term interest of their populations. The European Union, like Canada and parts of the USA, has adopted a number of directives in favour of a broad definition of family and in favour, too, of according legal rights and recognition to most personal living arrangements and equalizing the status of those involved in them. Some of these changes may well be irreversible, and indeed, few people rooted in the traditions of the liberal democracies would want to set the clock back to an era when people were seriously disadvantaged and discriminated against as a result of their status in relation to sexual or family matters. Nor would many people want to see the return of laws to police and control the varied and unpredictable relationships of adults. They may well be ready, though, to acknowledge that there are aspects in which change has proceeded without adequate consideration, and that this raises a number of philosophical and ethical questions, some of them conceptual, others practical. It is clear, for example, that the concepts of marriage and family are now seriously contested. At the same time, the ethical basis of marriage, the vow or promise, has been significantly diminished and indeed is now legally nullified. Perhaps the most striking shift of all, however, is the dwindling importance attached to biological or genetic relationships.

It is these topics that are the concern of the following chapters. I begin by considering matters from a personal and individual point of view, in which only the felt need of two people for each other is involved. Here I seek to explore some of the underlying philosophical tensions in this basic relationship, first limiting the enquiry to situations where only the interests, rights, and goods of adults are involved. But philosophical views of love and friendship, permanence and exclusivity in relationships, are sometimes given substance in the lives of philosophers themselves, and I illustrate this by reference to three famous exemplars—three philosophical couples who pioneered new approaches to partnering. I then go on to consider the broader picture of the family in its conventional role as a setting for having and raising children. I consider the influence of feminism, the impact of the new reproductive technologies, and the implications for the family of legal change (especially easier or no-fault divorce) and of state intervention in the area of tax and benefits policy. I look separately at some of the issues that have been raised from the point of view of the children affected by them, and consider finally the wider cultural and political perspective, including conceptions of identity and community, in which the whole debate about the family is set. What I hope to show is that, in the longer term, as the intimate focus of hearth and home becomes a source of contention in the public world, the personal becomes the political and the threat to human communities and their continuity represented by the decline and fragmentation of the family poses the greatest long-term challenge facing Western communities.

ℰ 2

Permanent relations?
Love, marriage, and philosophical lives

Being single is, for some, a lifestyle choice. Indeed, the very idea of the couple relationship can meet with reflective philosophical opposition from those who believe that, in a couple culture based on sexual exclusivity, authenticity is at risk for the coupled, and that their preoccupation with each other rebounds on those who are alone: a world of couples, they argue, imposes on the uncoupled the risk of social isolation and loneliness.[1] For others, though, the need for intimacy and security can best be met in a relationship that offers some guarantee of continuity. The prime example of this kind of relationship is marriage, and in this chapter the philosophical framework for marriage and other quasi-marital relationships will be considered apart from any connection these might have with the desire to have children. Marriage is currently a highly contested concept, and attempts to define it have a long history. Roman law referred to 'the joining together of man and woman, which we call marriage' (*maris et feminae conjunctio, quam nos matrimonium appellamus*). The canon law of the medieval church, based partly on Roman law, made consent and consummation the only conditions that needed to be satisfied for a marriage to be recognized, but the Council of Trent (1545–63) added the requirement that consent had to be witnessed before a priest in the presence of other witnesses. In the English legal tradition, marriage has been described as 'the voluntary union for life of one woman and one man to the exclusion of all others'.[2] But even where no explicit mention of children is made, most European legal systems have not separated marriage and family, and, in international statements of human rights, the two are invariably found together, as in 'a right to marry and found a family'.

The contemporary period has brought some new conceptions of marriage, including challenges to the assumption that it is a relationship between a male and a female. But, even apart from the gender challenge, the role of marriage has evolved in ways that require a broader specification, given that it is in practice also an economic and a legal arrangement. While it may still include the traditional elements of free consent, public recognition, and at least some degree of ritual that is often, but not always, religious, it also functions as an institution offering each partner certain specific expectations. Ideally, these expectations need to be secure enough to justify some personal sacrifices. In today's urban and mobile society, for example, one partner's career plans and prospects might be affected by marriage, and sometimes progress in one partner's career may involve further adjustments, such as a change of neighbourhood and social setting for both. For both of them, too, marriage may mean the sacrifice of other friendships or other potentially enriching personal relationships. Behind such adjustments, and the reason why people may be willing to make them, lies the need for marriage to be secure enough to justify making long-term investments, whether in material matters such as housing and other joint possessions or, of course, in children. For many people, marriage remains an institution that provides some solidity for the project of building a coherent life plan. Paradoxically, it gives expression to a desire to create bonds that transcend the legal, and to use the medium of law itself to do this.

Amongst these varied aspects of marriage, many of them concrete and practical, two abstract ideals stand out as primary defining features. One is the quest for permanence in the relationship, the other the ideal of sexual exclusivity or faithfulness. As far as the first of these is concerned, the aspirations of human beings for permanence and continuity have a long philosophical history outside and beyond the narrow focus of personal relationships.

The quest for permanence

The search for permanence in a world of change found expression in some of the earliest philosophical records, even before the time of Socrates. The contrast between continuity and change was already implicit in early metaphysical and cosmological theories. It was there in the division between the followers of Parmenides, who emphasized the permanence, unity, and continuity of the universe, and those of Heraclitus, who saw it as a state of constant flux—a theory expressed in a famous surviving fragment of his teaching: 'You cannot step twice into the same river; for fresh waters are ever flowing in upon you.' But, if these very general metaphysical claims provided the background, it was the Stoics who brought theory to personal practice in their recommendations for the cultivation of a mindset that has abandoned any expectation of permanence. Epictetus (c.55–c.135) asked his followers to try to imagine what it would be like to be immortal and condemned to a situation in which, as he put it, 'we all stayed tied to our roots like plants'. 'Surely,' he said, 'it is high time that we grew up and reminded ourselves ... the time must inevitably come for one thing to give place to another; that some things must break up and new things come along, some things stay the same and others change.' His recommendation: 'Remember that you ought to behave in life as you would at a banquet. As something is being passed around and it comes to you, just reach out and take a portion of it politely. It passes on; don't try to keep it.'[3]

The Stoics, then, held that the path to peace of mind lies through philosophical detachment from close personal ties. The aim was to try to break the bonds that shackle the individual, and so to avoid the pain and distress of their inevitable ending. If you do not want something when you have it, you will not miss it when you do not. In another passage, Epictetus makes clear how this detachment from bonding could lead to peace of mind. He wrote:

Whenever you grow attached to something, do not act as though it were one of those things that cannot be taken away, but as though it were something like a jar or a crystal goblet, so that when it breaks you will remember what it was like, and not be troubled. So too in life; if you kiss your child, your brother, your friend, ... remind yourself that the object of your love is mortal; it is not one of your own possessions; it has been given you for the present, not inseparably nor for ever, but like a fig, or a cluster of grapes, at a fixed season of the year, and that if you hanker for it in winter you are a fool. If in this way you long for your son, or your friend, at a time when he is not given to you, rest assured that you are hankering for a fig in winter-time.[4]

In contemporary terms, there is an unconscious drift towards the acceptance of flux and change as a condition of modern living. Applied to human relationships, the goal of achieving emotional detachment translates into not trying to hold onto a relationship that has gone stale—something that has become almost an article of faith where relationships between adults are concerned and is reflected in changing partnerships and easy divorce. In contrast, though, the unequal relationship between parent and child is more intense and unconditional than it has ever been, so that, when adult relationships break down, children can become pawns in a post-marital gender war that cannot ultimately be won by either sex.[5] Some see the transition from a focus on adult relationships to one of parent–child relationships as an irreversible and broadly welcome development. Indeed, the American legal theorist June Carbone sees it as a legal revolution. She writes: 'Across the academy, the courts, classrooms, and election campaigns, the code of family responsibility is being rewritten in terms of the only ties left—the ones to children.'[6]

There are, of course, many kinds of human relationships apart from family ones: those generated by work or leisure activities, by national loyalties, or by the fellowship of faith communities; in terms of emotional relatedness, too, there is a continuum from casual acquaintance, through friendship, to love, loyalty, and devotion. Some of these relationships are temporary and fluctuating, subject to change with circumstances, while others have a claim to be regarded as permanent. For people who live under non-authoritarian political systems, the closer and more intimate bonds between people often have the most natural and immediate force, and the broader more widely shared bonds, the weaker. Indeed, many see it as the mark of fanaticism to give priority to broader groupings—religious, political, or racial—over the more intimate ones of family and friendship.

Philosophical opinion, however, has always been divided, and philosophers' views have sometimes been reflected in their lives as much as in their writing. The poet Percy Bysshe Shelley, first an admirer of the philosophical anarchist William Godwin, and later his son-in-law, could be taken as a spokesman for those who are addicted to change in personal relations. In an essay 'Against Legal Marriage' Shelley deplored the 'despotism of marriage'—the attempt of law to govern 'the indisciplinable wanderings of passion'—asserting: 'Love withers under constraint; its very essence is liberty.'[7] Shelley's own short life brought tragedy in its wake, both for those he loved, or who loved him, and for those he married. No doubt it is true that poets and prophets are, as the British philosopher Roger Scruton has suggested, the best authorities on sex—true, too, that it is they who offer us the richest and most full-blooded account of human sexuality, when, as Scruton rightly observes, they 'present us with desire, shame, lust, love, obscenity, arousal, modesty, jealousy and all the many things that have "problematized" the course of sexual union, and made it the thing that it is'.[8] But perhaps it would be more illuminating in the end, in weighing the rival claims of constraint and liberty, to turn aside briefly from both philosophers and poets, and to look for comment from one of those most directly affected in practice—a philosopher's wife, rather than a philosopher. For someone like Alys, the first wife of Bertrand Russell, the bonds of a long-term human relationship may be hard to break. Forced to accept their divorce as a legal reality, it never became, for her, a felt reality. At the age of 82, describing how she had looked through the windows of his home and seen Russell with his later wife and children, she wrote to him: 'I am utterly devoted to thee, and have been for over 50 years ... but my devotion makes no claim, and involves no burden on thy part, nor any obligation, not even to answer this letter.' Explaining her inability to meet him face to face after their break-up, she wrote of their marriage: 'I was neither wise enough nor courageous enough to prevent this one disaster from shattering my capacity for happiness and my zest for life.'[9]

Today, the prevailing vision of necessary transience is embodied, whether intentionally or not, in new legal provisions for temporary forms of quasi-marriage, especially new civil unions or partnerships. Sometimes this is promoted simply as a way of offering a legally recognizable form of relationship to same-sex couples, but in some jurisdictions, for example, Holland, they are available to heterosexual couples as well. In this case, instead of opening up the possibility of a traditional marital-style relationship to gay men and women, the arrangement seems to offer legal transience to all—relationships that can be dissolved in months at the request of either partner. The argument is that what adults choose for themselves alone is their own business. However, the flexibility of the situation, which is part of its attraction, is confused when long-term financial commitments or the sharing of assets is introduced into these partnerships. Institutionalized arrangements of this sort may also depart even further from the 'consenting-adults-alone' principle by bringing in taxpayer support. Pension and housing concessions, including, for example, the waiver of inheritance tax, commonly receive backing either directly from the public purse or indirectly from the consumer, who must pay when firms are obliged to extend privileges, such as survivor's benefits or travel concessions, originally devised for the protection of women of a bygone era who had large families and no independent opportunity for a working life, to adult couples who have simply been together in a shared relationship for a period of time that may be as short as a few years. Defining the nature of that relationship remains a legal minefield for the future, but it seems it must include a sexual element, since otherwise so many other domestically based relationships would be able to claim the same privileges.[10]

The ideal of exclusivity

Civil partnerships, whatever the intention, and especially when they are open to heterosexual couples, are seen by many as involving a lesser commitment to permanency than marriage. But, if not permanency, they may still be seen as involving the ideal of exclusivity—the second of the twin pillars of marriage as an institution. It would not be surprising, however, if the crumbling of one of these pillars were rapidly to undermine the other. Some might regard this double erosion as a welcome development, creating a possible new ideal of marriage. The anthropologists Nena and George O'Neill opened up discussion of this new approach in the early 1970s, in a book with the title *Open Marriage*.[11] Taking up the theme from a philosophical point of view, Joseph and Clorinda Margolis forecast that, for many people, marriage would become a relatively transient institution. They wrote: 'It would be a source of continuing personal freedom and renewal for competent parties, weaving in and out of contact with more permanent and more fundamental family relations.' [12]

A short generation later, what they had put forward as a radical proposal had become a standard notion and, as if in partial confirmation of the Margolises' prophecy, the sociologist Anthony Giddens was able to report that 'coupling' and 'uncoupling' now provide a more accurate description of the area of personal life than 'marriage and the family'. He comments: 'A more important question for us than "Are you married?" is "Are you in a relationship?" ... In the 1960s no one spoke of "relationships". They didn't need to, nor did they need to speak in terms of intimacy and commitment. Marriage at that time *was* the commitment.'[13] Giddens's assumption of the death of marriage is shared by many of those who approach the issue from a socio-legal point of view. Summarizing what they regard as a standard assumption of contemporary life, Mavis Maclean and Martin Richards comment that 'marriage is now one form of a committed personal relationship which persists only as long as the relationship provides emotional satisfaction for both parties'.[14] Not the least remarkable aspect of this statement is the failure of the authors to notice that it is a contradiction in terms. To describe a relationship as committed is to say that it is *not* unpredictably dependent on each individual's feelings.

But the intention that a relationship should last is only part of the notion of commitment, and the question of whether the relationship should also be exclusive still remains. What can be the objection to individuals in a couple relationship enjoying other concurrent relationships that might be important and enriching for them? What is wrong with an 'open marriage'? Can just one person provide a focus for another person's life? One response would be to say that the notion of an 'open marriage' is a conceptual confusion, for it is hard to make sense of a formal arrangement that leaves both parties as much freedom as they had before. But this may be too simple a response. A more complete answer to questions like these is more likely to be reached by trying to glean such understanding as we can from human history and human experience—events that form the 'stuff' of poetry, myth, and literature. Much of this carries the message that to preserve the primary relationship while engaging in others is too demanding for many people, and more so for their partners. Relationships are corroded by lying and deception, or even by a failure to disclose. This is also an area where the saying 'What you don't know can't hurt you' often turns out to be wrong.

Contemporary writing is often more tolerant of diversity. The British philosopher David Archard describes the opposite presumption as a 'conservative prejudice'. He writes: 'it is the inability of one or both partners to tolerate infidelity rather than the infidelity itself which is the relevant factor here … . What surely matters is that unconstrained choices can be made in the light of what is felt to be best for each and every partnership.'[15] But, while jealousy and possessiveness may be bad, they are also amongst the 'facts of life' that play such a key role in human relationships. It is true that anthropologists have discovered some societies where sexual sharing is the pattern of living. In the end, though, it may be unrealistic to seek to introduce what are naturally occurring patterns of life in some primitive societies into complex and fluctuating Western societies. There is, too, a certain illogicality about the idea of institutionalized unfaithfulness; it may not be a contradiction in terms, but marriage with the *intention* of such a limited commitment comes close to being one.

There is also the risk for those who find monogamy unappealing that the kind of tandem arrangement sketched out by the Margolises may turn out to be equally untenable and that the many-partnered person may turn out in practice to be in much the same situation, emotionally and practically, as the no-partner person. It is a lifestyle that may in the end appeal only to someone willing to avoid the partner connection altogether—a person who is able to set the freedom of living alone over its risks. But there are risks involved. If too many people make this choice, it is a risk to society as a whole of the *anomie* and rootlessness that communitarian critics see as an inevitable consequence of the kind of preoccupation with self that might lie behind their choice. But there are risks for the individual too. Whether it is a result of someone else's decision or of natural events such as illness, death, or protracted separation, people who suddenly find this kind of freedom thrust upon them often find it is a false freedom: the freedom of a ship in a storm-tossed sea. There is a well-documented risk to the 'freed' individual of loneliness, mental breakdown, or illness triggered by the collapse of the network of dependency.[16] Marriage itself may have created the conditions for this—in the words of the writer Jonathan Gathorne-Hardy, 'a physical structure in the brain, a pattern of itself in the language of the cells'. Gathorne-Hardy believes that this might help to explain the peculiar and devastating quality of the loneliness ensuing upon divorce, which he describes as 'that quality of amputation, of having been ripped apart, of internal bleeding.'[17] Variety and choice, then, may be less accommodated to human nature than many people today have chosen to believe. And, while enrichment is valuable, it can be found in other ways. Psychologically, it may also have a lower priority than stability—not only for the children of a relationship, but also for the central parties themselves.

While some philosophical thinkers have struggled with these oppositions in their personal lives, the roll-call of celibate philosophers is extensive, and many appear to have avoided the closest of human relationships by remaining unmarried. Nietzsche, who remained unmarried himself, offered in *The Genealogy of Morals* (1887) a catalogue of unmarried philosophers, starting with Heraclitus, through Plato, to Descartes, Kant, Leibniz, Spinoza, and Kierkegaard. Of these, Plato gave his name to the concept of love without sex—the Platonic relationship—illustrated by Socrates' description in the *Symposium* of a night passed in company with the desirable young Alcibiades. The dialogue reveals that he chose to use the occasion for companionship and conversation rather than a togetherness of a more physical nature. In other dialogues, however, Plato portrays Socrates as recognizing the dangerous force of passion and its power to overmaster its victim. In the *Phaedrus*, the image is of a charioteer trying to control two horses pulling in different directions, one representing physical desire and uncontrollable passion, the other a love that is love of a *person* expressed in a more intellectual and companionate way. The real Socrates was himself a husband and father. Indeed, the desire of his family at the time of his trial and execution to plead for his life suggests that this was not an unsuccessful relationship. But the lives and relationships of philosophers have not always fulfilled their aspirations, even when, as in some cases, the philosophers concerned have taken up their pen in serious reflection and reasoning about the marriage bond itself. Their very iconic status would suggest that it is worth taking a closer look at three couples who did this either together or separately. Of these, William Godwin and Mary Wollstonecraft did marry, as did John Stuart Mill and Harriet Taylor, while, in a later and more tolerant age, Jean-Paul Sartre and Simone de Beauvoir chose not to marry, although their long intimate relationship was widely recognized both during and after their lifetime.

William Godwin and Mary Wollstonecraft

William Godwin's (1756–1836) anarchist political philosophy led naturally to a rejection of what was in the eighteenth century one of society's most rigid institutions, and it was perhaps not surprising that, when he met the author of *A Vindication of the Rights of Woman* (1792), the pioneer feminist Mary Wollstonecraft (1759–97), they shared with mutual appreciation their revolutionary conception of how men and women might relate to each other as independent individuals who rejected the need to take on the yoke of matrimony. Godwin had written of 'the evil of marriage', describing it as a system based on property and as the worst of monopolies: 'It is absurd to expect that the inclinations and wishes of two human beings should coincide through any long period of time. To oblige them to act and to live together, is to subject them to some inevitable portion of thwarting, bickering and unhappiness.'[18]

Mary Wollstonecraft's critique of marriage focused on other negative aspects of the institution, which she denounced as 'legalised prostitution'. She had personally experienced the darker side of relations between the sexes, first in a childhood home dominated by a choleric and violent father, later as the mother of the child of a man she had loved but who had then abandoned her. She had also once daringly, and for her time and situation rashly, unsuccessfully proposed an intellectual and aesthetic *ménage à trois* to the painter Fuseli and his wife. As she struggled in unpropitious and unsympathetic times to cope with her own personal situation, seeking to write and also to earn a living for herself and her daughter, she twice attempted suicide.

However, by the time she met Godwin, she was herself a much talked-about author. She had been in France during the Revolution, and subsequently in Scandinavia. Her travels had broadened her perspective on the world, and she was, though with difficulty, supporting herself and her daughter. Intellectually, then, if not emotionally, she was ready to join Godwin in rejecting the idea that anyone might need a 'companion for life'.[19] Nevertheless, in 1797, when she became pregnant with his child, they married, though, as Godwin put it in a letter to a friend, 'We do not entirely cohabit.' Indeed, Godwin undertook some extensive travels at that time, and Mary's letters to Godwin throughout her pregnancy reveal the depth of her care for him and betray her increasing wish for his presence as the time of the birth drew near and his return was repeatedly delayed. When he finally returned just before their daughter Mary was born, he was in time only to witness his wife's slow and painful death as a result of complications following the birth. They had married in March. She died in September, and any experiment in shared living was forever postponed.

Ironically, this tragedy, contrary to the views they had formed together, continued to haunt Godwin during his life, and, for him, the strength of their bond was closer after her death than it had ever been in life. Years later, he wrote: 'It is impossible to represent in words the total revolution this event made in my existence. It was as if in a single moment "sun and moon were in the flat sea sunk". Nature that had been so beautiful, so resplendent, so fascinating, lost at once the soul to which it was indebted for all its charms.'[20] There was, however, a philosophy behind the tragedy that is very recognizable in today's terms. Godwin and Wollstonecraft had rejected matrimony as an institution embodying joint commitment and a shared life, but both had bought freedom at a cost that was for each, separately, hard to pay. Had they known the brevity of their future, they might have valued their previous freedom less.

John Stuart Mill and Harriet Taylor

While the approach of Godwin and Wollstonecraft to marriage and personal relationships was libertarian and individualistic, that of John Stuart Mill (1806–73) and Harriet Taylor (1807–58) was more qualified and conditional. This despite the fact that their close personal relationship was widely seen by their contemporaries as an assault on the institution of marriage. At the time when their association began, both were in their twenties, and Harriet was already married to John Taylor, with whom she had three young children. It was eighteen years before the death of her husband made it possible for Mill and Harriet to marry and throughout that time they incurred much social disapproval for a relationship—albeit almost certainly Platonic—that so publicly transgressed the mores of Victorian England. Some of Mill's own family broke with him, although Harriet's husband, on the other hand, managed his difficult situation with considerable dignity. That it was not easy for him slips out, quietly and privately, in some of his correspondence with his wife—for example, when he wrote to her to say that it would not be appropriate for her to accept the dedication of Mill's *Principles of Political Economy*, published in 1848. Insisting that it would display a want of taste and tact, John Taylor wrote: 'It is not only "a few common people" who will make vulgar remarks, but all who know any of us—The dedication will revive recollections now forgotten and will create observations and talk that cannot but be extremely unpleasant to me.'[21]

Nevertheless, the history of this triangular relationship could in fact be seen as revealing an underlying respect for marriage, albeit as it ideally might be, rather than as it was in mid-nineteenth-century England. It could be seen, that is, as a public demonstration by Mill and Harriet Taylor of the fact that it is possible for a man and a woman to have a more than superficial friendship and to relate to each other as friends and intellectual equals. Both were early supporters of feminism, and opponents of the prevailing subjection of one sex to the other.[22] Their own long association was one in which they fostered and developed their common intellectual interests, and Harriet Taylor was inclined to dismiss as 'tittle-tattle' criticisms of their relationship, both in her correspondence with Mill and also in correspondence with her husband, John Taylor. Appearances, however, were indeed against them. As their friend Thomas Carlyle described the situation in a letter to his brother: 'It is the fairest Mrs Taylor you have heard of; with whom, under her husband's very eyes, he [i.e. Mill] is (Platonically) over head and ears in love.'[23]

It is easy, of course, to see a connection between this personal story and the general philosophical position that Mill defended in *On Liberty* (1859), his classic defence of liberalism—a work that he dedicated to Harriet, claiming her as co-equal and inspirer of the ideas it embodied. Mill's essay offered a reasoned if qualified portrayal of liberty and toleration, setting its limits only where one person's liberty could bring harm or hurt to somebody else. For Mill, then, and presumably for Harriet too, other people count, and harm to others sets a limit to the freedom principle famously summed up in the words: 'The sole end for which mankind are warranted, individually or collectively, in interfering with the liberty of action of any of their number is self-protection. ... The only part of the conduct of anyone, for which he is amenable to society, is that which concerns others. ... Over himself, over his own body and mind, the individual is sovereign.'[24]

But this had implications for the view that both took of the marriage bond and of their own claim to freedom in their relation with each other, although, perhaps surprisingly, they failed to apply the 'harm' test to the third person involved in their own situation, Harriet Taylor's husband, John. The most striking instance of this lacuna came at the end of his life, when he was ill with cancer and asked Harriet not to leave England for France, where she planned to stay for three or four months. She replied to his request: 'Your saying that you are sorry I am going has given me ever since I read your note so *intense* a headache, that I can scarcely see to write—However, it is only one of the vexations I have to bear and perhaps everybody has.'[25] She departed in late December and when finally, at the end of March, she accepted that his condition was indeed serious, she wrote that, while she would have been willing to come back in other circumstances, she had to wait for Mill, whose own health was not good, to join her in late April for a three-week holiday. It was not, then, till mid-May, after a five-month absence, that she returned in time to give her husband care and attention for the last two months of his life. It is reasonable to guess that the unexpressed emotional pain that John Taylor felt must have weighed as much with him as the physical pain of his illness. However, the relevance of the 'harm principle' to their situation was lost not only to Mill and Harriet Taylor, but also to most subsequent commentators. This may well be because it is a different and more historically significant practical application of their views that has impressed philosophical historians. This came later, when they were finally free to marry.

For here, Mill sought to renounce the privileges that nineteenth-century English law gave him over his wife, writing a formal renunciation of the rights vested in him as a husband by the laws of the period. These rights extended, not only to a married woman's property, but also to any children of the marriage. As a demonstration of his dissent from the prevailing situation, Mill drew up a formal, although at the time not legally enforceable, document in which he said:

In the event of marriage between Mrs Taylor and me I declare it to be my will and intention, and the condition of the engagement between us, that she retains in all respects whatever the same absolute freedom of action, and freedom of disposal of herself and of all that does or may at any time belong to her, as if no such marriage had taken place; and I absolutely disclaim and repudiate all pretension to have acquired any rights whatever by virtue of such marriage.[26]

As it turned out, their long wait for the chance to formalize their relationship meant that their eventual married life together was almost as truncated as that of Godwin and Wollstonecraft. Both had reached a stage in life when they suffered various health problems, for which doctors prescribed extensive European travels. Their recommended therapy seemed never to coincide, so that their married life was a relationship of enforced separation and long-distance correspond-ence. Marriage itself, however, remained unchallenged by either Mill or Harriet Taylor; in their respect for Harriet's own marriage, they implicitly recognized the norms of faithfulness, exclusivity, and permanence. They also attempted—albeit possibly misguidedly—to include John Taylor in their conversations and interests. They did not seek the kind of emotional and psychological independence that had originally appealed to Godwin and Wollstonecraft, and indeed Harriet, in a draft essay on women, marriage, and divorce sent to Mill early in their relationship, wrote eloquently of love: 'Love in its true and finest meaning, seems to be the way in which is manifested all that is highest best and beautiful in the nature of human beings.'[27] But, in terms of practical policies, they were more concerned to promote, for women and men alike, a number of more purely political goals: legal rights, equality of opportunity, freedom of choice—especially the choice for women of either marrying or not marrying—and economic independence. Their own relationship was an equal and permanent intellectual and spiritual partnership.

This prompts a rather ambivalent judgement. Admirers of Mill and Harriet Taylor will argue that there *are* special relationships and that people can indeed find each other too late, when they have already taken a decisive step involving someone else, and they may be justified in choosing to pursue it. But, even if this were to be conceded in some circumstances, it must be said that many more deceive themselves about the importance of their later 'special relationship' than can genuinely claim it, and there is usually a price to be paid in other people's happiness. In the case of the Mills, John Taylor's position must have deprived him for life of most of what he might have expected from his marriage. Mill's later statement, then, renouncing the exploitative and controlling elements of marriage, has an irony of which he himself was clearly unaware; it was an eloquent statement of the weight to be attached to the competing rights of other people by one who was blind to the situation of one of the persons most closely involved in his own life.[28]

Jean-Paul Sartre and Simone de Beauvoir

The philosophy of sexual relations espoused both in their personal lives and in their writings by Jean-Paul Sartre (1905–80) and Simone de Beauvoir (1908–86) was a mid-twentieth-century libertarian one, although it pre-dated the sexual revolution of the 1960s and 1970s. Their lifelong relationship began in their student days, but they lived independent lives, never sharing a dwelling and never contracting a formal marriage.

The picture of their relationship that was formed by their contemporaries during their lifetime was an idealized one: here were two existentialist philosophers who, flouting conventional norms, agreed to accept each other's liaisons, to discuss them openly with each other, but nevertheless to maintain the priority and intellectual strength of their relationship to each other. Ultimately, however, the publication of de Beauvoir's letters to two of her lovers, Nelson Algren (letters from 1947–64) and Jacques-Laurent Bost (letters from 1937–40), revealed a very different picture in which she confided to Algren the limitations of Sartre as a lover and the weakness of their relationship.[29] These and other third-party revelations also showed the downside of what had seemed to intellectuals of the period so admirable: that their openness to other relationships was essentially exploitative of their young and vulnerable admirers, who often seem to have been used as no more than material for literary or philosophical exploration. Some of these brief lovers later came to see themselves as having been used as playthings, rather than, as they had, perhaps naively, expected, valued for themselves and as partners in a relationship of equals. But this was in fact a natural consequence of a philosophy that made a moral ideal out of the notion of the self-created personality—being yourself. As far as the area of sexual relationships is concerned, the self-created free personality independent of emotional ties who is at the heart of existentialist philosophy will, almost inevitably, give primacy to immediate inclination, and this is likely to mean moving from relationship to relationship. In place of serial monogamy—a popular option for some—the concept here is that of a multiplicity of relationships—one primary and many peripheral. While possibly satisfying for the key figures, it would be hardly surprising if the fringe participants—the invisible 'others'—were to see this as the product and practice of the emotionally anaesthetized, for whom they were 'non-persons'.

This is all the more surprising since the idea of the invisible 'other' was an important aspect of the philosophical position of both Sartre and de Beauvoir. De Beauvoir had sketched the concept in her novel *She Came to Stay* (*L'Invitée* (1943)): ' "It's almost impossible to believe that other people are conscious beings, aware of their own inward feelings, as we ourselves are aware of our own" said Françoise. "To me, it's terrifying when we grasp that. We get the impression of no longer being anything but a figment of someone else's mind." '

Although men can, of course, have this experience, it is on the whole women who are more likely to be ignored or dismissed as persons by other people. But de Beauvoir was also a feminist who had noted and disapproved of the fact that the lives of most women were defined by a male relationship—a father, or a husband. In *The*

Second Sex (Le Deuxième Sexe (1949)), she compares a woman's passive acceptance of her role in life ('immanence') with the existentialist ideal of freely creating your own. Like Sartre, she advocated the principle of authenticity, condemning the 'spirit of seriousness' that takes over when people allow their identity to be expressed in fixed values, qualities, and prejudices. In practice, however, this seemed to mean that a woman might be just as neglectful of the personhood of another woman as men are often accused of being.

For Sartre, too, the notion of self-creation was fundamental. As he put it in *Existentialism and Humanism (L'Existentialisme est un humanisme* (1946)): 'Man makes himself; he is not found ready-made; he makes himself by the choice of his morality, and he cannot but choose a morality, such is the pressure of circumstances upon him.'[30] For Sartre, too, this was linked to a division between self and others, and the view that 'others' might be unreal to the active self-creating existentialist self. To other people, he pointed out, I am myself just an object. This is how *they* see *me*. In other words, for other people, *I* am Other. This point, which de Beauvoir, too, had recognized, is expressed by Sartre with reference to 'the look'—being caught in someone else's gaze. It leads to a feeling of alienation and separateness from others that we would like to overcome but cannot. Each of us, then, is ultimately alone in the world. This means, too, that we can never recognize each other's freedom; the Kantian principle that others must be treated with respect as ends in themselves cannot be followed, and we must live with the conflict that entails. As one of the characters in Sartre's play *No Exit (Huis Clos* (1943)) puts it: 'Hell is other people.'

But if our perspective on others is limited and constrained, our concept of self is intoxicatingly untrammelled. In Sartre's famous phrase, 'existence precedes essence'. As far as morality is concerned, the bad thing to do, according to Sartre, is not to take advantage of this freedom, but to follow the crowd—to conform. We have, he said, 'neither behind us, nor before us ... any means of justification or excuse. We are left alone, without excuse.' We are 'condemned to be free'.[31]

Sartre died a philosophical icon, 50,000 people filling the streets of Paris for his funeral. De Beauvoir, too, was no less venerated for her life and work. It would be difficult to claim that their ideas for living had not worked well for them personally. But the existentialist ideals, together with the lifestyle they embodied, particularly in their implications for sexual and personal relationships, passed to a whole new generation. Supported by another existentialist influence, Niet-zsche's 'revaluation of values', the ultimately relativistic moral theory of existentialism that can be expressed in the slogan 'right for me' engendered a hedonistic sexual lifestyle that was transmitted as both ideal and routine by Western literary and artistic media aided by an entertainment and communications technology that swept the world.

Both its philosophical roots and its potential consequences were most clearly demonstrated in a courtroom in California in 1970. A cult had grown up around a charismatic but murderous individual, Charles Manson. Although in no serious sense a philosophical movement, it embraced the idea of liberation from conventional norms and pressures. At Manson's instigation, this was acted out in a peculiarly horrific mass murder. A party of friends, including the film actress Sharon Tate, who was nine months pregnant, were murdered by four members of the Manson 'Family' in the Los Angeles house of Tate's husband, the film director Roman Polanski. It is unlikely that any of those who carried out the killings did so with philosophical theory in mind. Nevertheless, the value-reversal embraced by some European intellectuals had become, by some subtle transformation, part of the Zeitgeist—the spirit of that time—and in words that were strangely evocative of the relativist root of existentialist moral theory, one of the accused did indeed declare in her defence: 'What I did was right for me.'[32]

Love and friendship

The contribution of philosophers, then, to reflection on the sexual and personal life of free and unencumbered adults—couples alone—has been mixed, and philosophers' own lives, as these famous examples show, often throw as much light on their views of sex, marriage, love, and friendship as their published writings.[33] In much contemporary philosophical discussion, in contrast, the themes of friendship and love are approached in a relatively detached and analytic spirit. The focus is on how such concepts are to be defined. How far, for example, is it the nature of romantic love to be exclusive and particular? Does 'love' behave like 'patriotism' in the sense that, just as patriotism is neces-sarily particular—there is no obligation to love other similar countries equally—there is one kind of love whose necessary object is just one particular person? If so, it follows that there can be no obligation to love equally anyone else who happens to share that person's desirable qualities—indeed, quite the opposite is the case. Once given to one person, this kind of love closes the door to other possible candidates. But most commentators would agree that friendship is different. There is no problem about having more than one friend, and neither is there any strong obligation to maintain casual friendships, although there are some friendships, especially same-sex friendships (not the same as same-sex sexual relationships), that generate a strong loyalty comparable to that of lovers or spouses. In the *Nicomachean Ethics*, Aristotle considers other aspects of friendship: at one level, friendship means wanting prosperity and happiness for a friend; at another, it is simply valuing one's friends' company and empathizing with their moments of joy or pain. Ultimately, there can be little doubt that friendship of this kind is a strong support for members of the human species and that Aristotle was right when he said: 'The human being is a social animal, and the need for company is in his blood.'[34]

Despite some similarities, then, love and friendship do seem to generate different moral expectations, with love undoubtedly the more powerful in its potential and its demands. Love, however, may seem to go beyond the purely personal and to make universal claims, of which some at least can be expressed in terms of duty and obligation. There is a respected ethical tradition that emphasizes the commonality of human beings—the liberal doctrine that all human beings are one family and all owe an equal debt of love and care to all the others. There is much to be said for this tradition. Indeed, the contemporary philosopher Raimond Gaita sees the love of persons—especially those who are the most difficult for us to love—as the foundation of universal human rights. He argues: 'Were it not for the many ways human beings genuinely love one another—from sexual love to the impartial love of saints—I do not believe we would have a sense of the sacredness of individuals, or of their inalienable rights or dignity.'[35]

Nevertheless, where love and loyalty are concerned, room has to be found for an alternative, or more partialist, view that recognizes the possibility of special and particular bonds. As Bernard Williams observes:

such things as deep attachments to other persons will express themselves in the world in ways which cannot at the same time embody the impartial view, and ... they also run the risk of offending against it. They run that risk if they exist at all; yet unless such things exist, there will not be enough substance or conviction in a man's life to compel his allegiance to life itself.[36]

Both Gaita and Williams are expressing a subtle but incontrovertible truth. People are not atoms in a void. Invisible bonds weave them into the social tapestry of groups and communities, fostering interdependence, mutual support and a willingness to join in common projects. But, whatever the nature of the bond, whether that of a co-enterprise of limited significance, a deep bond of friendship, or the strongest of love relationships, it opens up further challenges and choices for the individual: it may provide opportunities for heroism, but also for cowardice; for loyalty as well as for betrayal; it may be a burden, but it can at the same time be a support; a source of grief and pain, but also the door to the greatest human happiness.

Sometimes people find this too restrictive and want their freedom—from an unhappy marriage, a tyrannical political system, the demands of dependent children, or the tight demands of conventional employment; and sometimes, too, from religious, class, or ethnic allegiances that they want to renounce because they can no longer subscribe to their ethos or teaching. But the bond of marriage has several distinctive features. While some relationships come about through the accident of birth or as a result of social and economic pressures, this is a voluntary union created by the two partners. Once formed, it *becomes* a kind of quasi-biological bond, but one that gains that concreteness and substance by legal and social recognition. The law that creates marriage, then, can be seen as an artificial means of changing what was originally a non-binding and voluntary relationship into the same unrelinquishable category as biological family relationships, like those of parent and child. Marriage as an institutional arrangement is a legal creation, but, while biology may not determine the relationship, the pair-bond once formed is deeply biological. It is a natural phenomenon to be found in some members of other species, who share the same grief at parting or separation from their partner. The American philosopher Santayana hinted at this ultimate commonality of human and non-human animal when he speculated: 'if the beasts could speak they would give us, no doubt endless versions of the only joy in which, as we may fancy, the blood of the universe flows consciously through their hearts.'[37]

Love may well be, for many people, the special human expression of the pair-bond, and Santayana described its symptoms in a vivid passage: 'the joy of gazing on the beloved, of following or being followed, of tacit understandings and avowals, of flight together into some solitude to people it with those ineffable confidences which so naturally follow the outward proofs of love.'[38] Nevertheless, the elaborated concept of love familiar to Western traditions is not always recognized in other cultural traditions. Some are inclined to dismiss it as a by-product of Western individualist capitalism interwoven with its Christian, predominantly Puritan, inheritance. Other traditions, they argue, may recognize the occurrence of irrational passion, but they would not regard it as a basis for marriage. Indeed, there is within the Western tradition itself a perspective that sees romantic love as something more like a madness struck by the dart of a playful or malicious god. But, from the classical period to modern times, there has been a wealth of romantic poetry celebrating the idea of love as a timeless and transcendent emotion. Even in the more hard-wired context of contemporary poetry and popular songs, it is possible to find convincing and moving poetic expressions of this concept of love, as in this lyric of Ewan McColl: 'The first time I ever saw your face | I felt your heart so close to mine | And I knew our joy would fill the earth | And last till the end of time.'

Passion or promises? Ethical boundaries

For some people, however, the only principle that seems relevant to a couple relationship is that of pursuing personal pleasure—a hedonistic ethic that can easily become pure unadulterated egoism. But egoism works here only in the short term, for a person's sense of self is built, to a very considerable extent, on that person's sense of others in relation. Without that sentiment of care for close others, the sense of self-hood itself can shrivel away. Perhaps this was what Kant had in mind when he said: 'The sole condition on which we are free to make use of our sexual desire depends upon the right to dispose over the person as a whole—over the welfare and happiness and generally over all the circumstances of that person.' This is a stringent condition, but Kant adds the compensating thought: 'If I yield myself completely to another and obtain the person of the other in return, I win myself back.' [39]

The idea of what is due, however, cannot be limited simply to balancing shallow pleasures against longer-term more significant satisfactions. There are pressures of duty as well as of inclination, and passion often comes into conflict with principle, whether the principle involved is that of promise-keeping or that of loyalty, or even a Kantian respect for persons. It seems an unavoidable feature of human existence, at least when reflection on life takes the place of unreflective engagement with it, to experience the pull of these two poles, often felt as an ethical dilemma in which Kantian rigour in sticking to principle whatever the consequences comes into conflict with the calculation of ends and utility.

On the one hand, there is the fact that a good deal of human misery can be traced to the harsh and uncompromising application of principles in those intimate and private areas of life that are dominated by emotions and feeling. Marriage is based on a promise. But promises concerning personal feelings are exceptional, since they seem to involve a commitment to what is outside the promisor's control—continuing love and affection for another person. In all other circumstances, such a promise would be held to be invalid. But the uncontrollability of personal feeling has to be balanced against the fact that an intimate relationship is not one-dimensional—it is multifaceted. Fairness, honesty, and the degree of commitment involved in *intending* to keep a promise have a place. Without these, pure sexual hedonism would create a Hobbesian state of 'war of every man against every man' and, of course, every woman.

It would be possible to look for a solution in judging matters on a standard utilitarian basis—the basis, that is, of weighing the interests of some against those of others and opting for the most benefit-maximizing decision. This may seem to offer a route away from conflict, but its implications may not be what its defenders often assume. Even the individual may be best served by thinking less of immediate and short term satisfaction than of physical, emotional, and intellectual satisfaction from the perspective of a whole lifetime. But the utilitarian is committed to calculating benefit on a wider basis than just that of the central agent or even those few people most immediately concerned. Indeed, a utilitarian perspective should take into account the consequences for the wider community of the choices people make in their personal lives when these have unavoidable ripple effects.

But here the boundaries of the narrow focus on the couple and their relationship with each other begin to reveal themselves. Sexual morality has a broader social function that is connected to its orientation to the future, and it provides a reason that might not otherwise be compelling for people to be willing to sacrifice some of their own goods for the sake of future generations. As Roger Scruton observes: 'Sexual feeling acquires a solemn character, for the very reason that the unborn and the dead have an interest in it.'[40] As it happens, that is also the ethical consideration most relevant to marriage when it involves, not only the two principals, but also wider and broader family relationships.

ৡ 3

From philosophy to law

The idea that children make a difference is hardly new. Tradition has it that, when the Buddha was told of the birth of his child, he responded with the words: 'A fetter has been forged for me.' Nor is the idea that the difference may not be entirely positive—a view the idealist philosopher Arthur Schopenhauer certainly shared: 'Happy marriages are well known to be rare; just because it lies in the nature of marriage that its chief end is not the present but the coming generation.'[1] In this, he believed he saw a fairly tricky, indeed even malevolent, manoeuvre of nature itself: 'the sexual impulse, although in itself a subjective need, has the knack of skilfully assuming the mask of objective admiration and thereby deceiving our consciousness; for nature requires this stratagem to achieve its own purposes. But whenever two people fall in love, however objective and touched even by the sublime their admiration may seem, nature's sole intention is the procreation of an individual of specific qualities.'[2]

Others, however, can accept the possible (or metaphorical) purposefulness of nature without seeing this as detracting from the primary relationship of the two people concerned. Indeed, accepting the need to see our own role as humans in the wider context of nature as a whole is increasingly a point of view to be found in both environmental and feminist philosophy. It is also common to many religious traditions, and the Catholic philosopher John Finnis was setting out a widely held view of the matter when he wrote: 'The reason why marriage requires not just "a commitment to each other" but commitment to permanence and exclusiveness in the spouses' sexual union is that … it is fundamentally shaped by its dynamism towards, appropriateness for, and fulfilment in, the generation, nurture and education of children who each can only have two parents and who are fittingly the primary responsibility (and object of devotion) of those two parents. Apart from this orientation towards children, the institution of marriage, characterized by marital *fides* (faithfulness), would make little or no sense.'[3]

Finnis's point has very general force quite apart from the religious viewpoint from which he writes, and it will be understood by most of those who have experienced the close bond of parent–child relationships in their own lives, whatever their religious or metaphysical beliefs. It may also be understood by those who have for one reason or another missed out on that experience, especially when either the random blows of fate or the untrustworthiness of another person have deprived them of the experience of a parent–child relationship. There are a number of compelling reasons, then, for accepting the idea that children make a difference, and for many people the desire to have children is, in any case, a strong inner imperative. But this expansion of the aims of marriage beyond the couple to a family unit that includes their children expands the concept of family in other ways, too. It becomes the locus, not only of a socially recognized sexual relationship, but also of a wider network of connections, often economic, and usually involving a shared home. Sometimes the common roof alone can embody the conception of family, as Amy in T. S. Eliot's play *The Family Reunion* explains:

> If you want to know why I never leave Wishwood
> That is the reason. I keep Wishwood alive
> To keep the family alive, to keep them together,
> To keep me alive, and I live to keep them.

In general, though, other factors, more political than personal, are involved. This has made the issue of families as the locus for child-raising a matter of interest for politicians, family lawyers, and judges, as well as a fruitful field for research for sociologists, social anthropologists, and psychologists. Some of this research will inevitably form an important element in this discussion.[4] But the idea of marriage as a setting for the having and raising of children was a matter of philosophical and ethical interest long before humans began to see themselves as subjects not only for science, but also for social science, and it is best to recognize this priority by looking briefly first of all at what some of the most important philosophers in the Western tradition have had to say on this subject.

Philosophers' views have not always followed the conventions of their own time, let alone ours. The challenge that Plato offered to both of the two root ideas of family, the pair-bond and the relation between parents and their offspring, has echoed down the centuries. John Milton was an early advocate of divorce. His view of marriage was that it was for 'the apt and cheerful conversation of man with woman, to comfort and refresh against the evil of solitary life'. He entirely rejected the idea that it was for procreation, dismissing this as a 'gross and boorish opinion'.[5] Locke's conception of marriage as potentially a temporary contract that could come to a natural end when any children had grown up was revolutionary for his day, but it planted a seed that matured and flourished from the mid-twentieth century. The ideas of Kant and Hegel, in contrast, offer more support to traditional views, Kant seeing marriage as an example of an unbreakable promise, and Hegel regarding the family—parents and their children—as a mystical unity. Contemporary philosophers have approached the issue from a number of equally diverse viewpoints, some claiming that intimate and personal arrangements for having and raising children have no ethical or moral implications, some that it is a matter of utilitarian calculation—of estimating the social costs and benefits of different arrangements, others that the state should remain neutral on matters involving moral judgement or religious belief. Because the framework for today's debates has been set by these arguments, some long distant, it is worth stepping back, if only briefly, to gain a more complete picture of this philosophical background in order to see how it is reflected in the conflicting positions of today's opinion-formers and policy-makers.

Of all the philosophers of earlier times who have engaged with this issue, Plato undoubtedly held the most radical views. In the *Republic*, a portrait of his ideal political structure, he rejected the family structure altogether, at least for the ruling class. In their case, he proposed abolishing the notion of the parental pair in favour of state-directed mating festivals in which participants would be selected apparently by lot, but in fact on a eugenic basis, secretly ensuring that the fittest would have most opportunities to reproduce. And in order to allow women a full role in the government of the state, not only was marriage to be abolished, but the mother–child bond was to be broken as well. This was to be achieved by arranging that babies, who would be looked after in publicly provided nurseries, would be fed on a random and anonymous basis by women who had recently given birth and who would simply interrupt their professional duties for these nursing visits. Inevitably, there could be no father–child bond any more than a mother–child bond under these arrangements, which would eliminate altogether the power of the blood tie. In his old age, when he wrote the *Laws*, Plato seems to have given up these radical plans and to have accepted rather more conventional arrangements in which couples would be allowed the link with their offspring. In the *Laws*, eugenic goals were still important, but they emerged in a different way: in what was probably the earliest of state health and safety proposals, Plato recommended the appointment of inspectors to regulate couples' sexual behaviour and make sure that they did not conceive their offspring in a state of drunkenness.

Plato's picture of personal and procreative life had to wait till the contemporary period to find real-life models and actual experiments in group living. But before the new radicalism of the late twentieth and early twenty-first centuries saw practices that in many ways instantiated Plato's more extreme ideas, the modern era brought a number of new philosophical approaches more attuned to the needs of people in newly urbanized communities. Some philosophers were prepared to place a primary emphasis on the contractual element in marriage. The pioneer of this approach was Locke.

Lockean liberalism and the marriage contract

Adventurously for his time and setting, Locke was prepared to view marriage, which he regarded as a procreative venture, as potentially only a *temporary* contract for child-raising purposes, so that it would be right in principle to release the contractors from their obligations when their child-rearing duties came to an end. (The same idea also occurred to Hume, who thought that chastity as a moral ideal for the middle-aged woman could be justified only as setting a good example to the young, and not for its intrinsic merits).[6]

Locke's brief account of the family—conjugal society—was an integral aspect of his liberal individualist political philosophy, and it meshes surprisingly closely with some common contemporary perspectives. For Locke, the marriage partners retain their own individual identity throughout their relationship. They are not obliged to share a special 'pair' or 'couple' identity. The limitations placed on them as individuals are set only by the legitimate rights-claims of others: first each other, and then their children. Locke writes:

Conjugal society is made by a voluntary compact between man and woman, and though it consists chiefly in such a communion and right in one another's bodies as is necessary to its chief end, procreation, yet it draws with it mutual support and assistance, and a communion of interests too, as necessary not only to unite their care and affection, but also necessary to their common offspring, who have a right to be nourished and maintained by them till they are able to provide for themselves.[7]

Following the 'state of nature' when an anarchic and arbitrary individualism prevails—a starting point common to all the social-contract theorists—Locke spoke of two kinds of association as developing between these initially isolated and egotistically oriented individuals: conjugal society and civil society. For Locke, conjugal society, as a natural relationship, comes first, and civil society follows. His account of the basis of conjugal society is explicitly biological. Indeed it was Darwinian in a pre-Darwinian era. Locke makes a number of comparisons with the animal kingdom, explaining the brief pairing and parting of grass-eating mammals by the speed with which their offspring become self-sufficient, while, in the case of hunting and flesh-eating animals, the male's lengthier involvement with offspring and mother is explained by the longer time it takes for the young to be self-sustaining. In turning to the case of the human animal, Locke regards the continuous and hardly interrupted series of pregnancies that were the usual lot of the human female in his time, and the long period needed for raising and educating children, as the two factors that combined to make the survival of human offspring dependent on the long-term interest and participation of the male.

But here Locke's foray into sociobiology gives way to the fundamental political and ethical beliefs that his writings on government are designed to defend. Despite the frequent charge that these writings, as well as those of other contract theorists, have a male-oriented perspective, Locke advances a surprisingly egalitarian view of gender roles. Indeed, his general view of family relationships—not only those of husband and wife, but also those of parent and child—is generously inclusive. Men and women jointly share the headship of the society that the human species forms for procreative purposes, and the rights of parenthood belong to mothers as well as to fathers. As for parental power, that is 'nothing but that which parents have over their children to govern them, for the children's good, till they come to the use of reason'.[8] The power of the father, then, is by no means absolute, nor does the wife sacrifice her own rights in marriage but is left 'in the full and true possession of what by contract is her peculiar right, and at least gives the husband no more power over her than she has over his life'.[9] Other things being equal, though, and admitting that both partners will be older by this time, Locke suggests that the contract might be thought to have served its purpose and to come to an end when the youngest child reaches an age to be self-supporting.

This suggestion, however, transforms the picture Locke has painted up to this point. A modern commentator, Brian Trainor, points out that, if the roles of husband and wife are treated as merely 'outer' social roles to be taken on for a limited period and then discarded, like outworn clothes, when they no longer fit, it may turn out that 'the notions of "husband and wife as one in marriage" and "mutual lifelong fidelity" have been analysed out of existence and discarded along the way'.[10] Trainor's own view is that: 'The marital contract entered into by two individuals establishes the boundary of a shared universe which is *their* own and in which they subsequently live, move and have their being. The good of this shared world is their common concern ... .'[11]

Trainor's portrait of marriage will strike some readers as a description of a vanishing and possibly hypothetical golden age, and it is true that it is Locke's, rather than Trainor's, perspective that has come to represent the current state of marriage and the family. What Locke so tentatively advocates is a fact of life of contemporary society—and it raises now in reality, as it did then implicitly, new moral questions. What, for example, of the obligation of gratitude? For, whatever their respective roles in caring for and raising their children, or providing for their financial and practical support, the two individuals of Locke's conjugal society have incurred a mutual debt. This is something that Locke himself and those who share his view today seem to have overlooked. For Locke and his modern successors, the concept of lifelong union is an artificial legal imposition on individuals who should be free to separate when they wish. The 'default' position for this conception of family relations is change, choice, and continuing consent. For their critics, the default position is reversed: breakdown, separation, and divorce are artificial legal devices designed to modify a strong conception of marriage. But it is the Lockean perspective that is increasingly reflected in contemporary perceptions of the central family roles—particularly the view that sees the roles of husband, wife, parent, and child as socially constructed and mutable, rather than natural and immutable. Indeed, modern advocates of this view have gone further, changing the names themselves to reflect and reinforce their view: 'partner' replacing 'husband' or 'wife', 'parent' replacing 'mother' or 'father', while 'carer' may be preferred to any of these progenitor terms, since they all imply a biological status. In formal language, it is a shift from status to contract. The basic challenge is also considerably reinforced with the possibilities opened up by new reproductive technologies that separate first conception from sex and then parenting from genetic relationships.[12] But, if Locke was the historic originator of the flexible family, Kant is the unbending standard-bearer for the idea of the promise-keeping basis of marriage, and, given these spreading implications, it would be useful to compare Locke's theory with the very different view of the marriage contract developed by Kant.

Kant and the marriage promise

In contrast to Locke, Kant appears to have regarded marriage more as a sexual than a family-founding arrangement. He also saw it as a paradigm instance of an unbreakable promise. For Kant, as for Locke, the partners in a marriage are independent contractors (technically, juridical parties to a formal contract). But whereas, for Locke, the conjugal relationship arose out of the state of nature and provided a foundation for civil society, Kant regards the existence of civil society as a prior condition for the possibility of the marriage contract. This is because the marriage contract is only one instance, although perhaps the most important instance, of the institution of promising—something that makes sense only within, not outside of, civil society. For Kant, the notion of promise-keeping is very strongly construed, and the argument by which he supports his conception of promising has as much the force of logic as of morality. It is tested by a thought experiment in which would-be promise-breakers test the coherence of their own intentions by trying to conceive of promise-breaking as a universal policy of others as well as themselves. Kant argues that the thought experiment breaks down in contradiction, for it is just not possible coherently to conceive of making a promise while at the same time allowing for the possibility of deciding later on not to keep it.

Kant's argument is often dismissed as an error—indeed, something not even to be taken seriously, especially when he suggests that the marriage contract establishes each partner's ownership of the other's 'sexual attributes' and that a runaway spouse could rightly be brought back by force. The fact is, though, that the present state of marriage in the Western world offers some empirical justification for Kant's argument. Kant regards the engagement to marry as 'the most serious and the most inviolable engagement between two persons and binds them for life'.[13] But it is now legally impossible to make such a binding commitment—divorce is available whether the partners want it to be or not—while the prenuptial contract is the *reductio ad absurdum* of today's legally limited contract. Its very existence appears to nullify the promise that is being made. Compare this approach to marriage with, for example: 'Lend me that large sum of money and I promise I will repay it unless, of course, circumstances change and I decide not to.' Possibly the reason that the logical force of Kant's argument is not more widely recognized is simply that in practice an institution can maintain a precarious survival for as long as deviations from it are confined to a few. But it may be that, if the balance shifts too far, and many people deviate from the norm, there comes a point when the logic of the situation imposes itself and the institution itself collapses. This point may well have been reached in some Western societies today.[14]

Kant also moves further from Locke on another issue. Like Locke, he is prepared to accept that the two persons in a marriage do still keep their separate identity and their individuality in some respects. Indeed, he argues that it is only in the framework of a marriage contract that a person can retain his or her bodily integrity. However, he believes this produces a 'unity of will'. For sex is only one aspect of a human being, and 'If one devotes one's person to another, one devotes not only sex but the whole person; the two cannot be separated.... In this way the two persons become a unity of will. Whatever good or ill, joy or sorrow befall either of them, the other will share in it.'[15]

Nevertheless, Kant, too, has some largely unrecognized claim to be seen as a proto-feminist. He decries the partial and narrow view of a man who sees a woman just as a woman—as a sex object—and not as a human being. On the contrary, he says that there is an absolute equality of the two partners, for each gives as much as the other. Each may use the other as a sex object, just because this very mutuality of use makes it non-exploitative. It is not a one-sided contract, although Kant recognizes that there are other, more exploitative, kinds of sexual relationship that are indeed one-sided and so, from a moral point of view, unsatisfactory. But it would be a mistake to divorce Kant's perspective on marriage from its broader context in his whole moral philosophy. And perhaps in the end his most important contribution on the subject of marriage lies in the fundamental principle of respect for each human person, that he expressed in the rule—the categorical imperative—that no one should be used simply as a means for someone else's ends.

There are different ways to interpret the idea of contract as a fundamental feature of marriage, and different consequences can be drawn from it. Nevertheless, it is understandable that critics might see the idea of contract as an intrusion into the personal world of trust and affection, and it seems that this was the reaction of some of Kant's contemporaries, including, in particular, Hegel.

Hegel and the 'Mystical Union' of the family

Hegel was amongst the first to argue against a narrow and legalistic interpretation of the marriage contract, and he set out to develop more fully a holistic and organic view of marriage and family. While he saw the family as a natural biological entity, he also saw it as an ethical and spiritual entity imbued with purpose and direction. It is the family, with its ceremonies and observances, that enables people to transcend their own death and that of their loved ones, seeing them as stages in the life of the family.

Recapturing as it did what was in effect the traditional account of marriage as expressed in the Christian marriage ceremony, the picture painted by Hegel was of two people who, through marriage, surrender their individuality to forge a common identity. In his words, 'though marriage begins in contract, it is precisely a contract to transcend the standpoint of contract, the standpoint from which persons are regarded in their individuality as self-subsistent units'.[16] The process of transcending contract is at once both self-restricting and liberating. But, while it describes what should happen in the case of the couple's relationship to each other, it is not meant to apply to their children.

They retain their claims as individual persons. They are not things and cannot be anybody's property—whether of their parents or of anyone else. As Hegel sums up his own position in an Addition to *The Philosophy of Right*:

Marriage is in essence an ethical tie. Formerly, especially in most systems of natural law, attention was paid only to the physical side of marriage ... This is crude enough, but it is no less so to think of it as only a civil contract, and even Kant does this. On this view, the parties are bound by a contract of mutual caprice, and marriage is thus degraded to the level of a contract for reciprocal use. A third view of marriage is that which bases it on love alone, but this must be rejected like the other two, since love is only a feeling and so is exposed in every respect to contingency, a guise which ethical life may not assume. Marriage, therefore, is to be more precisely characterized as ethico-legal [*rechtlich sittliche*] love, and this eliminates from marriage the transient, fickle, and purely subjective aspects of love.[17]

This summarizes the views set out more substantially in the main body of *The Philosophy of Right*:

In substance marriage is a unity, though only a unity of inwardness or disposition; in outward existence, however, the unity is sundered in two parties. It is only in the children that the unity itself exists externally, objectively, and explicitly as a unity, because the parents love the children as their love, as the embodiment of their own substance ... a process which runs away into the infinite series of generations, each producing the next and presupposing the one before.[18]

Hegel's recognition of the way the family functions as a chain linking generations has led to criticism from several different directions. Postmodernist feminist writers and critical theorists reject what they see as his biological essentialist views both of the family and of the function of women within the family.[19] But there is something very modern about Hegel's portrait of women's bond with nature and their function in the ongoing process of death and regeneration, their mediating role between the living and the dead. So some feminist writers are more sympathetic to Hegel's holistic view of the family as an ethical and spiritual entity with a unity of purpose.[20]

Unlike Kant, and surprisingly, given his strong view of marriage as a quasi-mystical union, Hegel says that marriage is not an absolute state. It is potentially dissoluble, but 'legislators must make its dissolution as difficult as possible'.[21] Although he does not say this explicitly, the fact of children must be at least part of the reason why divorce should be made difficult, for, he says, 'the parents possess in their children the objective embodiment of their union'.[22]

Nevertheless, Hegel, like Kant and Locke, was ready to agree that there is a contractual basis to marriage, even if he differed in thinking that it went considerably beyond this. Indeed, of these three philosophers, only Locke seemed prepared to adopt a minimalist view of marriage as contract. Given his position as the founding father of the form of liberalism that seeks to minimize legislative interference with individual choice, and as the author of a formulation of the rights of individuals that subsequently came to be embodied in a number of international declarations, it seems likely that Locke, in common with some liberal theorists today, may have judged a minimalist view of the marriage contract to be necessary as a matter of consistency.

From theory to actuality

Philosophical thinking about questions of sexual and family relationships in more recent times has followed these underlying currents in different directions. Some contemporary philosophers place human sexual behaviour outside the realm of ethics and morality, although they may allow that general moral principles such as honesty, loyalty, kindness, and consideration apply, or alternatively that utilitarian calculation has a place. In some cases, this backing-away from moral judgement may be based on broader ethical and political grounds. These might include, for example, the libertarian belief that the state should not interfere in the private life of individuals—a principle that has led some democrats to hold that the state should be neutral in matters of values and morality. On the other hand, some socialist thinkers who take Marx as their starting point favour value neutrality in this area, because they connect sexual ethics with bourgeois morality and an oppressive social class. Critical social theory, described by Anthony Giddens as a movement that sets out to 'outflank Marx from the Left', may see the issue primarily in gender terms and so take as one of its major aims the feminist goal of eliminating sexual oppression.[23] As Giddens sees it, this means recognizing marriage and the family as no more than 'shell institutions'—institutions, that is, whose basic character has fundamentally changed, even though they continue to be called by the same name.[24] The contemporary spectrum of views, then, includes some who want to maintain a distance from judgement or who look for more flexibility in the way sexual life is lived and others who aim at a complete rewriting of the concept of the family.

But most of these positions are based on taking the wishes of adults as central, and they fail to address one important question: what are the implications of these philosophical views for the least powerful individuals who make up the family—the children? Childhood is a stage of vulnerability through which everyone must pass in order to reach adulthood, and even the minimal state—for example, that described in Robert Nozick's *Anarchy, State and Utopia*—has a responsibility to protect the vulnerable.[25] So, if it seems that children's rights and interests are ignored or set aside either by liberal theories about adult relationships that treat choice as a free-standing phenomenon, or by Marxist doctrines based on a class-based analysis of society that discount the importance of small institutions like the family, this is something that should play a major, rather than an ancillary, role in the debate about the family.[26]

However, as I argue later, a considerable body of research confirms the view that formal marriage, recognized and preserved through time, is the best protection children can have in their growing years. A large body of research, which controls for such variables as income, race, and family background, has been assembled from the 1970s on, leading to a broad consensus amongst a majority of family theorists from widely diverse parts of the political spectrum that children do better when brought up by their natural parents who are married to each other. Not only that, but communities in which children and parents are living together in this formal relationship are better places to live.[27]

But, if it is not true that all child-raising alternatives have equal validity, the institutional aspect of marriage—the fact that it is a relationship entered into publicly, and authenticated by legal arrangements that have been carefully considered, understood, and accepted by the parties concerned—creates a gap between this and a purely transitory sexual encounter that needs some explanation.

Marriage as a Ulysses contract

One way to account for the difference might be to reorient our thinking about the commitment involved in marriage and to conceive of it as a kind of Ulysses contract—a contract, that is, that includes relinquishing the right to change your mind. Ulysses, warned against the dangers of sailing past the legendary Sirens who lured sailors to their death by the beauty of their singing, but anxious nevertheless to hear that wonderful sound, asked his crew members, whose own ears he had stopped with wax, to tie him to the mast and, no matter how he might signal to them to be set free, to leave him bound by those cords. This voluntary binding, which is intended to hold in all the contingencies of life—sickness or health, wealth or poverty, is the kind of foundation that indissoluble marriage vows can provide. Most have, in fact, accepted it in the past. But a shift has taken place from recognizing the need for divorce as a ground for relief in difficult situations, or when one partner is gravely at fault, to one in which the wish of just one of the partners to end the marriage can prevail in a relatively short time. This change, which has a much weaker ethical basis, may well be due more to the advocacy of social leaders, lawmakers, and intellectuals than to any slowly accruing pressure from public opinion. But, if the idea of law as an active agent of change would be welcome to some political and legal theorists, there are grounds for taking a more conservative view.

One early expression of such a countercurrent was famously provided by the British judge Patrick Devlin. Devlin insisted that law should not attempt to lead public opinion, but to follow it, and that slowly. He regarded the institution of monogamous marriage as foundational for English law, arguing that it is part of the fabric of British society, and part of the Judaeo-Christian heritage in which English law is ultimately grounded. He did not see this as meaning that divorce should be impossible in all circumstances. On the contrary, he wrote: 'I believe that our morality still dislikes the idea of marriage not being taken very seriously. It expects the parties to intend a lifelong union and to be willing to sacrifice much to the fulfilment of that intention, but it thinks that spouses who have done their best and failed should be allowed to try again.'[28] Nevertheless, for anyone who might wish to reject the foundational assumptions of marriage as an institution, Devlin's answer was: 'if he wants to live in the house, he must accept it as built in the way in which it is.'[29]

Public opinion has moved forward in the succeeding half century to a point where even Devlin's liberal opponents at that time might have hesitated. The narrow claim, though, remains. A conception of marriage that leans more towards Ulysses-style impregnability provides a framework within which not only the two principals, but children too, can be secure in their role and confident in their future. Objectors may point out that this presupposes a good relationship between children and their parents—something that can never be guaranteed—and may produce a conflict between the state and its representatives, on the one hand, and parents on the other. That is an argument that must be taken up later. First, though, there is a second and distinctive source of theorizing that has influenced contemporary perspectives on personal relationships probably more than any of the views described in this chapter. For these views, mainly of male authors, have made assumptions about the roles of men and women that are now radically challenged from a feminist perspective.

ℰ 4

Feminist aims, family consequences

The portrait of today's family is a mosaic built up from a variety of ingredients. But one major contribution to the changing fortunes of the family that must be added to this picture is the contribution made by developing philosophical perspectives on the role and position of women, spearheaded in the Western democracies by an emerging body of feminist thinking about gender roles and reproductive choices. Some of this philosophical thinking has been radical and rejectionist. It has taken the form of a demand for equality that cuts across traditional structures and expectations, especially those embedded in the concept of family, although there are other tendencies, too, within the feminist movement, that involve a more cautionary attitude to social change.

Women's oppression: The original diagnosis

Since militant feminism is often depicted as a force that has appeared only in the last few decades—perhaps only since the 1960s—and then mainly to be a thorn in the flesh of the conservative right, it is worth recalling that it is, as an ideology and a movement, very much older than this. Already in the fifth century BC, Plato had recognized that women could be men's equals in capacities and potential. Significantly, too, Plato also understood that, if that potential was to be released, this might have dramatic implications for the restructuring of society. And while he had other broader reasons for prescribing communal living for the Guardians of his Republic, Plato clearly believed that equality for women was incompatible with individual family life and indeed with individual homes and possessions. In other words, children would have to become the business of the state if the state was to become the business of women.

It is true, though, that Plato's ideas remained in the realm of philosophical fantasy until the modern period, when feminist reflection on the respective roles of women and men took, as its starting point, some rather more practical concerns than any desire to exercise power in a Platonic utopia. Dominating these concerns was the central fact that, because they were not easily able to earn a living independently, women were, with few exceptions, confined to roles determined by relationship, especially those of daughter, wife, or mother. The focus of a woman's life was the family into which she was either born or married. As Mary Wollstonecraft, the pioneer of the Western feminist movement, noted, this meant that a woman's view of the world she lived in was necessarily restricted: 'Females ... denied all political privileges, and not allowed as married women, excepting in criminal cases, a civil existence, have their attention naturally drawn from that of the whole community to that of the minute parts.'[1] Mary Wollstonecraft was herself an exception to this rule. Indeed, it may have been the claim to be recognized as an equal in potential to men in matters outside the family, as much as her own financial needs, that encouraged her, in the society of eighteenth-century London, to struggle with the challenge of being the sole support of herself and her daughter.[2]

Early feminism, then, was already familiar with the idea that women could achieve genuine equality only if the path to providing for their own economic needs by other means than marriage was not arbitrarily barred to them. But it was the claim to political rather than economic equality that led later feminists—in America, the women who gathered in Seneca Falls, NY, in 1848 at the birth of the American Women's Rights Movement, and in Britain, individual activists such as Harriet Taylor and John Stuart Mill, followed later by the suffragette movement—to focus on achieving political change through the narrower goal of equal voting rights. Many of those who sympathized with the cause of women's advancement at the time, including some feminist activists themselves, shared this goal, and a core element in the liberal agenda continued to be the belief that women's liberation was a matter of political justice and rights, especially the right to political recognition at the ballot box. It is one of the ironies of history that it was the economic rather than the moral argument that ultimately won the battle for recognition of women's claims to equality, for it was the need to use women's labour and capacities to maintain the home front in wartime that ultimately demonstrated that women could in fact take on many of the roles that had, until then, been the unique preserve of men.

These broader political moves, though, did not affect perceptions of the more personal and intimate aspects of relations between the sexes, and marriage could still be seen, as indeed Mill and Harriet Taylor did see it, as an equal and permanent intellectual and spiritual partnership between the sexes. Arguments for the emotional independence of women from men, and of men from women, had to wait for the twentieth century, when feminist analysis began to identify itself with the existentialist idea—for which in this context Simone de Beauvoir was the most eloquent advocate—that the freedom that women were seeking was an individual trophy—a prize that could be achieved only by a self-creating free personality, focused on self-development, inward-looking, and independent of emotional ties beyond those of immediate inclination.[3] For earlier feminists, love and loyalty, not to mention romance, retained their psychological appeal. Indeed Mary Wollstonecraft herself had both bravely and eloquently committed herself to these abstractions when she wrote: 'It is far better to be often deceived than never to trust; to be disappointed in love than never to love.'[4]

But, if the perspective of liberal feminism retained the basic framework of family relationships intact, even as Mill was challenging Victorian England's assumptions about the status of women another and very different analysis of the family was taking shape. This was the Marxist account of the family as a weapon of bourgeois domination: an essential tool for the political and economic structuring of a class-based society and the keystone of an ideology that was summed up in the phrase 'capitalist patriarchy'. The picture painted by Engels in *The Origins of the Family: Private Property and the State* was of the family as an institution in which women and children were assigned the status of property, with ownership vested in their male relatives.[5] The point of the system, according to Engels, was to benefit men by enabling them to hand down their property to offspring they could identify as their own. In this context, he argued, women's position was that of an exploited underclass whose role was the reproduction of further generations of workers and their capitalist exploiters.

Both these rival analyses from the nineteenth century have extended their influence to the present day. For some feminists who accept at least the spirit of the socialist analysis and for some, too, in the liberal tradition, they have led to the conclusion that the key to freeing women from the cycle of servitude is their liberation from economic dependence on individual men. They see two interlocking policies as a way of achieving this: one is the transfer of unavoidable dependency to the state, the other, the introduction of legally enforceable equality and anti-discrimination policies. The goal is a society in which private domestic cares, obligations, and ties are transferred to the public sphere, and all doors in public life are open to women. In practical terms, the first of these aims can be translated into a demand for the public provision of childcare and the all-day crèche, while the second involves significant changes in workplace practice and employment law. In both cases, it is easy to overlook the question of how these policies stand up in terms of broader and wider feminist interests. But it is worth considering the issue briefly from this point of view.

Transferring dependency

There are times in the lives of most women when they cannot easily be financially independent themselves. Of these, the most obvious is when they are having children and caring for them. So it is understandable that women might see substituting dependence on the state—the body of taxpayers—for dependence on a husband or partner as a short cut to achieving personal autonomy. But, as early as 1929, Bertrand Russell realized that this might have broader political implications. As he noted in *Marriage and Morals*: 'If the State were to adopt the role of the father, the State would, *ipso facto*, become the sole capitalist. Thoroughgoing Communists have often maintained the converse, that if the State is to be the sole capitalist, the family, as we have known it, cannot survive.'[6]

Russell's insight into the implications for families of social and political change along these lines were remarkable in anticipating the consequences of much legislation not even conceived of at that date. He noted: 'It would...with a slight change in our economic institutions, be possible to have families consisting of mothers only...It may be—and indeed I think it far from improbable—that the father will be completely eliminated before long, except among the rich...In that case, women will share their children with the State, not with an individual father.'[7] He went on to speculate about the psychological impact this might have on men. Men would, he thought, be less interested in the past, losing their sense of the continuity of historical traditions; at the same time, their perspective on the future would change and they would find it difficult to take an interest in anything after their own death. Sex would become a trivial matter, wars of defence less of an imperative, and work would lose its appeal. All this he attributed to the loss of the biological purpose of fatherhood, which he saw as being to protect children while they were growing up. When this biological function is taken over by the state, he said, 'the father loses his *raison d'etre*'.[8]

What Russell might have added, but did not, is that the transfer of responsibility for the family from the individual to the state does not in fact make women *independent*—it merely makes their dependency more diffuse. They are still being supported by others, but no personal relationship is involved. So, as far as the transfer of responsibility is concerned, recourse to the taxpayer only obscures the real issues, for the inevitable and natural stage of dependency around childbirth and early child-raising—inevitable at least under modern conditions—is something that affects all but a small minority of women who are wealthy through inheritance or through their own high earning capacity.

Nevertheless, most governments in the Western democracies have taken steps in this direction, whether for ideological reasons or because of genuine sympathy for women and children caught up in poverty or hardship. Social commentators have only recently come to challenge the policy by recognizing the risk that it involves, for women and children themselves, of trapping them in a cycle of dependency.[9] The principle involved here can be put quite briefly: that compassionate assistance in solving the individual's problems can destroy the rules of socially acceptable conduct that keep down the overall number of cases. Appealing to the social principles that John Stuart Mill set out in his *Principles of Political Economy*, Norman Dennis writes: 'Individual assistance must be rendered to all "hard cases", but never in a form that attracts people into the conduct that created their problem in the first place.'[10] Dennis argues that, when problems are created by misfortunes over which the individual has had no control, family and friends will rally round to help. But 'those who have created their own problems by making choices they need not have made must never be put in a position of being able to count upon assistance from the community in general which will make them as well off as those who have prudently and perhaps with difficulty acted in conformity with the requirements of institutionalised conduct'.[11]

Added to this is the fact that divorce was at one time a recourse only of the rich, but, when the state steps in to support a first, or even a second, family, it is not surprising that it becomes an easy and popular option. But, while it frees the primary earner from responsibility, the vast majority of the families left behind following divorce do suffer adverse social and financial consequences.[12]

Equalising opportunities

If the transfer of dependency is something of a two-edged sword as far as women are concerned, the case for opening up opportunities for women by anti-discrimination legislation and equal-opportunities policies in employment seems less problematic. It can be put in these terms: opposition to unfair patronage and preferment has a long and distinguished history, and privilege by reason of birth is just as objectionable if it is sex based as it would be if it were based on the more ancient and traditional preferments of social caste, connection, and class. Freedom can indeed be breached if someone finds herself consistently unable to work, or repeatedly passed over in appointments in favour of inferior rivals, on no other basis than a set of assumptions made because those rivals are male. Mill called this the problem of 'ascribed statuses', and it is this that constitutes the *prima facie* case for women's rights. But, while the *principle* is unassailable, the fact is that today a huge and expanding anti-discrimination industry has grown up, imposing heavy financial costs on society in general and, in effect, turning the principle on its head. For, while the complacent and open operation of prejudice is wrong, and being prevented from earning a living is indeed a significant harm in itself, laws intended to protect individuals from this harm may turn out to have unintended adverse consequences for women themselves, through the risk that employers will see them as a potential burden to an enterprise. Another less often recognized risk is that they may also impose costs on another and less high-profile class or group—the single or childless workers who may be asked to cover for unpredictable absences or to work unsocial hours and accept unfavourable holiday arrangements.

There are other practical considerations, too, to be brought into the picture. Advocates of equal treatment too easily assume that the claimants *are* bringing an equal contribution to the workplace, but this is, for good and obvious reasons, very often not the case. Women with family responsibilities are very often *not* in as strong a position as the unattached. They will often prefer less money for less responsibility, less workplace stress, shorter hours, the ability to be absent at short notice or no notice at all. Men, too, sometimes find themselves in situations in which they would be willing to make a trade-off in these terms. A sick wife or child, dependent elderly parents, partner desertion or death, or personal psychological or physical difficulties are all situations in which a rigid absence from home from eight in the morning to six at night five days a week—or, worse still, shift work or unsocial hours—may be just as much of a problem for a man to cope with as is the typical 'woman's' problem of caring for young children. Simple considerations of fairness would suggest that it should be possible for people of either sex to negotiate an employment contract that takes needs like these into account, but at whatever reduced rate of pay the employer would consider fair compensation for agreeing to take on an employee whose contribution to the enterprise is likely to be handicapped by personal factors.

The claim that what a person is offering is as good as what someone else is offering must in any case be distinguished from the very different claim that, while that individual's contribution is of lesser value, no fault attaches to that fact, and that person should not be cut off from the possibility of earning a living. This, after all, was the thinking that lay behind legislation to compel employers to take on a percentage of disabled workers in Britain following the major wars of the twentieth century.[13] There was no pretence that a man who had, for example, lost a leg in military service could function just as efficiently in every occupation as a man who had survived the war without injury; nevertheless, there was a strong public will not to leave people who had made such sacrifices for their country on the scrap heap of unemployment.

To recognize this is not to abandon the basic axiom of equality, and, where subsequent equality and antidiscrimination legislation is concerned, the principle that women who *are* prepared to offer genuinely equal work should be guaranteed equal treatment is ethically incontestable. But the understanding should be that the equality of input offered is the same as that offered by many men, who would regard it as their own and their partner's, not their employer's problem, that households depend on shopping and cooking being accomplished, and that sick children need to stay home from school; that the school day is shorter than the typical working day, and so on. Some women *will* want to have these special needs taken into account, and that is also a valid choice. But what is *not* reasonable is to ask for special consideration *and* equal pay. This even applies to the issue—often regarded as sacrosanct—of maternity leave: it is unreasonable to deny that a prolonged absence at an unplanned time can leave an organization in disarray, and unreasonable, therefore, not to acknowledge that there is a cost to be attached to this. The issue is not whether or not maternity leave should be available, but how the cost of predictably interrupted service should be calculated, and also how it should be met.

Some advocates of affirmative action, though, ignore or brush aside such considerations. Of course, if 'affirmative action' simply means taking steps to encourage diversity of applicants for a job or a training course, then there can be no objection. But, if it is taken to mean preferential treatment to correct an imbalance in numbers, this is a different matter. There is no need to assume institutional or personal bias if a group is not proportionately represented in every desirable occupation or training course. Personal choice also comes into the matter, and, as long as a significant number of women are willing to trade money or status for a more rounded life with room for personal and family time, statistics will show a lack of proportion in the number of women in prestige positions. The fact is, though, that it is as bad to choose someone because she is female (though not as good as someone else who is male) as to choose someone because he is male (though not as good as someone else who is female). It is doubtful, in any case, whether women actually *need* affirmative action in order to progress in today's world; and true that, as a policy, it can in fact harm women who achieve success through their own efforts and abilities by casting doubt on that achievement.

Here a striking paradox has to be recognized—that many of the freedoms sought by today's feminists turn out either to be constraints themselves, or at least to generate other constraints. Very often, too, these freedoms incur costs that must be paid by others—the vulnerable groups old and young whose well-being is on the whole more likely to be protected by a secure family structure. It is right to be wary of freedoms that generate either hidden constraints for those who claim them, or unintended costs for others. This is particularly so where the demand for individual freedom becomes a demand for the state to take over the traditional role of the family. Feminist demands for female freedom often run counter to traditional liberal demands for a reduction in the involvement of state agencies in personal and private life. In this case the price paid for the freedom of one sex may be too high if bought at the cost of important freedoms of both sexes.

This debate has broader political implications. Given the permanent tendency of human beings to construct hierarchies of power, and given pressures for conformity, there is an important role for institutions that cut across political, economic, and social hierarchies. Of these institutions, the family as a biological and natural network is one of the most powerful. While it can itself be repressive in some cultural contexts, it nevertheless remains the ultimate bulwark again depersonalized totalitarian regimes.

Reclaiming motherhood

One feminist interpretation of the family is incompatible with this account of the social role of the family, because it leans towards an interpretation of gender equality and gender roles that largely discounts its biological structure. Although it has grown out of the Marxist analysis, this more radical feminist account tells a different story about the nature of women's subjection. Where Marxists see it as class based, this feminist position detaches the patriarchal thesis from its broader historical and economic roots to offer an analysis that is wholly gender based. The case that is made is that in *all* forms of social organization, not only bourgeois capitalism, men have exploited and dominated women. Antoinette Stafford summarizes the position and its exponents in these terms: 'Via a complex "genealogy" of women's oppression, such thinkers as Andrea Dworkin, Adrienne Rich, and Mary Daly point out how, in cultural phenomena ranging from pornography and prostitution to religion, marriage, motherhood and heterosexuality, the patriarchal culture has imposed male power on its female victims.'[14] The practical conclusion to be drawn from this is, in the words of another feminist commentator, that 'any definition of feminism must see it above all as a social and political force, aimed at changing existing power relations between women and men'.[15]

This form of feminism paints a picture in which the care of children is seen as an obstacle to a woman's self-fulfilment, and the domestic sphere as, at best, a gilded cage. At its most extreme, the rejection of motherhood takes the shape sketched out by Shulamith Firestone in *The Dialectic of Sex,* in which the mystique of motherhood has been drained away by a technology that has turned childbirth into a detached and impersonal technical procedure.[16] While the technologizing of childbirth is indeed an anti-woman development of the modern age, Firestone takes her argument further and challenges even the claim that there is a natural tendency for men and women to form close personal bonds, whether with each other or with their offspring. And, far from condemning technological reproduction, she offers as an ideal a society in which artificial reproduction has released women, and men too, not only from their bonds to each other, but also from the deep bond of the parent–child relationship. This is part of a broader thesis that finds the ultimate solution to exploitative gender relations in androgyny—the elimination of gender differentiation.

Given that this so conspicuously fails to fulfil the psychological need many people feel for relationships of deep intimacy—to find, if they can, for as long as they can, the love and trust of another human being, whether partner or child—it is hardly surprising that a new wave of feminist theorists has begun to take a more sympathetic view of the family, even if it is one that is qualified by a degree of reinterpretation of the concept itself. For whatever reason, by the 1980s revisionist feminists had already begun reappraising the feminist programmes of the 1960s and 1970s in relation to the family. Perhaps this was to be anticipated, for, as Hilde Lindemann Nelson points out, most feminists were themselves raised in families and go on to form families of their own in adult life.[17] This marks a shift in the feminist perspective towards a more considered view that recognizes the centrality of children in many women's lives. Nor does women's relationship with their children end with their early years. Indeed, the fact that women have a long span of life after their biological procreative role ends has prompted research that suggests that there is an identifiable practical value to grandchildren of an involved grandmother. All this helps to support the claim that the campaign of some feminists to reclaim motherhood has some basis in sociobiological reality. Reviewing this bid historically, Diana Tietjens Meyers writes: 'Central to the overall critique developed at the beginning of second-wave feminism was a critique of motherhood. The economic disadvantages were documented, the missed opportunities for personal fulfilment were chronicled; the undercurrent of social contempt for motherhood was exposed.' But, she says, motherhood was later reconceived and revalued partly through feminist counterfigurations. She continues: 'For motherhood to be reclaimed, it must be refigured in ways that express auspicious meanings, like gladly bestowing life on and/or caring for a precious child.'[18]

Others, too, including some of those who had provided the original inspiration for the feminist movement of the 1960s and 1970s contributed their voice to this critique. Betty Friedan, whose book *The Feminine Mystique* had been a seminal influence on that movement, was now prepared to define the family, not as a reactionary relic, but as 'that last area where one has any hope of individual control over one's destiny, of meeting one's basic human needs, of nourishing that core of personhood threatened by vast impersonal institutions and uncontrollable corporate and government bureaucracies'.[19] Germaine Greer, too, redrew the portrait of women's destiny that she had painted in her iconic publication of the 1970s *The Female Eunuch* in *The Whole Woman*—a publication that just caught the close of the twentieth century. [20]

These revisions have done little, though, to mitigate the impact on the family of some legislative responses to pressure for gender equality. The consequence for many working mothers has been that work is no longer seen as an option, but rather as a necessity, while the psychological sense of security of family members, especially but not only the children, is undermined by escalating figures for divorce and family breakdown.

The global perspective

At the same time, in other parts of the world, and in other subcultures within the Western democracies, the family as a child-centred unit remains robust, and it is hardly surprising that Western feminism is viewed with suspicion. For this, the feminist movement itself is partly to blame, even if this unsympathetic view is partly only a matter of perception and based on an outdated view of what Western feminism involves. But even later feminist reappraisal of the family remains a localized rethinking within a movement that did indeed initially tend to ignore the position of women in other parts of the world. It had paid scant attention, for example, to the situation of women in Eastern Europe under communism, or in China with its one-child policy, or in other parts of the non-Western world where religion and cultural traditions have a dominant influence. The fact that feminism is itself culturally influenced—by place, politics, and religion—became impossible to ignore at the beginning of the 1990s, following the changes in Eastern Europe as the former communist countries threw off the yoke of centralized economic control and prepared to draw deep breaths of the heady air of market freedom. For not least of the expectations current at the time were those of a small number of women in Eastern European countries, including, for example, Poland and Czechoslovakia, who, with minimal attention or publicity, supported nascent and low-profile feminist movements in their own locality. Their expectations, however, may well have been coloured by the picture of the lifestyle of women in Western countries projected by Hollywood and by internationally marketed TV soap operas. It would have been natural for anyone with only a second-hand acquaintance with life in the USA, for example, to assume that what capitalist plenty brought for women was freedom from the burden of combining domestic and family life with a full-time 'real' job in the outside world. Indeed, there was for a moment a sense of confusion as feminists of the Eastern bloc met feminists from the West, and found to their surprise that they were confronting a very different political agenda, and different preoccupations. As they quickly discovered, the freedoms sought by Western feminists were precisely those already enjoyed under communism: freedom to work outside the home on equal terms with men; ready access to abortion as a means of family limitation; and access to state-provided childcare facilities from the child's earliest months—arrangements designed to meet parents' needs to cover for long and demanding adult working days rather than children's needs for a little early social and educational stimulus outside the home. And behind all this, for couples or families in the Eastern bloc countries where such arrangements were routine, lay the hard reality of the economic impossibility of living on a single adult wage.

Both Russian and Chinese communism did allow women a form of equality, although one that made few concessions to any domestic needs or aspirations—women could certainly work, but they worked hard and long. In contrast, in other areas, where religion rather than politics held sway, and particularly in India and the Arab nations, the position of women was, and in many places remains, deeply rooted in male domination and in reproductive control. This cultural contrast, looked at in more detail below, is of interest in itself. But it also provides a stark illustration of a major cultural conflict within Western feminism, throwing an unexpected light on some of its internal difficulties and ambivalences.

The chinese experience[21]

The egalitarian gender politics of twentieth- and twenty-first-century China grew from a very different soil from that in the West. The Chinese ideal of womanhood was traditionally summed up as three obediences. That is to say, when a woman was unmarried, she was to live for and obey her father, when married, her husband and, as a widow, her son. Throughout the 5,000-year history of China, Chinese women lived in a male-dominated culture that confined women to the domestic sphere and gave them a marginal role in society. With one or two notable exceptions of women who held power through their imperial connections, they were oppressed, powerless, passive, and silent. But, from the second half of the nineteenth century, partly inspired by Western cultural influences, the idea of gender equality gradually took root. The issue of women's liberation was first raised in a modern sense by Chinese male reformers such as Kang Youwei and Liang Qichao, leaders of the Reformist movement of 1898, who set women's liberation in a nationalist context, arguing that China's own strength was dependent upon the strength of Chinese women. The revolution they inspired was, however, short-lived, lasting only about 100 days and brought to an end, ironically enough, by a woman: the Dowager Empress Cixi.

However, the establishment of the Republic of China (1912–49) brought significant steps towards women's liberation. The May Fourth Movement of 1919 promoted women's suffrage and opposed such practices as foot-binding, sex segregation, and arranged marriages. Later, Chinese women began to acquire further rights in relation to education, marriage, and property. And, in 1949, the birth of the People's Republic of China brought legal moves to guarantee women's political participation. With formal recognition of the equality of women and men, China has, from 2000 on, successively enacted or revised laws and regulations to provide a guarantee of equality. As a result, women hold leading posts in many areas of government and political organization and are probably closer than most Western nations to achieving the goal set by the United Nations of holding 30 per cent of political posts. However, China's burgeoning population has led to other moves, adopted for demographic reasons, which have affected the lives of all but a small number of women in rural communities in ways that may be less attractive to individual women themselves. Most striking of these is the one-child policy introduced in 1979. Combined with the possibility of fetal scans and abortions and a strong preference for male children, by 2005 it had resulted in a sex ratio of 119 newborn boys for every 100 newborn girls. In some areas the number is even higher, with 133 boys to every 100 girls, and this has led to moves to ban sex selection by law, and to advertise the useful virtues of daughters.

The diverging sex ratio, which so conspicuously favours males, is not, however, the only aspect of concern to women. While the policy is a courageous measure to keep population within bounds, it carries with it the loss of a freedom that people in most societies have taken for granted—the ability to choose for themselves their preferred family structure. But, with only one child per couple, most family links necessarily fall away—first, sisters and brothers, and then, within a single generation, cousins, aunts, and uncles. On the one hand, then, the one-child policy has been a contributory factor in making possible greater political equality for women than that available in many Western countries, where the same goal is approached by more pragmatic measures such as all-women shortlists for government positions and positive discrimination in employment. On the other hand, that freedom is counter-balanced by the loss of what Chinese society in the past valued most—the complex and generally supportive structure of wider family bonds.

The muslim experience

In contrast to the situation of Chinese women, women in Muslim societies may, as some Muslim women commentators themselves argue, find themselves confined to the single role of bearing children. This role, too, may have a further internal gender bias, because of the preference of husbands and families for sons rather than daughters. As far as that aim is concerned, in many of the countries where, whether for religious or purely economic reasons, the male preference is strong, what had earlier been associated with female infanticide has subsequently been brought about at an earlier stage, as a result of fetal scanning and sex-selective abortion.[22] The overall effect of this gender bias, taken together with a similar preference by other religious and cultural groups, has been a calculable loss in the number of women in the parts of the world affected. According to the economist Amartya Sen, writing in 1990, this loss may amount to more than one hundred million women.[23] A more recent study suggests that this trend has continued and indeed is increasing.[24] As in the Chinese situation, but without limiting births per couple to the same extent, it has created an imbalance in the relative numbers of adult men and women. Another more immediate consequence is that education for girls may be undervalued, while the aspirations of individual women to independence can be held in check by forced marriages, or by the threat of honour killings for those who look outside the expected framework of their community in their life choices. For women living under the more conservative Muslim regimes, either local or national, and imprisoned under modes of dress that conceal not only identity, but beauty and personality, and sometimes trapped as well under a tyrannous domestic regime, the goal of equality in political and public life can be, for many, no more than a distant aspiration.

Paradoxically, these tensions came to a head in the West in what is arguably the most tolerant of European societies, and the one with the best-known record of respecting cultural and religious difference: the Netherlands. A key figure in the Dutch debate was Ayaan Hirsi Ali. Ali was born in Somalia in 1969 and brought up as a devout Muslim. However, faced with a marriage she was unwilling to accept, she found refuge in the Netherlands, and in 2003 became an elected member of the Dutch Parliament. Influenced by her own personal experiences as a Muslim woman who had resisted her prescribed destiny, she became also an author and a film-maker. Her book *The Son Factory* painted a picture of women in Islamic culture as confined to the role of baby-making machines, while her film *Submission* featured a message about women's oppression in the home.[25] This film was illustrated by some highly contentious images, interpreted by some as sacrilegious, and it was followed by the murder in Amsterdam of its Dutch director, Theo van Gogh, and threats to the life of Ali herself.

Ali received a number of international awards for her work to promote freedom of speech and women's rights, including a nomination for the Nobel Peace Prize. But in 2006 the Netherlands Government issued a challenge to her citizenship status, and she was offered a political research role in the USA. Ali's campaign had, however, already challenged the sexual politics of Islam in the forms it has taken in the many Muslim countries but also amongst Muslim communities in the West.

While Ali is perhaps the best-known feminist critic of Islam, it is possible to find other and less controversial Muslim feminist viewpoints that interpret Islam more sympathetically as far as women's role is concerned and seek to define a position that is set within rather than outside Islamic traditions. The sources of a contemporary Islamic feminist movement of this sort can be traced back over at least a century, and feminist scholarship has flourished in various Asian and Middle Eastern countries including Egypt, Turkey, and Iran. Indeed, according to the feminist Islamic scholar Margot Badran, the term Islamic feminism, coined in the 1980s, now has currency as a movement for full equality of all Muslims, male and female, in public and private life.[26] Nor is this a matter of moving from a religious to a secular perspective or adopting a particular local interpretation. On the contrary, according to Badran, it is possible to locate Islamic feminism within religious belief and practice and to see it as having very broad application. She writes: 'Islamic feminism is a global phenomenon. It is not a product of East or West. Indeed, it transcends East and West.'[27]

Women in western traditions

While interpretations of these important global movements may differ, Western feminism has much to learn from the contrast between the two conceptions of women's role that they seem to embody. In both China and the Muslim world women's family role is strongly determined by economic and demographic factors, and this carries a message for women's advocates in the West. In particular, it brings into sharp focus the often-conflicting goals of the contemporary feminist movement in the Western world. While Chinese aspirations can be seen as centred on securing for women a political and workplace role in a context in which they have a drastically reduced family role, the Islamic direction still embodies an ideal in which, for all but a few exceptional women who achieve high prominence in the political sphere, a domestic rather than a public role is the expected norm. The contrast between these two approaches, with their differing emphasis on political and private roles, throws light on a deep ambivalence in Western feminism. While there are always some individual women who will find it possible to resolve the antithesis between public role and private life definitively in one direction or the other, the majority of women in Western countries live with these competing aspirations in their day-to-day lives. On the one hand, they want the recognition and fulfilment a public role can bring, on the other, the warmth and continuity of the deep attachments of intimate family life, and time and space for these to flourish.

This suggests that it is worth looking again at the sources from which Western feminism has sprung. Feminism often defines itself in revolutionary terms as a breach with the repressive habits of the past, and it is true that Western societies, like those of other parts of the world, have been built on the pattern of male dominance, which is reflected in the long-held principle that the male is the head of the family. Even so, at the root of the Western view of marriage there is a belief in the complementarity of male and female that is, at its best, fundamentally egalitarian. It is a belief that is deeply embedded in the Judaeo-Christian tradition, and that tradition has thrown up many examples of a female role in which submissiveness itself is not powerless but can even be used as a weapon in a different kind of trial of strength. The portrait of the female as initiator of change and influencer of events can be traced back to the tradition's origins. For, while Eve's creation as the product of Adam's rib is usually taken to confirm her secondary status, the more remarkable point is that it is Eve, not Adam, who plays the dominant role in the Genesis story.

While the Judaeo-Christian tradition has recognized women's individuality in various ways that are reflected in stories in both the Old and New Testaments, this individuality is also part of the classical tradition of Greece and Rome. In neither of these important sources were women invariably shown as mere ciphers. Often they were portrayed as important agents and key influences on the course of events. Strong female roles are to be found in Greek legends and drama, and both the Greek and Roman worlds of gods were peopled with male and female divinities who were more or less equal in powers and strengths and owed equal respect. Until the dawn of the scientific era in the twentieth century, it was these early traditions that formed the principal content of Western education, and they provided a familiar and well-understood backdrop to the lives of the women, as well as the men, who shaped Western society in modern times. But, if their historical and cultural traditions lent credibility to the idea of women as partners in at least some aspects of life, period and place necessarily affected the form that their participation could take. For example, the demands made of women in settler societies such as America and Australia in the eighteenth and nineteenth centuries were very different from the expectations of the women of that time who remained in Europe. In pioneering situations there was a partnership based on a tacitly agreed, but logical, division of labour that took account of different capacities, and women needed to draw on very different virtues and strengths from those they had relied on in the domestic world they had left behind.

Historical perspectives on those pioneering episodes differ, and they are no longer viewed simply from the point of view of the newcomers, but also from the perspective of women in the indigenous societies they encountered. All the same, whatever broader judgements are involved, the fact is that, whether they were sharing hardships and dangers in foreign countries, or influencing society and politics from a European drawing room, women within the Western tradition were not always victims of a form of patriarchy that confined them to their child-bearing role. On the contrary, their broader contribution was needed and often welcomed. If novels and plays of Victorian times are peppered with helpless heroines awaiting rescue, it is possible to find other female characters who are strong or even dominant. Fiction is often more true to life than is theory in revealing tacit assumptions. Novels that centred on the upper classes often took for granted the respect paid to female roles and female conversation, while pictures of family life in the lower classes often showed husband and wife joined in a common fight against poverty and hardship. Of course, the reverse is also to be found—foolish prattling women, harridans, profligate wives—but even these are strongly painted characters, and in a different way convey the same message: that women were not negligible, they made a difference, whether for good or ill. They were not stripped down, as they often are in current times and current literature, to a purely bodily description and identity.

Literary figures, however, were in some ways less remarkable than some of the real women who ignored or transcended the boundaries of their time. Famous individuals of the Victorian era such as Florence Nightingale, Mary Seacole, or Elizabeth Garrett-Anderson saw needs that their society had assumed were beyond the competence of women. Generally indifferent to both advice and criticism, they ignored the opposition of their contemporaries to nurse in battle zones or to found hospitals for the poor. It was in this same period, too, that intrepid women travellers set out on journeys no less incredible than those of their better-known male contemporaries who mapped continents and seas. The nineteenth-century African journeys of Mary Livingstone, both with and without her celebrated husband David Livingstone, were astonishing for the courage and endurance they demanded, particularly as she often had to bring those qualities to bear in situations when she was pregnant and caring alone and unaided for herself and her small children.[28] But Mary Livingstone was by no means unique in the challenges she met. Other independent-minded women undertook remarkable travels, often alone. Daisy Bates (1859–1951), born in Ireland, lived for most of her adult life amongst the Australian aborigines, inspired by a determination to record their stories and traditions for posterity.[29] Her chronicle *The Passing of the Aborigines* was published in 1938. Fanny Bullock Workman (1859–1925) left her birthplace in Massachusetts to travel in India, China, Central Asia, Russia, and Cuba. The Yorkshire woman Isabella Bird (1831–1904), although disabled by spinal problems, travelled first for her health, but nevertheless found her way to the Rocky Mountains in the USA, to India, Iran, Korea, China, Japan, and Morocco. The English woman Freya Stark, once described as a female Lawrence of Arabia, was a worthy twentieth-century successor to these nineteenth-century pioneers. Fluent in Arabic, she understood the political map of the Middle East and travelled in dangerous wartime conditions in Arabia, Egypt, Palestine, Syria, Iraq, and Iran.

This record of female independence could be paralleled in other spheres, educational, artistic, and scientific. Pre-dating, as it does, the dawn of any formal feminist movement, it suggests that there may be a need to think again about the common assumption that Western feminism is at odds with its own cultural heritage. The ground that Western feminists today are claiming is not as new as all that. Rather than marking a shift from heritage and tradition, many aspects of the new movement stand in a long historic line in which female strength, spiritual, moral, and intellectual, and even occasionally physical, has often, if not always, been both asserted and respected. This recognition may lead to some further reflection on modern feminism—on where it has come from and where it should be aiming to arrive. This in turn may affect the way we think of feminism, what it is and what it can hope to achieve.

Rethinking feminism

Although often portrayed as the preserve of Western women, feminism might less contentiously be interpreted as a political campaign for bettering the position of women under all cultural, religious, and political regimes. This is to see it as a movement rather than an ideology, and one that has women's lives as its focus. Woman, like man, is a biological creature, and, though there can be exceptions, women tend to put human, often family, relationships first. This is not to say that men do not value family relationships, but that, forced to choose, women are more likely than men to prioritize the personal over the political. Some indeed would go further than this, claiming that men's interest in their children is indirect and that, as two American commentators, June Carbone and Naomi Cahn suggest, this has the authority of science. They write: 'Evolutionary psychology suggests that women have a direct relationship with their children; men are more likely to see their relationship to children mediated by their attachment to their mate.'[30]

Such claims need to be set in particular contexts, and it would be wrong to suggest that men do not take seriously their relationship with their children. Nevertheless, support for the claim that there is a difference in approach between the sexes was an interesting and unexpected finding from Carol Gilligan's well-known research based on Lawrence Kohlberg's theories of moral development. Gilligan found that women's approaches to moral dilemmas often showed them as rebelling against impersonal principles of morality, preferring to make sympathetic concessions, and to opt for mercy rather than justice. In the responses they gave, Gilligan identified a special moral conception characterized by a distinctive use of a particular vocabulary: a vocabulary of selfishness and responsibility, of morality as an obligation to exercise care and avoid hurt for particular others. She saw this as a stage of moral development in which the tension between selfishness and responsibility was dissipated and replaced by a morality that involved respect for the detail and texture of personal life that comes with knowledge of particular people and particular circumstances. Male respondents, in contrast, more often gave priority to the moral, legal, and social aspects of the decision.[31] In a separate study of women who had been faced with abortion decisions, Gilligan found that women in those real-life situations did not usually appeal to issues of rights or justice, or to

legal or moral aspects of their situation, but rather to their own personal responsibilities for close others who would be affected by their
decision—other children, or sick or dependent relatives.[32] Contrary
to Kohlberg, who had seen this kind of approach to a moral issue as
representing a 'lower' stage of moral development, Gilligan identified
it as a distinctive and different 'voice'—an approach to moral issues that
could be shared by men, but which was most characteristic of women.

Whatever the current approach of men to such issues, and acknow-
ledging that some men would share the women's perspective, some
significance might be read into the fact that the deliberate individual
choice of the reverse priority—the political over the personal—is
something that has traditionally been associated in story and legend
with men. It was, for example, in the ancient Greek story, Agamem-
non who was willing to sacrifice his daughter to appease the gods and
produce a fair wind for setting sail for Troy; it was Abraham, in the
Jewish scriptures, who was prepared to prove his obedience to God's
command by killing his son Isaac; and it was Stenka Rasin who, in
the Russian legend, cast his young bride to her death in the Volga's
foaming waters in order to inspire his men to courage in battle and
demonstrate his own willingness to sacrifice everything for their cause.
These are stories from three different traditions in which men sacrifice
those they love for the stronger claims of duty or religion. While it
is true that generations of women, too, have 'sacrificed' husbands and
sons in war, myth and legend do not seem to offer many examples
of women making this kind of choice deliberately, on an individual
basis, although there have been some notable exceptions. One of the
most striking examples of this is provided by a memorial to Japanese
pilots in the Second World War that records the story of the wife of
a Kamikaze pilot who, when she found that her husband would not
have been allowed, as a family man, to join his comrades in choosing
the patriotic death he desired, had chosen to free him for that role by
killing herself and her young children.

Such stories suggest that, if Western feminism has seemed to favour
a reversal of what are very often seen as women's values, it may need
to recognize that it cannot speak for all. It may also need to recognize
that there is a central conflict in women's aspirations that needs to be
resolved if the attempt to forge a common agenda from the diverse
aspirations of women's groups under different economic and political
regimes is to succeed. One aspiration that has won less than universal
acceptance is the idea of the genderless family advocated by feminist

writers such as Susan Moller Okin. For Okin, a just family would be a family in which both paid and unpaid work in the public arena, as well as childcare in the home, would be equally shared by men and women. She writes: 'A just future would be one without gender.'[33] While some couples in the Western democracies have achieved a harmonious arrangement on the basis of sharing rather than dividing roles, and while it is even a common presumption in, for example, the Scandinavian countries and the Netherlands, it requires adjustments that many are not able, or not willing, to make. In particular, as another commentator observes, liberal feminists who equate mothering with fathering, preferring to use the term 'parenting', are 'neutering' motherhood, and the result is the creation of the two-parent family, which, she argues, is 'an institution with potentially NO available caretakers'.[34]

One reason that so many contemporary Western feminists do see equality in terms of gender identity or sameness could be that those in a position to define what women want often occupy a privileged role in which they can themselves accommodate the oppositions other women must struggle with. They may, for example, be in academic or journalistic occupations that allow them to control their time, their working hours, and their energies. And the solutions they seek are more likely, where very young children are concerned, to involve employing a substitute carer in the home rather than making use of a ten-hour daily crèche. For others—the majority—the choice is starker, since it has to be based on accepting the inevitability of the absence of both parents from the home for the whole of the working day, and the financial impracticability of providing a substitute in the home. The feminist movement in both the USA and Europe did a disservice to the vast majority of working-class women in failing to appreciate this fact or to register its implications.

So, if the contemporary feminist movement is to play a more inclusive role, it must define itself in more general terms, repositioning itself as a movement for improving the lot and position of women of all social classes and, if it is to have a global influence, under all political regimes. But this is not an easy transition, and the wish to respect cultural or religious pluralism can itself produce conflicts. There may, for example, be a reluctance to condemn policies such as sex-selective abortion and infanticide, female circumcision, or forced marriages, for fear of violating some principle of cultural autonomy. The philosophical influence of postmodernism, which many Western feminists have made central to their own theorizing, tends to reinforce this tendency to cultural and moral relativism, and to affect its application to practical issues. But the postmodernist approach fits ill with the goals of a broad international women's movement, since, in rejecting Enlightenment rationalism with its claims to universal truths and values, it makes any attempt to provide a universal analysis of women's needs across differences in culture, class, and ethnicity fundamentally inconsistent. A comment by the feminist writer Hester Eisenstein vividly expresses the struggle to unite these conflicting ideals:

Finally, there is the option of entering the world and attempting to change it, in the image of the woman-centered values at the core of feminism... [This] means associating feminism with the liberating traditions of Western thought, from Locke and Rousseau to Marx and Engels, tending in the direction of greater equality, shared decision-making and justice. But it means, too, transforming these traditions, by imbuing them with the woman-centered values of nurturance and intimacy, as necessary and legitimate goals of political life.[35]

The argument of this chapter has been that the overall impact of feminism as currently interpreted has been on the whole negative, at least to the extent that it involves an analysis of the family as a source of women's oppression. The option remains to reinterpret feminism in a way that can more realistically reflect women's broader needs and aspirations, as well as those of their children, whose happiness is often an integral part of their own. But, despite the new wave of feminism, which is more willing to recognize the value of family, this response has been muted—perhaps even distorted—by another issue. This is the move to broaden the concept of family to include a wide range of alternative structures. Susan Moller Okin describes this more inclusive position in this way: 'most contemporary feminists ... have not rejected all forms of family. Many advocate that "family" be redefined so as to include any intimately connected and committed group, specifically endorsing same-sex marriage and parenthood; almost all, certainly, refuse to choose between accepting women's double burden and abolishing the family.'[36]

But is this debate about 'variant families' necessarily a feminist issue? No doubt feminists will sympathize with the wish of some lesbian and separatist feminists to have children in their relationships, but they may well accept that the implications for those children must also come into the picture. And, in the age of gender equality, they will need to reflect on the implications for males as well as for females. Families without men are common, but do they also wish to endorse families without women? Would they be concerned about children, male or female, without mothers? Accepting that some people living with same-sex partners already have children from a heterosexual relationship, creating children for these situations raises different and novel questions, especially since the biological involvement of women will continue to be essential, however indirect. This debate would have been, until relatively recently, largely theoretical. The possibilities, however, have been enlarged and extended through advances in reproductive medicine. The question of non-standard families, then, is best considered in the next chapter in this broader context. The implications for feminists, however, are clear. Before embracing a non-biological constructivist view of what parenting and family involves, feminists should reflect more carefully on what their deep prior interest in the family means for women. Women may not want, as individuals, to be written out of the picture. Both women and men are, biologically speaking, products of the past. Only women, however, carry from birth the future within their own bodies.

PART II
Shaping families: Science's contribution

5

Having and not having children

Many of the new developments in medicine and reproductive technology have been welcomed as holding out the promise of help to families, whether they want to limit the number of their children or whether, on the other hand, they have problems of infertility or subfertility. Medically, the new technologies can be used to filter out serious genetic diseases, while, socially, they offer new kinds of choice, although not all of these choices are regarded by everyone as ethically or legally desirable. The more problematic possibilities include, for example, being able to choose whether to have a boy or a girl or whether to try for other more general characteristics through donor or embryo selection. It is not difficult to see the more widely available and legally sanctioned opportunities as family-friendly developments, and this is no doubt the way many people see them. Contraception, for example, was originally termed 'family planning', and abortion was often promoted as a way to avoid bringing into the world children who would either lack a family (in the sense that they would be born to a woman on her own) or add an unwanted burden to an existing family. The object of fertility treatment, in contrast, is to create wanted families where nature has made that difficult. But it is possible to look at these developments from a different point of view. Looked at in this other way, far from fulfilling these family-oriented goals, they can be seen as contributing to the current crisis in the social stability of the family. This may seem a paradoxical claim. How could enlarged possibilities be counterproductive as far as the family is concerned? To understand how greater reproductive control could have family-*un*friendly consequences, it would be useful to look briefly at the short history of these developments.

Contraception

Many aspects of contraception are fraught with contention, and opinion continues to be divided, especially from some religious perspectives, about its ethical standing. Practice, though, has long seemed to ignore the theological objections—something adequately demonstrated by Italy, where the Roman Catholic Church might be thought to have the greatest influence, but which has one of the lowest birthrates in Europe. Even so, religious concerns mean that the issue remains a live one internationally in relation to some important areas of policy. For example, political decision-making about aid to developing countries is affected by the fact that some large donors will not give financial support to work that involves population policies promoting contraception and abortion.

It is worth asking why the Catholic Church should have taken such a strong stand against the most popular and reliable methods of contraception. Part of the answer was supplied by the Cambridge philosopher Elizabeth Anscombe in a paper that was, in the main, a reaction against the new contraceptive freedom of the 1960s.[1] In this paper, she cites a distant debate that has cast a long shadow on Catholic thinking on the matter. The debate was initiated by the followers of an ascetic Christian sect founded by the Persian prophet Mani (216–c.275) in the latter half of the third century. Known as Manicheanism, and influenced to some extent by Buddhist notions, the cult emphasized the struggle between good and evil. On the side of good were light, God, and the soul. On the side of evil, darkness, Satan, and the body. This led the Manichaeans to hold that sex was evil, but that procreation was an even greater evil. For this reason, those followers of the cult who were either not able or not willing to give up sex used primitive methods of contraception and resorted to abortion when these failed. As a final step, if a child was born in spite of these precautions, it would be put out to die.

Reacting against this philosophy and the practices it brought in its train, St Augustine defended the principle that sex should be open to procreation and set within marriage—a position, later endorsed by St Thomas Aquinas, that was destined to become the key to Catholic thinking on sex and marriage. In the twentieth century, following the papal encyclical *Humanae Vitae* (1968), Catholic doctrine accepted this focus on the intention of the couple and, in particular, on whether or not they were positively aiming to avoid conception. It was this idea of the linkage between act and intention that led Anscombe to argue in broader philosophical terms that the nature, and in particular the morality, of an act changes with the nature of the intention. With the negative intention of avoiding conception, she argued, sex becomes a shallow indulgence, stripped of the profound significance that it can and should have in human life.

This historical background explains to some extent the reason why the Catholic Church, while it sanctions the use of the rhythm method, a natural means to limit families, remains hostile to artificial methods of contraception. The debate itself may seem to be of no more than academic interest to non-Catholics, and even to some Catholics as well who do not see it as relevant to their personal lives, but it has a continuing importance because of the way in which it continues to influence broader population policy in an international context.

What I want to consider here, however, is not so much theory as practice. In the context of today's world, and particularly in urban Western societies, a more pressing question is what effect the advent of more efficient and reliable contraception has had on the family. Simply to be willing to look at this question with an open mind is not, of course, to suggest that the genie can be put back in the bottle. The availability of contraception is here to stay. It has been hailed as a major beneficial advance, and it is promoted by pictures of smaller families and of happy mothers, possibly rejoining the workforce after the birth of their (ideally two) children. But it would be foolish to deny that there have been more problematic consequences from a social point of view.

Perhaps the most important of these adverse consequences are, first, its potential for removing a cautionary attitude to sex and, second, the fact that it makes short-term living together a viable and often preferred alternative to marriage. There are also some more immediate consequences that may ultimately come to be seen as against the public interest and also against the interest of individuals. These are less fundamental in the sense that they are easier to correct by personal choice, public policy, or scientific advance. As things currently stand, however, these adverse risks stem from the fact that, of the various alternatives available, the contraceptive of choice is the pill, first introduced in the 1960s and now used by more than 100 million women worldwide. It is often preferred because of its convenience and its low failure rate, and also, as far as women are concerned, because it places contraception in a woman's own hands and allows her to take control of her own fertility. But the pill, along with injectable or implantable contraceptives, provides no protection against infection and so, having removed one of the main reasons to avoid multiple partnering, it is also indirectly responsible for a major increase in sexually transmitted diseases, including the escalating rates of invisible chlamydia infection that have become a leading cause of infertility in women.[2]

Taking all these elements into account, what is individually often taken as an unqualified benefit has had a number of unforeseen consequences, and some of these affect not only individuals but also societies and communities. As birthrates in parts of the developed world fall to below replacement rate, the demographic aspects, too, take on a new significance.[3] These must be considered later, but at this point it is worth looking more narrowly at some of the more personal consequences that are the unintended byproduct of apparently beneficent interventions of science and legislation. Central amongst these is the fact that, while the risk of unplanned pregnancy is widely recognized, it is equally possible to fall into the trap of unplanned infertility simply as a result of the ability to delay child-bearing. This is not to say that it is necessarily a good thing for a woman to have a child before she feels ready to do so, but that the idea of 'readiness' can be overinterpreted. Many people can accommodate to circumstances that were not originally intended, particularly when the reward for doing so is something as valuable as a child. Nevertheless, the idea of pregnancy as an avoidable or remediable error has become part of current social assumptions. For a woman, an understandable and wholly rational reluctance to accept pregnancy until some ideal moment later in life may lead to a series of childless partnerships that take her beyond her child-bearing years.

Caught in this sociobiological trap, many look to science and technology to make good what may turn out to have been an error of personal, or perhaps communal, judgement about the ideal path of a woman's life. While not all women feel this in the same way, the sense of having left founding a family too late is a pervading aspect of twenty-first-century culture; as a result of this, a multi-billion-dollar fertility industry has sprung up to respond to the personal consequences for women of effective reproductive control. A century ago, the loss of millions of young men in the First World War left many women without hope of family life or parenthood. The era of fertility control has produced a comparable effect, with similar loss and regret for vanished possibilities for the individuals concerned.[4] In this case, though, the men, too, share the loss, but, while the missed opportunity is a matter of biology for women, for men it is a matter of the arithmetic of gender relations. This is because the natural harmony that seems to produce near-equal numbers of male and female at birth is disrupted by shifting patterns of sexual partnering: numerical equality is not enough on its own to produce a match between the number of young women of child-bearing age and the number of men who might be ready to found a family. In the past, men and women tended to marry and have children at roughly the same age. Today, though, the number of women of child-bearing age is reduced by the pattern of postponed child-bearing and this problem is compounded by the phenomenon of second marriage, since this often means that men of grandparent age raid the shrinking pool of women young enough to become the partners of men of their own sons' generation.

It is not necessary to draw from these observations the conclusion that people should—even if they would—give up using contraception to shape and protect the family they have undertaken to raise. The well-being of children already born is itself a factor here. While the ability of parents to care for their family may be limited both financially and in terms of time and effort, sex can be the cement that confirms a relationship, reinforces affection, and so protects and maintains the family unit. It must be able to do this without threatening that stability. Even so, it is worth recognizing that the law of unintended consequences has forced itself as a factor into the equation, often affecting people's long-term dreams and aspirations, particularly where the initial decision to found a family is concerned. However, contraception alone cannot be blamed for this. In practice, the ability to control fertility has been buttressed and supported by abortion used as a fallback for failed or neglected contraception.

Abortion

Even more than contraception, abortion has divided ethical, political, and social opinion. Again, the issue here is not how the moral issue should be resolved so much as what the impact of access to abortion has been on the family. As one prominent feminist writer on medical ethics, Christine Overall, has observed, abortion has changed attitudes to pregnancy, so that it is increasingly seen as voluntary.[5] So, while a man cannot compel a woman to continue with a pregnancy, even if he is her husband and wants his child to be born, he may resent parenthood being imposed on him without his agreement. A woman, on the other hand, may feel under pressure to terminate an unintended pregnancy when she might otherwise have preferred to go ahead with it. In other words, she may feel obliged to choose abortion simply as a result of the fact that a man who might in times past have bowed gracefully to the inevitable may feel he cannot be held responsible for a child whom he sees as the result of the mother's, rather than his, voluntary decision.

Like contraception, abortion has been a popular option. In Britain, the Office for National Statistics reported 190,700 abortions in England and Wales for the year 2003. In the United States, abortions have averaged 1.5 million per annum since the crucial *Roe* v. *Wade* legal decision in 1973 gave women an unconditional right to decide on termination in the first two trimesters of pregnancy.[6] Some estimate this as a loss to the American population of perhaps fifty million people if most of those pregnancies had in fact been continued. Eighty per cent of the terminations were for social, not medical, reasons, nor did they involve serious situations such as rape or incest. It is not always realized, however, that the unqualified freedom to choose established in the United States by the case of *Roe* v. *Wade* is not recognized in most other democratic jurisdictions. British law, for example, appears at first sight to be more restrictive, setting out carefully the conditions that would need to be satisfied for an abortion to take place and requiring that two doctors certify that these have been met. In spite of this, the outcome is similar to that in the United States, since women can readily be referred to doctors who have a liberal approach to abortion. In practice, then, Britain does have abortion on demand in the first two trimesters of pregnancy. More stringent conditions are set for late abortions. Those after twenty-four weeks are bound by the conditions set out in the 1967 Abortion Act, which require two medical practitioners to certify in good faith that there is a substantial risk to the child, if born, of serious handicap.[7] The terms 'substantial risk' and 'serious handicap' are not defined in the Act and so disputes continue as to whether they apply in the case of particular medical conditions such as, for example, cleft palate or Downs' Syndrome. Women can, however, travel to clinics abroad for late terminations even when they would not be legally available in the United Kingdom.

The broad picture, then, is one of ready availability of abortion, and this fits with a widely held view that a woman's own choice should prevail in these matters. This view is part of a broad feminist position that emphasizes women's rights and gives a lower priority to any putative claims of a fetus. The feminist claim is for women to have control of their own bodies, combined with a moral judgement that no one has an obligation to support another life at serious cost to herself (although she may be morally admired for doing so).[8] This emphasis on the woman's position, as against the claims of the fetus, is strengthened by the consideration that some of the exceptions the law already allows are not based on anything to do with the status or rights of the unborn child, but are rather a matter of the circumstances surrounding conception. But it is possible to concede that very strong claims of a woman (for example, the claim of a 13-year-old victim of gang rape not to have to continue a pregnancy) can outweigh the claims of a fetus, without allowing a mere preference to do so. It is also possible to argue that, while the child at a significant stage of pregnancy merits the protection of the law, freedom to reject child-bearing within days or even weeks of conception can reasonably be left to individuals, as the early conceptus, whatever its ethical status, has not yet acquired sufficient standing, morally or legally, to justify the involvement of the state.

All the same, as argued in the previous chapter, the case for abortion on feminist grounds is not as clear-cut as is often assumed, if feminist grounds are grounds that give priority to the interests of women. For outside the wealthy nations, abortion often works *against* rather than *for* women's interests, as it did in Eastern Europe under communism, when free access to abortion meant that women could experience repeated abortions throughout their child-bearing years, with adverse consequences for their own health. On a gender basis, too, the argument that a valuable life is lost in abortion is strengthened by the sheer scale of the disproportionate loss of female lives in countries where male offspring are valued more highly than female.[9] And, as Western societies become more diverse and include communities that, whether for religious or other reasons, share the values of those societies, it is no longer possible to discount the *ad feminem* argument in those societies too.

On the other hand, some commentators ground the right to choose to abort a fetus in broader political considerations. According to the American legal philosopher Ronald Dworkin, 'the principle of procreative autonomy, in a broad sense, is embedded in any genuinely democratic culture'.[10] In the American context, he believes, it is implicit in the Constitution, even though, of course, given its time and setting, the authors of that Constitution themselves would never have conceded such a right. Nevertheless, Dworkin argues that, while abortion would indeed have struck these Puritan pioneers as abhorrent, freedom of choice to terminate a pregnancy is part of the religious freedom they sought to guarantee in the First Amendment. Apart from the peculiarly paradoxical nature of this derivation, it unfortunately helps to reinforce a common error: that is, to see the issue as a uniquely religious one, rather than as an ethical and social issue of much more general significance.

This more general significance is a function of the importance of the family for social and personal life. As far as the family is concerned, it is impossible to avoid the conclusion that, not only has abortion limited existing families; it has also closed the door to many potential ones. For a woman who does not later succeed in creating or setting up a family situation or having a child, this may come to be viewed in retrospect as a matter of lost opportunities—for some, indeed, as a personal tragedy. Some difficult situations will, of course, have been avoided, but some not necessarily unhappy compromise ones will also have been lost. It is arguable, then, that women's interests have not always been served even on a personal level by easy access to abortion. What is more, if a woman later comes to regret an abortion decision, or to see it as a moral error, the error is disproportionately bad as compared with other possible moral errors—for what she may come to regret is that she herself was responsible for bringing about the loss of her own child. This aspect of later regret, particularly when there are no future children, is well known and forms a part of the counselling women are offered when they are considering a termination of pregnancy. But it is not only the central figure—the woman herself—who may later come to experience this kind of shift of perspective. Dworkin reports that some prominent male Republican politicians in the United States, seeking to distance themselves from their party's anti-abortion position, declared that in certain circumstances they would support their own daughter or granddaughter if she decided to have an abortion. He goes on to comment: 'They would hardly do that if they really thought that abortion meant the murder of their own grandchildren or great-grandchildren.'[11]

But what if they later *did* come to see it in that way—especially, perhaps, if their daughter had no later opportunity to become pregnant, for example, or had become infertile, or died? There is no need to see the issue in terms of murder. What they would have suffered would certainly have been a loss—a loss of a more than potential life and more than potential posterity. It would not be the same as a situation in which their daughter simply decided not to have children. In that case, they might regret the fact that they lacked grandchildren. They could regard this as a lost opportunity, but not as an actual loss—the ending of something that already had a place in their world. The politicians' comments, whatever they intended, reinforce the point that abortion can be looked at in two ways, and most especially so when viewed retrospectively—that is, after the event rather than at the time of the decision. It resembles those trick diagrams used by psychologists in which the same picture, looked at in one way, shows a vase, in another, a pair of human faces. A mere blink of the eyelid can effect the transformation. Similarly, looked at in one way, abortion is the termination of an awkward or unwelcome condition; looked at in another way, it is the snuffing-out of an independent life rich in possibilities.

Since the creation of new life has always been a central concern of the family, it is difficult not to see this as an issue whose true focus is the family, rather than the individual. And, whatever ethical or religious perspective is brought to bear on it, the judgement from a family perspective is that abortion should never have become, as it has in many countries, the remedy of first resort for an untimely or unintended pregnancy. If help is available within days or weeks of conception to protect the wish many women feel to direct their own life plans, abortion clinics could be places of last resort. If, politically, abortion seems unlikely to be relinquished as an important option for twenty-first-century living, it should nevertheless be recognized as being, in many ways, socially counterproductive, and this recognition could affect government policy in ways that stop short of compulsion or regulation.

While most people agree that births to young teenagers are best avoided, sex education in schools could promote alternatives to either contraception or abortion by ceasing to make the basic assumption that very early sexual activity is inevitable, and by encouraging an approach to pregnancy that sees it as something only to be initiated in the context of security and commitment. So far, however, education policies have contributed to the deteriorating picture, in that health educators have echoed the message of media and entertainment in promoting the idea that multiple partnering is the standard lifestyle. They have been reluctant to be straightforward about what its consequences are likely to be. In general, there has been a perverse but widespread reluctance to acknowledge the role of sexual choices in preserving health, fertility, and prospects for parenthood.

These issues have shaped the area of reproductive choice from the second half of the twentieth century. But the questions they raise have now been overtaken by other developments in reproductive medicine that have introduced yet more dramatic options into family life, opening the way for the evolution of new and unfamiliar social structures and new ways of having children.

The IVF era

While it is not difficult, even if disputable, to see contraception and abortion as negative developments as far as the family is concerned, the burgeoning area of assisted reproduction is generally regarded as positive, since it makes the family its focus and goal. For many people, the birth in 1978 of Louise Brown, the first baby to have been born by IVF (*in vitro* fertilization), is regarded as a watershed—a development that ushered in a new family-friendly era.

First it must be conceded that assisted reproduction has indeed brought wider choice in the area of reproduction, and, in the context of a free society, it is hard to see choice as anything but a good. But an often overlooked question here is, whose choices are enlarged? Those of adults or those of the children who result from those choices? Human reproduction has until the very recent past been linked to two apparent immovables: one, the biological fundamentals of male and female; the other, the idea of the family as the basic building block of human society. It is hardly surprising then that, when in the 1960s it became possible to create embryos outside the womb, and then implant them in a woman to produce a normal pregnancy and birth, the ethical objections at first seemed overwhelming. Indeed, Robert Edwards, one of the pioneers of research in this area, is reported as saying: 'If rabbit and pig eggs can be fertilized in culture, presumably human eggs grown in culture could also be fertilized, although obviously it would not be permissible to implant them in a human recipient.'[12] That 'obviously' was soon abandoned, for humans tend to operate on the principle: 'If it *can* be done, sooner or later, somewhere or other, it *will* be done.' The use of the new techniques moved from the rare to the routine, while new uses were made of the ability to transfer human gametes, first sperm, then eggs and embryos, between individuals without the need for sexual intercourse. Reliable contraception, bolstered by relatively easy access to abortion, had made sex possible without reproduction. Now science had made possible reproduction without sex.

But each step in the new technologies of reproduction brought new and unfamiliar ethical dilemmas. Previously inseparable aspects of parenthood now had to be recognized: fathers could be defined as genetic, social, or legal, with motherhood facing a further possible division between the mother who supplied the egg, or even just the nucleus of an egg, from which the child developed and the mother who carried the child through pregnancy to birth. Embryos could also be frozen, to be born years after conception and even after the death of their progenitors. Welcomed by some, regarded with concern or suspicion by others, these developments generated other social options. They made possible new kinds of families: families founded by single parents, lesbians, gay men, by reproductively cooperating groups, and by people who had passed the normal reproductive years. Generous transfer of gametes also produced unprecedented numbers of half-siblings, most unknown to the others, and in some cases this has been taken to surprising extremes, as in the case of a Danish sperm donor who, as the Aarhus-based sperm bank Cryos International once reported, has unknowingly fathered more than one hundred children worldwide.[13]

This wealth of choice seems to assume a narrow view of family as no more than parent and child. The genetic family is, however, a broader notion than just two adults and a child. Some of those involved in fertility treatment still insist that, after donation, the source of a child's genetic material is irrelevant—that parenthood is a purely *social* concept. These practitioners would prefer to maintain the anonymity of sperm and egg donation and tend to resist moves to greater openness. Users of fertility services, however, favour on the whole innovations that allow them to have children to whom they are genetically related. And, as the science of genetics has begun to unveil its secrets, individuals born by assisted reproduction are increasingly concerned to understand their own complex genetic inheritance and to have access to the world of their genetic relations—a biological family that includes grandparents, aunts, uncles, and cousins, as well as forebears and descendants.

To break the genetic link at that first and most basic stage is to remove that important wider network of relationships. This is a loss that can be mitigated by openness and honesty on the part of family members themselves, but, when medical confidentiality is combined with legal secrecy, it can also mean the violation of what in some countries is regarded as a basic human right: access to *knowledge* of one's genetic or biological parentage. This is not to suggest that there should be intrusive official investigation of private relationships, but simply to say that, in the case of donors and donor-conceived children, the issue is not only whether a child has a right to know, but whether a government has the right to conceal. The fact that private deception can happen when people have secret liaisons is not the government's business, and the state's authorities, after all, are unlikely to have access to the facts. But the state does nevertheless have a duty in relation to those children whose creation it directly sanctions. The fabric of genetic connections has until now formed the webbing underpinning most known cultures and societies, and, for some people, knowledge of origins and heredity will be a significant matter. They will not willingly accept being deprived of the chance to locate themselves in a biological network that has until now provided individuals' deepest conception of their identity and offered them the social space within which to find their earliest sense of self.

This wish to know and to belong has been a central issue in relation to adoption. Advocates of openness in adoption like the Australian philosopher Trevor Jordan see this deprivation as a failure of justice. He writes: 'Just as the universalising, civilising British justice system could impose its values on an inhabited continent and declare it to be *terra nullius*, so too could utilitarian policies, formulated for the greater good of the greater number, define birth parents out of existence, bureaucratically rendering them invisible and legally inaccessible.'[14] The least that children born of donated gametes will want is what has now been generally conceded in the case of adopted children: to have later access to at least some part of that network of genetic relationships.

The conception of a social space of this sort has been an important aspect of the study of human societies; indeed, social anthropology has often taken the mapping of kinship lines as a way of defining a culture. Some cultures, like that, for example, of the Australian aborigines, recognize a much wider range of kinship relations than Western societies, but the broad lines of kinship have been at the heart of anthropological understanding of European communities as well. The social anthropologist Marilyn Strathern says of this broader historical picture: 'Until now, it has been part of most of the indigenous cultural repertoires in Europe to see the domain of kinship, and what is called its biological base in procreation, as an area of relationships that provided a given baseline to human existence.' She adds: 'It is an extraordinarily impoverished view of culture to imagine that how we conceive of parents and children only affects parents and children.'[15] These points remain valid even if social anthropologists are now more inclined to interpret kinship in cultural rather biological terms.[16]

The reasons for the importance given to the genetic link are complex, and may perhaps better be sought within the depths of the subconscious mind rather than in any reasoned judgement. The myth of the changeling has haunted literature and legend since the beginning of history. The 'Cinderella' experience, too—step-parent and stepchild relationships with their tensions and threats—has been a common and recurring theme. And, where doubts about paternity have long been a feature of human life, these new capabilities, which include egg and embryo donation, make it possible for people to experience doubt about their parentage on both sides in a radically new way. Is their mother really their mother? Are their parents really their parents? Is this person they are attracted to really a for-ever-to-be-unidentified halfsister or halfbrother? These questions could come to haunt even those to whom none of these doubts apply in reality. They have become possible because previously unified roles are now susceptible to division, and this opens up a much larger discussion about new issues of rights, obligations, and relationships.

ℰ 6

New reproductive technologies: *Whose human rights?*

As a new era of reproductive choice opens up, it raises many questions about where this expansion of possibilities may be leading. Some see a need for caution and would prefer to hold back on institutionalizing the untested social experiments made possible by novel progenitive procedures. Others welcome them as offering a new dawn for the family, which, they believe, has not been diminished, but renewed and regenerated in myriad new forms. They welcome the opportunity to create new kinds of family beyond the 'traditional' nuclear family—a man and a woman raising their own offspring. While they dismiss this as an outdated concept, they do not necessarily base their case simply on taste or preference: on the contrary, they may see it as grounded in basic human rights, in particular the right to privacy, and the right to found a family. As far as the first is concerned, appeal can be made to Article 8 of the European Convention: 'Everyone has the right to respect for his private and family life, his home and his correspondence.'[1] The second is supported by Article 16 of the UN Declaration of Human Rights: 'Men and women of full age, without any limitation due to race, nationality or religion, have the right to marry and to found a family.'[2]

But how should these rights be interpreted? Do they bestow an unqualified right to reproduce? According to some influential commentators, democracy itself entails and guarantees a broadly interpreted principle of procreative autonomy. Ronald Dworkin argues that a right of this sort can be derived from the US Constitution, since, in guaranteeing religious freedom, it protects choices based on moral and religious grounds.[3] Writing in a European context, John Harris supports Dworkin's claim that this is an area where the state should not intervene and has modified his own utilitarian position to describe reproductive choice as a basic human right. The attempt to combine utility and rights may appear contradictory. However, it is a viewpoint shared by Dworkin, who holds that the idea of rights is parasitic on utilitarianism, since the core of that theory is the idea of well-being as a collective goal of the community as a whole. But, while Dworkin was concerned with a right *not* to reproduce and was defending autonomy in relation to abortion, Harris takes the argument further, extending it to cover the right to reproduce in a variety of ways made possible by the new reproductive technologies.[4] The concept of a *prima facie* moral right to reproduce in this extended sense is also defended by the American legal philosopher John Robertson, who argues that control over reproduction is 'central to personal identity, to dignity, and to the meaning of one's life'.[5] Robertson uses the principle of reproductive choice to defend various kinds of 'collaborative reproduction' as well as commissioned pregnancies, paid adoptions, and similar contracts. He writes: 'An ethic of personal autonomy as well as ethics of community or family should … recognize a presumption in favor of most personal reproductive choices.'[6] Citing the outlawing of contraception and abortion in Romania under Ceaucescu and also China's one-child policy, he argues that the burden of proof lies on those who would limit freedom in this area.

But how strong is the case for extending the interpretation of reproductive choice in the way these commentators propose? First, there is the question of whether an appeal to rights can be justified at all. Some would follow Bentham in rejecting the notion of a right as an invented metaphysical entity. But, as Dworkin argues: 'Individual rights are political trumps held by individuals. Individuals have rights when, for some reason, a collective goal is not a sufficient justification for denying them what they wish, as individuals, to have or to do, or not a sufficient justification for imposing some loss or injury upon them.'[7] But whether reproductive rights of a novel sort can function as trumps in the contentious debates surrounding the new technologies must depend on whether or not there are other claimants with conflicting rights to be considered. It is for this reason, too, that the argument that moral and religious belief make this a no-go area for law and governance cannot be sustained. Whatever validity it may have in the abortion debate, it cannot be extended to situations that will at some later stage involve actual children. Nor is it possible to sidestep this issue by appeal to the broad international recognition already accorded to family-related rights. For what the authors of the international declarations had in mind was not technological assistance in child-bearing, but rather the possibility that a totalitarian state might attempt to *prevent* people having children by methods such as forced sterilization or abortion.

Three steps are conflated in the reasoning that has led so many philosophical commentators to stretch the case beyond this limited boundary. The first step, which the international declarations were certainly intended to support, is to defend the freedom of two individuals (who, prior to the new technologies, must have been a male and a female) to marry and have children together. The second step is to advocate a right to receive assistance from medicine and science to do this—something that, even if not necessarily included in the first freedom, is not incompatible with it. The third step is to claim a right to donor-assisted reproduction. It is the third step that has a more problematic status: it has come into the picture only because some of the resources and assistance that can be used to help people to have their own genetic offspring can also be used to help them have the genetic offspring of other people. This immediately expands the circle of stakeholders or concerned individuals and changes the role and responsibilities of the decision-makers.

A putative right of this sort, then, differs significantly from the right to found a family as originally conceived, first because the conventions apply only within a very specific framework—that of a couple who are in a position to marry. So neither a man nor a woman separately can find support in these conventions. As far as men are concerned, subsequent legal decisions have found that a man has no right to prevent his wife using contraception or having an abortion, and, since he certainly has no right to compel any woman other than his wife to bear a child for him, it would seem that Article 8 of the European Convention cannot be read as giving a man *as an individual* an enforceable right to procreate. But, unless a gender imbalance is accepted, this throws into doubt, too, a *woman's* right to reproduce. That conclusion seems to have been indirectly accepted in the United Kingdom, though possibly not in some other European countries, in relation to assisted reproduction involving artificial insemination, since, in situations where sperm has been stored or where sperm could be taken from a man who has died, the man's consent to the use of his sperm is judged to be essential to its use. Hence a woman's putative right, too, would seem to be qualified by her need to find a willing procreative partner.

But some would argue that the advent of the new reproductive technologies has changed all this. In the case of a woman, a voluntary sperm donation service does, after all, give her a practical way of exercising her right to have a child with the help of a consenting male person, and for men, too, a parallel might be claimed because of the possibility of obtaining the services of a surrogate mother and an egg-donor, whether the surrogate herself or another woman. This might seem to suggest that a right to procreate could, after all, be asserted and be enforceable outside the 'couple' framework. If so, it should be recognized that this would be a new right, and not an extension of an existing one. Some appear to see this challenge to the scope of the conventions as linguistic rather than pragmatic, and so amenable to being solved by an arbitrary and radical ruling on what the term 'family' means. An extreme instance of this is a definition suggested by the Human Fertilization and Embryology Authority (HFEA), a body set up in the UK to regulate fertility treatment: 'the woman to be treated and any person together with whom she is proposing to receive treatment, and any legal child of that woman or of any person with whom she is proposing to receive treatment, at the time at which treatment is to take place.'[8]

This is what might be called a 'snapshot' portrait of family relationships—an instant picture taken at a particular time and place. Reinterpretations of family that are as broad as this are striking in their willingness to break all reference to close or even continuing relationships. When the issue is assisted reproduction, they neglect the reasons for control of these developments in the first place. These reasons must include the rights and interests of the child who results from the 'treatment'. A child is not a mere acquisition, and children should not be viewed simply as commodities medically generated to satisfy the needs or desires of adults. This point was succinctly put by Maura A. Ryan in relation to the views of John Robertson mentioned earlier: 'the success of Robertson's argument depends on accepting the view that persons can be the object of another's right … he is asserting the right to acquire a human being.' Such a position, she argues, fails to respect offspring as autonomous beings.[9] This underlines the paradox in the position of those who advocate 'procreative autonomy'. In stressing the primary agents' autonomy, they neglect the autonomy of the human being, who, at that early stage, is only secondarily involved. What is more, since assisted reproduction involves the cooperation of other people—especially clinicians and other health professionals—these have a responsibility to consider that other perspective. This is especially so where donated gametes are involved, for then the situation is in a significant way analogous to adoption. This justifies at least some of the safeguards and public involvement accepted as reasonable in that case in order to see that fair consideration is given to the interests of the child. This is not, as is often suggested, to ask doctors to sit in judgment on would-be parents. It is simply to recognize that children are the most vulnerable of all human beings and that this places a special burden of responsibility on all those who play a part in the procreative process.

Future children, future rights?

In a situation in which a new and unfamiliar gulf has opened up between genetic or biological relatedness and social relatedness, it is easy to overlook the fact that the question of a child's interests is broader than a simple question of welfare. Indeed, since welfare is often, in these contexts, interpreted in purely psychological terms, it may give a deceptively reassuring impression, ignoring some real concerns. A striking example of this is discussion surrounding a proposal to solve the shortage of donated human eggs for use in fertility treatment by taking eggs from cadavers or from aborted fetuses. While accepting that the interests of children born in this way might be involved here, John Harris considers the relevant question to be how such children might *feel* about their situation. His answer is another question: 'Will this knowledge be so terrible that it would be better that no such children had ever been or were even born? It is difficult to be certain how to answer this question, but it is surely unlikely that the consequences would be unacceptably terrible.'[10] As far as objective assessment of the child's interest is concerned, he continues:

One question we should ask is whether the act of producing such a child is in the overall interests of the individual who is thereby produced, or is wrongful for some other reason. In the expectation that it will live a normal lifespan and have a reasonably favourable balance of happiness over misery in its life, it is overwhelmingly likely that the individual will have what would be objectively judged to be a worthwhile life.[11]

This is a powerful argument that may seem to trump any objection that can be raised in relation to the future situation that the child will experience. This is particularly the case if a preoccupation with the rights of adults to reproduce leads people to neglect the child's perspective altogether. The argument is that, under whatever circumstances a child is conceived, it would not otherwise have existed, and life is almost always to be preferred to non-existence. Hence regulation or constraint is both wrong and unnecessary except in the most extreme of circumstances.

In the case of children born by assisted reproduction, however, the argument is conducted in terms that suggest that they already have a kind of shadow existence in which they confront the alternatives of existing or not existing—it is as if there is a queue of children waiting in limbo for a chance to be born, so that the onus is on those who *stop* them being born to justify their decision. But this is nonsense. A child who may be born by assisted reproduction is in the same category as books that may be written, motorways that may be built, or laws that might be passed. Some assume, nevertheless, that, where a possible human life is at issue, existence is bound to be the better option, no matter what the circumstances. As Harris puts it, 'unless the child's condition and circumstances can be predicted to be so bad that it would not have a worthwhile life, a life worth living, then it will always be in that child's interests, to be brought into being.'[12] But no one is injured by not being conceived, and, while most people can imagine what it would be like to wish they had never been born, it is impossible to imagine regretting not having even been conceived.[13] It is worth noticing, too, that the people who put this argument forward in connection with donor-assisted reproduction—that it is almost always better to exist than not to exist—never seem to entertain that principle when discussing abortion, where even minor disadvantages, such as being born into too large a family, or possible poverty, or suffering from minor handicaps, are taken as acceptable reasons for not bringing a fetus to term. Nor are they usually opposed to screening embryos for serious disease and allowing unwanted embryos to perish. But it is inconsistent to favour either abortion or the selection of embryos for reasons like these, and at the same time to be opposed to thinking in advance about the future rights and interests of merely possible children.

For, while there is no waiting entity to benefit from mere existence, the claims of any actual future entity do need to be considered in advance. And, where donor-assisted reproduction is involved, those who stress the rights of adults but see no special human-rights issues as applying to the child may do so because they discount the significance of original genetic material—eggs, sperm, or embryos. Susan Okin puts this point succinctly: 'a human infant originates from a minute quantity of abundantly available and otherwise useless resources.'[14] But this is to ignore the extraordinary potential of these 'resources'. In particular, it suggests a blinkered view of what an embryo is. It has no thoughts, feelings, or expectations, so is 'morally insignificant'. As a result, the idea that an embryo might have future claims that could be affected even at this early stage is not taken seriously. Its moral claims are assumed to be nil.

But, while it is possible to make excessive claims about embryos, where an embryo is destined to become a person, the argument that its future claims may need protection does need to be taken seriously. There is nothing irrational in recognizing that, because of its capacity to mature into a rights-bearing individual, human genetic material has a unique and special status.[15] The idea of protecting future claims before their owner can assert them is well established in both law and ethics. For example, an infant's inheritance can be protected, and a child can apply for compensation for an incapacitating injury it has suffered at the fetal stage, providing it survives those injuries and passes the birth threshold. Of course, even if we recognize that a person's rights can be violated at the fetal stage, we might still hesitate to apply this principle to the embryonic stage. But, again, new possibilities bring new ethical considerations, and, in this case, there may well be a conflict between what some existing human beings want or appear to need and what another future person might be entitled to. The important point here is that some adults may find that rights they consider important, and that other people enjoy, were taken away from them by actions and decisions made by other people before they were born.

Designing babies

The possibility of such a conflict is brought strikingly into focus by the issue of designer babies. Two examples provide convincing illustrations of the way in which a person's future rights can be disregarded or even nullified at the earliest stage of existence.

The first is a purely hypothetical example that nevertheless has some practical application. It stems from the fact that deaf people often share a friendly and supportive community life; hence some deaf people wish to have children who are also deaf and so will be able to become full members of their own community. In one much-discussed case, this wish led to a deaf woman successfully seeking a deaf sperm-donor in the hope of having a child who would also be deaf. (In this case, a sperm-donor was sought because the would-be mother was a lesbian with a female partner.[16]) But, if it were possible to secure a deaf child by direct interference with an embryo as opposed to achieving this by selection of donor, most people would agree that, no matter how happy the resulting child might be in its later life, it would have been deprived of a right taken for granted by other human beings and one that most people would consider inviolable.

This consensus might be harder to find in the case of the second example, which is provided by the debate surrounding what have been called 'saviour siblings'. The background to this debate is that children suffering from certain rare inherited diseases may be helped by a blood or bone-marrow transfusion from a suitable donor, ideally a sibling. Parents may understandably hope that one of their existing children could provide a tissue match, and, if this is not the case, they may decide to have another child in the hope that it will be compatible as a donor for the sick child. But science can now assist this choice. The procedure involved is relatively straightforward, given the widespread use of assisted reproduction. It involves producing a number of embryos, which can then be examined *in vitro* to see if there is an embryo free of the condition that could become a child who is an ideal tissue match for the existing child.[17]

At first sight, this may seem a wholly benign approach. But, compassionate though it might seem, the question is whether the donor child is being fairly treated. In this case, both welfare and rights are involved, and it is doubtful whether either can be adequately protected in these circumstances. The strategy is initiated in the hope that all that will be needed is the newborn baby's cord blood. However, if the cord-blood donation fails, the new child is destined for a possible lifetime of pressure to donate whatever its ailing older sibling might need in the future. This could include not only repeated donations of bone marrow but even non-replaceable organs.[18] In practical terms, the result is a healthy child growing up alongside an older child whose medical needs it has been specifically selected to meet. Undeniably, and no matter how excellent its situation in other respects, this is a child who has been created in order to be used for a purpose that goes beyond itself and its own interests. In this case, both state and parents, in their understandable concern for an existing child, can be seen as combining against the second child's autonomy. Their decision and their choice, however, are made at a stage when it is impossible that the child's own voice could be heard.[19]

While the case of the deaf child and that of the savour sibling have a medical dimension, these are not the only kinds of interventions with future effects that may be experienced at the embryonic stage. Social rather than medical reasons for intervening are probably more common than medical ones, and these can result in future losses of a different kind. In particular, some reproductive choices can mean the exclusion from a child's life of a genetic parent.

Lesbian and gay families

The question has already been raised, is there a right to found any sort of family? In some circumstances single women, single men, and lesbian and gay couples can adopt children. Does it follow that people in all these categories should be able to create families of their own choosing? Many believe that there should be a right of equal access for all. But in opening the door to this possibility in the United Kingdom in the 1990 Human Fertilization and Embryology Act, it was judged necessary to add a legal requirement that the need of a child for a father should be taken into account. Since that date, technology has developed to a stage where the need of a child for a mother cannot be taken for granted either. For the first time, it is necessary to ask, do children have a right to a mother, a right to a father, or even a right to two parents one male, one female? This is a new and untrodden area for society. However, it is not difficult to find theorists ready to support this new plurality. Many would agree with the liberal philosopher Max Charlesworth when he said: 'We cannot ... in a liberal society set up the traditional mode of family formation as a paragon and see all other modes of family creation as deviant and subversive.'[20]

Some indeed would go beyond this to reject the traditional structure itself. There are two kinds of objections: first, from those who would simply replace the male and female presumption with a greater openness to same-sex parenting, while retaining the small-scale intimate structure of a unit centred on the having and raising of children, and, second, from those who would reject the underlying structure in its entirety. For this second group, far from long-term monogamous relations being the goal that lesbians and gays should aspire to, they are part of the old repressive family model in which women are no more than property. These objectors would prefer to reject the category 'family' altogether as an intrinsically oppressive structure rather than to try to redefine it as inclusive of lesbians and gays.[21] In place of the traditional heterosexual procreative unit, they propose new models of social living—informal groupings of adults and children unrelated by either blood or legal convention. This is the 'postmodern' or 'queer' family described by Cheshire Calhoun: 'By "queer families" I mean ones not centered around marriage or children, but composed instead of chosen, adult, supportive relationships.'[22] But Calhoun recognizes that, if gay families are equated with non-marital and non-parenting families, this might concede too much to those who regard gays and lesbians as unfit for bringing up children. And so she argues that these non-standard groupings should have access to the legitimate and protected private sphere of mothering, marriage, and family. Calhoun puts the position in these terms:

lesbians and gays who resist their construction as family outlaws are not bidding for access to one, highly conventional family form (such as the nuclear, two-parent, self-sufficient, procreative family). They are instead bidding for access to the same privilege that heterosexuals now enjoy, namely the privilege of claiming that *in spite of their multiple deviations* from norms governing the family, their families are nevertheless *real* ones and they are themselves naturally suited for marriage, family, parenting *however* these may be defined and redefined.[23] (emphasis in original.)

It would be easy to confuse the issue of lesbian and gay family formation with that of lesbian and gay partnerships. But the involvement of children in any arrangement raises distinctive social and ethical considerations, and, while gay and lesbian pressure groups have been largely successful in many Western countries in their demand for parity in law as far as adult unions are concerned, the intention to treat the partnership as one for bringing children into the world raises some additional issues. A distinction was drawn earlier between two functions of marriage, the first, individual—two people's emotional desire or need for each other—the second social—raising children who will later form the nucleus of society. But, once the two functions are considered separately, something it is easier to do today with greater reproductive control, some novel questions force their way into the equation. In particular, can two people of the same sex really substitute for a male and a female parent? It would be wrong to take this as a question about purely practical possibilities—two females can raise children and often do so very well; it is also possible for two men to do so, though not so many will have the sustained interest or the empathy needed. But then, if only possibility is in question, as opposed to desirability, it has to be recognized that others can raise children too: aunts, uncles, grandparents, foster carers, or simply unrelated kindly guardians. But many of these arrangements are *faute de mieux*—that is to say, they are ways to meet the needs and interests of existing children who, for one reason or another, cannot be cared for by their own parents.

There is, though, a further question. It is not about what can happen, but about which, if any, of the possibilities should be taken as a model, not for the adoption or care of existing children, but for bringing children into the world. There is a historic conception of mother and father common to most human beings that sits uneasily with recognizing one of two female partners as a legal father. Even more difficult, though generally undiscussed, is the question of whether one of two males in partnership can be regarded as, or fulfil the functions of, a mother. In spite of this, legislation for same-sex partnerships has gone ahead in many of the liberal democracies on the assumption that the right to officially recognized same-sex partnerships carries with it all the rights of heterosexual couples, including those connected with having and raising children. The principle widely applied here is that not to have equality in this respect amounts to unlawful discrimination. A number of European countries have amended their legislation on same-sex partnerships to reflect this, and the European Parliament in 2003 adopted a report recommending that unmarried partnerships, both heterosexual and homosexual, should be given the same rights as marriage.[24] Indeed, as far as adoption is concerned, once it is possible for a single person to apply to adopt a child, it is difficult to prevent men or women in same-sex relationships doing this. In the Netherlands, Sweden and the United Kingdom, same-sex couples may adopt children, while in Denmark and Germany, a person can adopt the child of a same-sex partner. In a case in Scotland, too, in which a handicapped child was placed with two gay men, the Court of Appeal ruled that each case should be treated on its merits.[25]

The new perspective represented by these legislative moves reflects a sea change in public and political opinion. But, in welcoming the new openness and acceptance of alternative lifestyles, it is possible to lose sight of the broader picture. Appeal is made, in particular, to the success of lesbian parenting.[26] But success can be gauged in different ways, and there are some less visible empirical considerations that are also relevant and important. For example, given the effects of family breakdown on children, it is not unreasonable to take into account the likely length of a relationship, and the fact is that same-sex relationships do not, on average, last as long as heterosexual cohabitation, and less time again than marriage.[27]

There is also an underlying ambiguity in these relationships that has begun to emerge in the law courts, following cases in which the custody of children has become an issue. So, while many continuing situations provide a happy context for children, it is when couples split up that the ambiguities implicit in the arrangements can begin to affect the children's lives. Much turns on how the parental or caring roles are interpreted. For example, in a case in Canada involving a lesbian couple, a woman succeeded in her claim that she had no responsibility, financial or otherwise, for the children she and her partner had brought into being using anonymous sperm donation. In another, a woman who wanted to maintain contact with a child whose upbringing she had shared was judged to have no claim in law, even though she was the child's genetic parent, having donated her own egg for her partner to bring to birth. In contrast to this judgment, in another landmark case in England, a woman was awarded shared parental responsibility for her former partner's biological children, two girls then aged 6 and 3. The two women had lived together for about eight years, but the mother of the children now had a new partner and wanted her previous partner to be seen as no more than an extended family member, and not as a parent. In a novel judicial interpretation of diversity, Lord Justice Thorpe was reported as saying: 'What has been said about the importance of fathers is of equal application in same-sex parents.'[28]

Many of those who sympathize with the wish of some lesbians and some separatist feminists to have children in their relationships may nevertheless believe that the implications for those children must also come into the picture, and the insecurities, both personal and legal, of their situation are a part of this assessment. The legal situation could, of course, be clarified, but this course would have wider implications as a result of laws already in place that outlaw discrimination between man and woman. However, the implications of gender equality are not always thought through to their logical conclusion. Where two women are bringing up children together, the children's early upbringing may not be so different from that of many others, since families without men are not uncommon, nor are families in which the man must leave the house for work during most of the child's waking hours. But it is not so obvious that the same can be said about families without women. What about children, male or female, without mothers? Accepting that some gay partners already have children from a heterosexual relationship and want to continue to care for them, and also that other men have given their children love and care after the death or loss of a wife and mother, accepting, too, that two men may be able to offer a caring home life to an existing child, it is another matter deliberately to create children for these situations. The motherless child is culturally regarded as a tragic figure in most societies, and it would require a psychological tsunami to sweep this basic human instinct aside. Questions about a child's need for its mother would have been largely theoretical in the past, but advances in reproductive medicine now present the issue in practical terms in a way that would have been inconceivable to earlier generations.

Strong sentiments are involved here, and it is not easy to resolve the tensions, for, where same-sex parenting is concerned, one harm is unavoidable. This is the harm of being deprived of one parent, even if a substitute is provided in the form of a second mother, or a second father. It is an important tenet of a free society that it is wrong to rule out social arrangements designed to satisfy people's strong desires where this involves no serious harm to others. The issue turns, then, on whether this deprivation is a *serious* harm, and this may still be too hard to establish. It is difficult to know, for example, how it would feel to have been deliberately denied the maternal relationship, as happened in a highly publicized case in which a male couple fathered three children using commercially purchased human ova and paid surrogates. It is too easy to generalize from the case of children born after the death of their father as a result of factors outside either parent's control to that of children born following the *deliberate* exclusion of a parent, especially a mother.

As for the broad ideological debate about diversity and gender neutrality, the gender-neutral notion of parenthood seeks to resolve conflict by placing on a par any two-person arrangement for raising children, whether male and female, male and male, or female and female. But the principle of equality requires only that like cases be treated alike, and it could be argued that heterosexual unions are in general intended as the foundation of families—in most human societies that has been their *raison d'être*—while gay unions appear, again in general, more commonly intended for adult companionship. If this diversity of purpose is accepted, then the anti-discrimination argument is not decisive. In other words, if there is a relevant difference between the two cases, based on a difference between the two kinds of relationships, then it would not, after all, be unfair to treat them differently. This would not mean that the state would place unreasonable obstacles in the path of same-sex relationships, nor would it rule out in advance any particular caring arrangements for existing children. But it would justify a slower pace of change and a more cautionary approach to the 'new-families' ideology. Instead of endorsing this ideology on the ground that the traditional, heterosexual family defined by marriage and blood relationships is dead, the 'new family', where it exists, would be regarded as the kind of exception that, as the old adage has it, actually proves the rule.

But, as one of the key exponents of reproductive choice himself concedes, in cases where multiple participants are involved, 'it becomes unclear which participants hold parental rights and duties and will function socially and psychologically as members of the child's family'.[29] It is tempting to ask whether contemporary organizations that seek to provide gametes for same-sex couples have fully appreciated the underlying reality of the situation when choosing misleading names such as WomanNotIncluded and ManNotIncluded—misleading because, as these names so eloquently demonstrate, the male or female element is not in fact eliminated. It is simply thrown into shadow by the impersonal transfer of sperm or ova. Even where there are no ensuing difficulties or disagreements, the children who result are necessarily deprived of one or other biological parent and also of a substitute of the same sex as that parent. Whatever compensation may be implicit in the situation, the remarkable fact is that what they are deprived of is something that, for the entire history of humankind, has been taken as a good and has so far not needed to be proclaimed as a right—in the one case to a father/male parent, in the other to a mother/female parent. And yet, as Jonathan Glover has observed: 'The normal state for a child is to have one parent of each sex. It is surely right to be very cautious about tampering with something so fundamental.'[30]

The failure to recognize this may be due to a loss of perspective—an unwillingness to look at matters the other way round. So how should we rate the loss (in the sense of deliberate deprivation) of either a father or a mother? From the examples cited earlier, it is clear that men and women who have brought children into the world without the direct involvement of the opposite sex are often ready to challenge each other's biological interest in the child who, as things currently stand, can be created only by the joint participation, no matter how distant or medically impersonal, of male and female. These new ways of constructing families do involve bypassing either a biological mother or a biological father. Does this matter? Should we recognize that children may be losing something valuable if the reproductive choices of others, supported by medical and scientific expertise, necessarily deprive them of an important genetic link? Admittedly, in these cases involving single or gay people, there will be one strong genetic link, and this must mitigate the loss of the second parent. How much this matters is not something that could be finally settled by empirical research or information, although this must be part of the picture. For, behind the contested viewpoints lie two more reflective and open-ended questions that perhaps people will in the end be able to answer only in the light of their own observations. How much does a child's biological mother matter? And how much do fathers matter?

Do mothers matter?

Literature, legend, and history have consistently painted the orphan— the child who lacks both father and mother—as someone to be pitied, and the early loss of either a mother or a father by death or abandonment would almost always be viewed as a tragedy. By 'early' loss, I mean loss before the child is old enough to understand, or indeed before the child is actually born. Of course, the later loss of either parent is likely to be deeply traumatic for a child who has already come to love that parent.

But what if the child has never had the experience of being cared for by a parent? Should it matter to a child that its birth has been arranged so as to deprive it of the near-universal experience of having a mother and father? Philosophers' views on this issue sometimes seem to reflect their own personal experience. Mary Warnock, whose Report on Human Fertilization and Embryology provided the basis for UK legislation in that area, has cited her own experience as a posthumous baby to support her own view that children can have a satisfactory upbringing and a happy childhood without a father. The case of Diane Blood, who sought to use her dead husband's sperm to have his children, received much support from an underlying assumption of that sort, although in that case it was Mrs Blood's husband's lack of formally established consent on which the issue turned, rather than the issue of whether to assist posthumous births, since this is provided for in the United Kingdom.[31]

But does a child have a special need for its mother that is stronger and more biologically significant than any other relationship? There is no reason to doubt the widely held view that a child who lacks the warm physical bond of mother love has lost something that can be only partially compensated for by others, if at all. A wealth of empirical research exists concerning that relationship. This ranges from Harlow's sad experiments on maternal deprivation carried out with monkeys to John Bowlby's observations on child development and the maternal–infant bond. [32] Contemporary studies of mothers who have themselves experienced institutional care in childhood have confirmed a picture of this leading later on to difficulty in handling their relationships with their own children.[33] So the separation of mother and child is something that should not be taken lightly.

However, the new era of cooperating procreation has brought new complexities into the picture, for conflicting claims may cast doubt on the notion of 'mother' itself. Where egg donation is involved, this does, in most cases, deprive a child of its genetic mother, whether this is in a heterosexual or a homosexual context. But, apart from when a surrogacy contract has been made to exclude this, it does provide someone else who has a close claim—and many would say a sufficiently close claim—to be a mother in another sense—that is, she has invested her own body in supporting the essential stages from embryonic to infant life, creating another kind of intimate biological bond. Indeed, this double claim has created another ambiguity that has been resolved in a number of countries, including the UK, by giving the birth mother legal recognition.

But, while that is perhaps a necessary decision in order to clarify the child's position and guarantee its home life, it should not obscure the biological reality accepted without question in the case of other living creatures, that genetic origin has a special and determining significance. This suggests that, at a minimum, a child is owed information about the special circumstances in which it came to be born, and parents and doctors are wrong if they conspire to conceal this. The arguments that have brought more openness in the case of sperm donation apply here as well. Both ethically and legally, it is a step too far to expunge from all records the genetic origin and hence ancestry and other relationships of the child. Given honesty and acceptance, however, a child's need for a mother may in some circumstances be met by another woman's longing for a child, and this may help to compensate the child for other lost relationships. There are good reasons, then, for saying that mothers matter. But does this mean that the case for helping single or lesbian women to have children is stronger than that for assisting single or gay men? This seems to imply that a father has a lesser role in the life of a child. But is this true?

Do fathers matter?

Contemporary confidence that a male relationship with a very young infant can be a satisfactory substitute for its relationship with its mother is largely untested. This does not necessarily mean that findings would be negative, but it is perhaps worth noting that men left with the care of an infant have almost always sought the help of an alternative female carer for their children.

Here some established psychological differences between men and women may need to be acknowledged. For example, while sperm-donors often express a wish not to be told if they have fathered children, women who donate eggs seem to have a deeper sense of involvement and concern, which may be based on a stronger sense that they are parting with their biological sons or daughters. In contrast to male donors, they are more likely to want to know if a child has resulted from their donation. This is likely to be the case even when, in egg-sharing arrangements, they may have had to agree not to be informed if their eggs result in a birth and may accept that it is better in such circumstances that they should not know.

But what of the children involved? Even if young children who are well cared for often appear little affected by the loss or absence of a male parent, fathers are generally acknowledged to have an important role with older children. Later still in life, there is ample evidence that, for some offspring at least, the desire for contact with a missing father can be overwhelming. In the case of children born by donation, many who are now reaching their twenties or thirties are asserting their own claims to information or contact with their natural father.[34] In one influential case, a young woman born as a result of fertility treatment, the records of which could not be found, claimed a duty on the part of the UK Government and the HFEA to assist her in finding out the identity of her natural father. The court found that her human rights were engaged and the Department of Health later set up a voluntary register (UKDonorlink) to help people trace relatives.[35]

Underlying discussion of this issue must be the acknowledgement that in practice children can be happily raised, at least in their early years, by a woman on her own, or by two women.[36] It must also be acknowledged that fathers' claims and involvement increase as children grow older. But, whatever the facts of the matter, there is a distinction between situations that arise from the ordinary circumstances of life and those that are deliberately brought about. In particular, there is a question as to whether it is right for medical science to be called in to create such situations *ex nihilo*. As J. David Velleman observes in a philosophical paper on the link between personal and biological identity: 'Creating children with the intention that they not have a custodial father, or alternatively a custodial mother, is potentially just as problematic as creating children divorced from their biological origins.'[37] Even if it is accepted that novel structures such as these can be rewarding for the adults involved, it is questionable how far it is reasonable to build that recognition into a new conception of family, to be widely imitated and promoted, rather than recognizing it as an exceptional situation that will necessarily involve some loss for the child. Other empirical findings may be relevant here, including the tendency of same-sex relationships to be of shorter duration than heterosexual ones, and the consequent possibility that they may later unwind into their original constituents in the law courts.

Trading in humans

While altruistic and personal transfers of gametes or embryos with adequate controls and forward consideration can be justified, the fact is that the new possibilities have brought about a commodification of human genetic material. This has been gathering momentum as the demand for the raw material of baby manufacture far outstrips supply, and it undermines the whole basis on which the biological family exists. Not surprisingly, one solution that occurs to people who, for whatever reason, have an interest in increasing the supply is to introduce a financial incentive into the equation. But a special moral objection has long been attached to the sale of human genetic material, and a number of declarations by international bodies have explicitly ruled out commerce in human embryos. These include UNESCO

(United Nations Educational, Scientific, and Cultural Organization), which has ruled that the transfer of human embryos can never be a commercial transaction, and the European Union, which has insisted that the prohibition on making the human body and its parts a source of financial gain must be respected.[38]

Individual countries, too, have adopted stringent laws on the matter: Sweden threatens up to two years imprisonment for anyone who seeks to profit from the transfer of biological material from a living or a dead human or tissue from an aborted fetus. Switzerland prohibits the gift of embryos and any commercial transaction involving human germinal material and any resulting products from embryos. The case of Australia, though, may be more typical of what can happen in practice. While it is an offence there intentionally to give or receive value for the supply of human eggs, sperm, or embryos, and a ten-year jail sentence may be imposed for trading commercially in human eggs or embryos, Australians are bypassing the law by travelling to the USA to achieve what they cannot access in their home country.[39]

Despite the international agreements that exist to ban such transactions, the fact that they are not outlawed in the USA is a significant factor.[40] There are, of course, other countries with a permissive regime. But even countries that would prefer to appear to be adhering to international agreements on the matter are seeking ways to sidestep the issue. Payment described as compensation plus comprehensive expenses may, for example, be a *de facto* way of achieving this if compensation and expenses are loosely and generously interpreted.[41]

Given that there is a demand, it is not surprising that the whole matter may be viewed by entrepreneurs in business terms. The Denmark-based Cryos International is the world's largest sperm bank. It markets its sperm throughout the world, shipping it to more than forty countries, including Spain, Paraguay, Kenya, Hong Kong and the United States. Denmark's laws protect donor anonymity, and the number of children a donor can father depends on where he lives and where his sperm is sent.[42] Some welcome these developments, because they see them as expanding reproductive choice and allowing people to have families who would not otherwise have been able to do so. They may even be families designed to fit their preferences, since the trade in gametes, particularly over the Internet, allows people to select for desired characteristics by the imperfect and only partially reliable method of selection of donor.

There are, however, a number of different reasons for challenging this. First, there is a general objection to the 'instrumentalisation' of the human body that applies, as well, to the sale of organs and tissue. It would be odd to object to the sale of kidneys but to have a *laissez-faire* approach to the sale of ova, sperm, and embryos. Second, there is a well-founded fear that financially vulnerable individuals could be exploited. This already happens in the case of kidneys, and countries that permit women to sell their eggs are likely to find that the same is true of many of the women who decide to go through the unpleasant and risky process necessary to provide these eggs. Israel, for example, initially had a very liberal approach in this matter, but drew back from this when it became clear that there was a risk of creating an exploited class of women. Finally, there is a general judgement that the sale of human eggs, sperm, or embryos is contrary to human dignity. Whatever the child-friendly goals of the practice, it evokes distant echoes of the sale of human beings in slavery. It is offensive to conceptions of the value of human life that it has taken millennia to establish and that we sometimes claim, even if a degree of self-deception is involved, as the foundation of our twenty-first-century civilisation.

Lost identities

The new controllers of the necessary ingredients of reproduction may well consider that their own responsibility ends with a pregnancy. But resulting from these global transactions are children who, taken from their genetic roots and their location in particular continents or ethnic settings, have become the new dispossessed. Certainly, the idea that children may belong within a cultural or geographic community is taken very seriously at the end if not the beginning of the gestation period. It has, for example, become harder for Western couples to adopt babies from countries such as China, despite the numbers of babies in need, because there is a sense that, whatever their situation, Chinese children belong within that community. Another comparison, which may seem extreme but is effective in underlining the idea of cultural and familial belonging, is the case of the children in Argentina who were taken from their parents at birth and given to childless supporters of the regime who then brought them up as their own. Some later discovered that they were children of the 'disappeared'. The fact that their parents had died as victims of a murderous regime tragically intensified their situation, but their alienation from their true family and community constituted a loss and a rights deprivation in itself. These children of the 'disappeared' had become a new 'disappeared'. Those they believed to have been their parents were not in fact so, and the cultural and kin context in which they found themselves were often completely alien. There are also other historical cases that, while they lack those malevolent overtones and indeed were often inspired by humanitarian motives, had comparable effects: for example, the 'Stolen Generation' of aboriginal children in Australia who were placed with European incomer families, or the children shipped to Australia from Britain and Ireland around the time of the Second World War who never saw their birth families or place of origin again.

But is it so different to be bartered and shipped before birth rather than afterwards? It may seem an excessive response to see today's global international commerce in genetic material in this way, but, where the overt or covert sale of gametes or embryos is involved, it is possible to see the resulting children as the victims of a similar kind of deliberate alienation from their ethnic and cultural roots. It is worth remembering, perhaps, that at least one of the wrongs involved in the historic slave trade, apart from the condition of slavery itself, was that tens of millions of inhabitants of West and Central Africa were taken to the Americas, and so deprived of their genetic and cultural inheritance. This is echoed, generations later, in the need some black Americans still feel to seek their personal roots in Africa.

It would be unreasonable to stretch these comparisons too far. Nevertheless, whatever the philosophical arguments deployed in relation to other issues concerning the status of the embryo, equity in the preservation of personal identity has not received as much attention as the rights of adults to fertility treatment. Another United Nations Convention does, however, appear to recognize a right of this sort. Article 8 of the United Nations Convention on the Rights of the Child specifies that: 'States Parties undertake to respect the right of the child to preserve his or her identity, including nationality, name and family relations as recognized by law without unlawful interference.'[43] Legally this might not be stretched to cover transfer at the embryonic rather than the birth stage, but, ethically and practically, it would seem that the same considerations that prompted it would apply in these cases too.

Evaluating the possibilities

These are, then, difficult issues, and fraught with contention. Nor is it clear that they are open to the kind of reasoning that is standard in either science or the social sciences. Perhaps indeed it will have to be accepted that argument cannot settle these matters, which are deeply intuitive. They bring into question conceptions of family, social and legal conventions, and a judgement about the value of nature versus human artifice. As the philosopher Leon Kass once put it: 'At stake is the idea of the humanness of our human life and the meaning of our embodiment, our sexual being, and our relations to our ancestors and descendants.'[44]

Whatever the situation, though, 'children of choice' have a right to at least one choice of their own: a right to choose *knowledge* of their parentage—not, that is, to be deliberately deceived about their origins by a medico-legal conspiracy. Without this, they are born as exiles from the kinship network and are orphans in a sense previously unknown to human beings. They may in fact have unknown half-siblings, cousins, aunts, or grandparents, but they will never meet them. Of course, there is every chance that they will be provided with an alternative family network that will provide love and security, but the subtle similarities of genetic relationships may come to haunt them in the future, particularly when they have children of their own and start to look for such things as shared resemblances, attitudes, interests, tendencies, qualities of character and physical features in their own offspring.

Given the choice, people seeking assisted reproduction overwhelmingly choose to have children who are genetically related to them. It seems, then, that while much public discussion is based on the assumption that alternative lifestyles and new modes of family formation are matters of popular demand, most people do continue to favour the security of reliable family relationships. Hume was surely right when, three centuries ago, he said that the relation of blood 'creates the strongest tie the mind is capable of in the love of parents for their children'.[45]

In enabling intervention at the embryonic stage, the new technologies of reproduction have created both new risks and new rights. A commitment to freedom of choice in this area means not only respecting the choices of adults, but also recognizing a responsibility to protect the welfare and rights of people at a stage when they are in no position to protect them for themselves. This means that the well-established right to found a family must not be interpreted in a way that would create a class of people—the 'donor-conceived'—who would be unequally treated in having their access to their genetic origins and their family relationships blocked by medico-legal rules of confidentiality or, more controversially, by depriving them of a specific type of parental or other intimate relationship. But equity in the preservation of genetic identity—particularly the rights of the donor-conceived—has not so far received as much attention as the rights of adults to fertility treatment. As the class of the donor-conceived has reached adult life, and as they have come forward with their own claims, the case they are pressing appears more compelling: not to be treated differently from those whose origins are more conventional and in particular not to be deprived of rights that are enjoyed by the naturally born majority.

In sum, then, how should we regard the new enlarged reproductive possibilities from the point of view of the family? Should the extended options be seen as helpful to families or the reverse? Fertility treatment can, of course, in the right circumstances be a valued good. It can make possible the happiness that founding a family often brings. But, where the transfer of gametes and the breaking of the genetic connection is a feature of the arrangement, and where this is not chosen for strong and compelling reasons such as the need to avoid passing on a serious genetic condition, it has other less acceptable features. I believe that in the end the less optimistic appraisal may be correct, and that the loss of genetic relatedness and the closing-off through this of all other genetic relationships strikes at the root of what has always till now constituted the human family.

Here it would be useful to return to the question how *should* the right to found a family be interpreted? And, while accepting the force of the very clear internationally endorsed statements about procreative rights, it is important to take care not to set foot on the escalator that leads to too broad an interpretation of these and the costs that involves. This is not simply a question of costs in money terms. More important are the personal and social costs of developments which are often superficially viewed as carrying only benefits. For when human gametes are regarded as no more than raw material for the medical manufacture of children, a whole dimension of human reproductive experience is lost.

PART III

New frontiers:
Family, law, and politics

7

Family choices:
What do children really want?

What many of the choices made about children, whether at the embryonic, infant, or teenage stage, have in common is that they are grounded in the preferences and needs of adults. The previous chapter illustrated the way in which possibilities inherent in the new technologies of reproduction mean that rights it has never before been necessary to claim can be nullified at the earliest stage of a person's life by adult choices. But these are not the only ways, and this is not the only stage, when children's rights and interests can be pre-empted by others before they acquire a 'voice' for themselves. Later stages of infancy, and even children's growing years, are vulnerable. Where education or health policy is concerned, some decisions must inevitably be made by adults, but even in these cases there can be serious disagreement as to whether or how the child's own perspective might feature. There may also be a conflict between parents and professionals about what is best for a child, and there is a further question as to how far either or both of these can speak for the older child as it begins to acquire a 'voice' and a perspective of its own. Increasingly, as far as welfare is concerned, judgement is being weighted towards professionals as the best-qualified judges of what is best for children.

But parents, even if not expert and even if prone to error, do have rights in respect of their children—rights based on the responsibility they have to care for their children. If this were not the case, the family structure would not hold in a world in which there is an increasing willingness to turn to outsiders for many decisions affecting children and young people. But, even if these outsiders were reliable judges of what is best for children's well-being, that would not be a sufficient reason for giving them ultimate authority. The child's interests matter, but if that was the *only* important consideration, the fundamental assumption that children belong with either or both parents would itself be under challenge. In other words, in the case of both parents and children, there are rights that are not covered by the notion of interest, benefit, or even choice.

The idea of a right—in the sense of a moral as opposed to a legal right—is sometimes regarded as problematic.[1] Many would share the view of the legal scholar John Eekelaar that rights are simply 'intellectual constructs'. This analysis, however, is not inconsistent with the view that a complex of rights and reciprocal obligations is indeed involved in the parent–child relationship, as Eekelaar himself points out, and that a right should not be confused with another person's judgement of where someone's interests lie.[2] If this were not so, and without ethical and legal presumptions about the relationship between children and their natural parents, there would be no reason for an intrusive state bent on social engineering *not* to consider a shift away from the tradition of parental care in the home to other arrangements less vulnerable to chance and the unreliability of individual human beings. Indeed, a number of assumptions that are already part of the social and political map, such as that it is the state's responsibility to provide round-the-clock crèche and after-school care for children, could be seen as steps in that direction. Although a necessary contribution to the common good where parents' personal circumstances are difficult, they are not the best way for children to begin their lives.[3] What is more, moves like these on any substantial scale could limit rather than extend freedom for family members. A state that takes on too much of the parental prerogative risks opening the door to an altogether different type of society—a new order of social living that is more in keeping with Plato's totalitarian vision of a state that, having all but eliminated family relationships, is free to pursue whatever political or educational objectives it chooses.

But, if the state and its representatives cannot be trusted with children's needs and aspirations, and if parents are sometimes indifferent to or careless of them, who *should* speak for children? One possibility is that they should, in some circumstances, be allowed to speak for themselves. This idea has a degree of acceptance, at least in the broader international context, and there is already some scope for children to express their own preferences in important decisions that affect their own care or well-being. It is a principle that has been embodied in some important public statements such as the United

Nations Convention on the Rights of the Child, and it is reflected in the Council of Europe's 1990 recommendation that there should be an ombudsman for children.[4]

These are some of the issues to be discussed in this chapter. However, a further set of questions is raised in the context of parental divorce or separation, when the parental 'voice' is itself divided. Of course, it is almost inevitable that, when a family splits up, what children want and what their parents propose may be hard to reconcile, but, when parents themselves are in conflict, especially in disputes over custody and contact with their children, it is parents' competing rights and interests rather than those of their children that can turn out in practice to be the hinge on which decision-making turns.

All these issues, then, bring into focus a picture in which there are a number of parties with potentially conflicting claims. Three of these are immediately identifiable: father, mother, and child. Then, as children move out into the world, teachers and other adults with child-care responsibility become part of the their world. As for the courts of law where conflicting legal claims are argued, the underlying assumption is that the court's role is that of an impartial adjudicator, but one that gives priority to the welfare of the child in decision-making. However, while they are the point of intersection for the three central figures, courts today introduce a fourth element into the picture: the professional adviser—social worker, doctor, psychiatrist, teacher, or other expert. Once this more complete picture is painted in, the child can be seen as uneasily located in the centre of several potential areas of conflict: in some cases, the struggle will be between parents and professional advisers, in others between the parents themselves. These areas of competing interests impinge in different ways on the position of the children caught in the middle.

Children, parents and professionals

The right of parents to make decisions on behalf of their offspring and in the light of what they, rather than their child, think is in the child's best interest was commonly taken for granted in the past. Even those political thinkers committed to the principle of individual autonomy saw no reason to extend it to children. They tended to assume that, if there is a role for paternalism anywhere at all, that place must be the family. Indeed, John Stuart Mill, in his classic advocacy and defence of individual liberty, found no difficulty in excluding children and young persons from the scope of the liberty principle. The reason Mill gave was that 'those who are still in a state to require being taken care of by others, must be protected against their own actions as well as against external injury'.[5]

Where philosophers' views on the family did take account of children, this did not usually mean looking at matters from their point of view. Both Kant and Hegel, for example, saw the interests of the child as included in that of the male head of the family, although Kant did insist that the members of a family retain their individual personhood and are not to be regarded as mere 'things' or instruments. Hume was almost alone in *not* assuming the patriarchal hypothesis, and his upbringing by a woman alone, his widowed mother, may well have influenced his views.[6] And, while Engels, in his classic text on the origin of the family, challenges conventional assumptions about power relationships between the sexes, he did not seem to think it necessary to challenge those between parents and children.[7]

This may well explain why it is that the issue finally came to the fore in a legal rather than a philosophical context. While every jurisdiction has its own distinctive aspects, the way in which thinking on the subject of children developed in England can be taken as reflecting more widespread evolving attitudes and assumptions about the position of children. The new focus came when the principle that there could be legal intervention to protect children began to take shape in the nineteenth century. A series of new laws limited the hours children would be allowed to work and tied this to requiring them to receive at least a minimal education. The first of these reforming Acts, sponsored by Sir Robert Peel in 1802, set the maximum daily hours of work at twelve, while another, in 1833, supported by the philanthropist Lord Shaftesbury, reduced this to forty-eight hours a week with two hours' education daily. In addition, two nineteenth-century legal cases, which were more directly concerned with the position of the child within the family, could be seen as embodying the germ of the welfare principle as it came to be used in later decisions involving children and their parents.[8] These cases, however, were concerned with welfare rather than autonomy, and a more visible and decisive change of emphasis came with the 1889 Act—sometimes known as the Children's Charter—which for the first time gave a 'voice' to children themselves by making it possible for a child to give evidence against its parents in cases of ill-treatment or neglect. Even so, it was only when a child's welfare was seriously at issue that a court would override parental right. And, as one commentator remarks: 'The State, when it took children away from parents, assumed the same rights over them as their parents had.' Reviewing the whole series of Children's Acts up to the 1970s, this writer continues: 'you can search through existing legislation as it affects children and not find a single sentence which enhances the dignity of childhood or recognizes that children are people in their own right and not just appendages of adults.'[9]

It was not till the latter part of the twentieth century that the idea that the interests and rights of children may need to be considered separately from those of their parents—that parental power is not absolute—began to be taken seriously. But the new weight given to the child's interest introduced a new factor into the equation and led to a new and much stronger role being assumed by professionals—teachers, judges, counsellors, social workers—in children's lives. Their role does not always have to be specific to their professional expertise, but can sometimes be a matter of interpreting and representing the child's own point of view.

Who speaks for children?

As far as this question is concerned, a case pursued through the English legal system by Mrs Victoria Gillick was a turning point. The London-based Department of Health and Social Security had advised that contraception should be available to all young people at risk of pregnancy regardless of age, and Mrs Gillick had written to her local health authority to ask for an assurance that her own daughters would not be offered abortion or contraception advice or treatment without her knowledge or consent. Unable to obtain this assurance, she brought a case against the DHSS and her Health Authority in which she sought a ruling that it was unlawful for doctors to provide advice on abortion or contraception or to prescribe the contraceptive pill to girls under 16 without the knowledge or consent of their parents.[10] The case went through a series of appeals but was in the end lost, although, of the nine judges who considered the case at its various stages, five favoured Gillick and only four were against.

This case was important in that it brought to the surface the potential conflict between parental and professional views about what is best for children, and also between parental rights and the rights of the state to intervene in children's lives. The view that ultimately prevailed was widely seen as defending young people's own autonomy against parental claims. One of the judges, Lord Scarman, said that 'parental right yields to the child's right to make his own decision when he reaches a sufficient understanding and intelligence to be capable of making up his own mind on the matter requiring decision'. This was consistent with the view of another eminent lawyer, Lord Denning, that parental right is a 'dwindling right', starting with a right of control and ending with little more than scope for advice. But, while it is clearly best that the law should support a model of decision-making in which children's views count, it would be a mistake to assume too readily that it is always the child's voice that is heard when it is mediated by professionals. As the family-law scholar Andrew Bainham comments: 'The wisdom of giving schools, the medical profession, employers commercial bodies, religious institutions and other outsiders a completely free reign to deal with adolescents without parental knowledge or approval must be doubted. ... the real decision-maker will be neither the parent nor the child, but the outsider concerned.'[11]

However, the Gillick case was not only about children's autonomy. It was also about their welfare. Judging welfare, however, is not as straightforward as it might seem. To begin with, it is possible to overlook the fact that what is good for a particular child at a particular time may not be good for children or young people in general or as a group. Secondly, even where an individual child is concerned, it is a mistake to base judgement on short-term rather than long-term considerations. The young teenager will later be a 20-year-old, a 30-year-old, and so on. Most people think it reasonable, often necessary, to overrule a child's own wishes when young in the light of what the later person is likely to have wanted. This is a presumption that is routinely made in the case of education, and compulsory education is regarded as a right rather than an imposition. A similar presumption is also implicit in many health-promotion strategies, including vaccination and screening for latent health problems, as well as in other relatively uncontroversial social or medical choices. It is widely accepted, in other words, that there are important choices that cannot be left to the child.

In these cases, the issue becomes one of deciding who best represents the true interests of the child—parents, or the state and its agents? But, if so, hindsight casts a different light on the Gillick decision. Figures for teenage pregnancies and abortions and for sexually transmitted infections have continued to escalate.[12] So, if the state was indeed seeking to take on the role of parent, the evidence suggests that it may unintentionally have chosen the role of the unwise or feckless parent rather than the wise and caring one. Child protection in Britain in the early twentieth century, as in other democratic countries, had been a matter of using the state's authority, buttressed by law and punishment, to fend off sexual demands on children until they had enough maturity to cope with them—with the age of consent set first at 14, then 16. But sex education programmes based on the assumption that many young people will engage in sexual activity from 12 years on or even earlier have relied heavily on damage-limitation strategies, and there is some evidence that they have been counterproductive, and may even be adding to the problem they were intended to solve.[13]

In spite of this, state-determined health policy continues to overrule the wishes of individual parents in this area, and in May 2005 two further cases were initiated by mothers of teenage girls, though neither was successful. In one case, Julie Kosmala sought to contest the application of national guidelines that had led her daughters' school to provide free condoms for boys and to offer young girls 'fast-track' appointments with school nurses to obtain the morning-after pill, in both cases without their parents' knowledge. In the other, another mother, Sue Axon, objected to school nurses or social workers referring girls for abortions without their parents' knowledge. It could be said that the judgement in these cases was consistent with advice from UNESCO that governments should make abortion available to all women and adolescent girls without restriction.[14] But it ran counter to a strong current of opinion in the United States, where 44 of the 59 states have parental involvement laws intended to ensure that parental guidance and support are available when minor children seek to obtain an abortion. This is not to give parents' authority to prevent their child ultimately deciding what to do, but is based on a robust opinion in America that turns the issue away from welfare arguments to a straightforward assertion that the state cannot simply ignore the parental role—a minor child is not 'the mere creature of the State.'[15]

The question of how best to promote children's welfare or well-being is, then, a controversial matter, as is the question of whether parents themselves are always the best judges. But, while it would be wrong to claim that parents always do what is best for their child, there is one powerful argument for settling the question in their favour. This is a political rather than an ethical argument. Indeed, it is a foundational principle of democracy, and it moves the issue in the direction of parental rights rather than leaving it to flounder in disputes about practical outcomes and welfare considerations. It is the argument that it is only by putting trust in parents that a democratic state can voluntarily limit its own powers and demonstrate its commitment to individual liberty. In the words of one commentator, 'The practice of entrusting children to their parents ultimately limits the control of society to determine the life-style and beliefs of persons.'[16]

There is a more practical reason, too, for weighting judgement in favour of parents rather than handing it unchecked to experts who are acting on behalf of the state. Child-raising and education are areas where fashions come and go, and experts tend to converge on a single dominant theory, at least during their period of influence. This means that, if they are wrong, they are disastrously wrong, and their wrong judgement affects a whole generation. The judgement of parents, on the other hand, is limited to their own children and is as individual as individual families themselves.

The conclusion this points to is that, while in general children are best served when parents and professionals work together on their behalf, in most situations where it is necessary for one or other of these to speak for children, parents are better placed than professionals to do this. That is not to say that there can be no exceptions to this rule. For example, parents who neglect, abuse, or ill-treat their children cannot be trusted with this function, and there may also be problems when parents themselves are divided or have strong personal interests to pursue. There can be occasions too, particularly in the context of medical treatment, when an older child's decision might rightly be better understood by the health professionals caring for the child than by parents, who may press for the continuation of extreme but futile and painful treatments.

There could be some extreme circumstances, then, in which it would be right to deprive parents of their right to decide on behalf of their children, or even to allow children to separate themselves formally from either one or both of their parents. One writer who has pursued this argument to its conclusion, the American philosopher Hugh LaFollette, believes that a formal 'divorce' of parents should be an option open to older children, and he argues that not to allow for this is to limit them to the uncontrolled and more dangerous option of running away.[17] Clearly, it would be only very rare situations that would justify such a step, involving as it would a breach by the state of parental rights. However, some compelling examples do occasionally occur.[18] For instance, in one American case, a boy sought to free himself from his father who was in prison for the brutal murder of his mother. Firmly settled in his own mind that he did not wish to have anything further to do with his father, the boy appealed to the courts to bring an end to his father's parental rights and to allow him a 'divorce' from his parent.[19]

While this is a highly unusual case, the idea that children might be allowed to reselect their own guardians or parental figures in certain circumstances is not novel.[20] Laura M. Purdy, discussing the case of another boy, 12-year-old Gregory K., who, in 1992, sought to terminate his legal relationship with his mother, proposes a potential way to handle those rare situations in which allowing children to separate themselves from their family is the only way to protect their interests: the creation of children's houses, analogous to women's refuges that provide a similar function for women in cases of domestic violence.[21] These, she believes, could provide a neutral base for children to stay while their claims are considered.[22]

For LaFollette, on the other hand, the case is stronger that this, and he argues that there should be a presumption in favour of the child's choice, particularly when it is the state rather than the parent that has taken on the parental role. He writes: 'I would not suggest that the children's say can never be legitimately overridden by a court exercising its role of *in loco parentis*. However, that judicial role should be exercised infrequently and then only when there is compelling evidence that these children's decisions are not only unreasonable but demonstrably imprudent.'[23] There are some rare cases, then, when it may be necessary to turn to the courts and their professional advisers rather than to parents to represent the child's own voice. The issue of parental rights *vis-à-vis* those of their children comes to a head, however, not so much in these unusual cases but in another situation children are far more likely to encounter: the turbulent field of custody disputes. In these situations, if the bond between parents has broken down and they cannot agree on matters that seriously affect their children's lives, there seems to be no option but to give a greater role to outsiders in resolving matters.

Mothers and fathers divided

When parents are divided and dispute centres on the role and rights of fathers and mothers in relation to their joint offspring, the noise of their competing claims can leave the child mute, exposed, and vulnerable. Until relatively recently, arrangements in England, like those in other Western countries, gave rights in respect of their legitimate children to fathers. Fathers had a right to the custody of their children until they reached the age of 21, a right to control their education and religious upbringing, and a right to punish them physically for misdemeanours. In an early case that involved three children whose parents disagreed about their religious upbringing, one of the judges declared: 'The right of a father to the custody and control of his children is one of the most sacred rights.'[24] On the basis of this right, fathers had been able to claim possession of their children from their mother, no matter how young the children. In one case in the early nineteenth century, an eight-month-old child was snatched from its mother's breast, placed in a carriage open to the weather, and carried away by force.[25]

Gradually, however, the tide began to turn in a rather different direction: that of the mother. Initially this was only a matter of empowering the Court of Chancery to give a mother custody of her children under certain circumstances but, following the Guardianship of Infants Act of 1925, it was established that, as far as court proceedings were concerned, neither parent should be regarded as having a superior claim. Half a century later, further legislative change gave equal and separately exercisable rights to both parents of a legitimate child.[26] The 1925 Act, however, had also made the welfare of the child the first and paramount, although not the sole, consideration in proceedings concerning custody or upbringing. More recent decisions have established that the welfare principle should take precedence over any principle of justice as between parents, and the Children's Act of 1989 states unambiguously that 'the child's welfare shall be the court's paramount consideration'.[27] It is now taken as a presumption that having contact with both parents may be part of that welfare.[28]

The risk is, however, that, far from avoiding parental conflict, the welfare principle may actually exacerbate it. For, if considerations of justice are set aside, the person who has been responsible for the breakdown of a marriage and the disintegration of the household may be given custody, while the parent who is not responsible for it may nevertheless lose the children if that is thought better for them.[29] Every case, then, is personal and individual, and yet argument is often conducted in terms of categories rather than individuals: what is due, for example, to women as mothers? To men as fathers? Ancient stereotypes intrude, or take new forms: while fathers in Victorian tales were often seen as dispensers of justice, disowning their wayward sons, or driving disgraced daughters from their door, mother love was regarded as more unconditional, and this assumption of maternal unconditionality lingers on, affecting both public and private judgement.[30]

But, although stereotypes risk misleading, they cannot be entirely rejected. It is hard to ignore the fact that having and raising children is an area of special concern to women. Up to now, a woman has been seen as the primary carer, even when not conceded any rights to her child, and, to date, only a woman can gestate and bring to birth a child. There is, too, a common perception, and some empirical evidence, that, while there are notable exceptions on both sides, women may be more sensitive than men to matters of human relationships and more ready to accept that children count in their own right, not merely as the appendages of adults. Even so, this is not true of all women, nor is it exclusive to them. Men, too, can show passionate devotion and self-sacrifice where their children are concerned. To take just one powerful example, the author Elie Wiesel's account of his own father's devotion and ultimate self-sacrifice on a death-march ending in Buchenwald concentration camp in the closing weeks of the Second World War paints a compelling picture of the devotion and tenacity of a father's love that kept one child alive in the most extreme of circumstances.[31] In desperate situations, then, there is really no contest between mothers and fathers—some parents, whether male or female, are capable of selfless sacrifice, some may not be able to live up to that standard, and a few will be indifferent to it.

Courtrooms, however, can bring out another side to human behaviour. Sometimes paternal devotion may be falsely paraded, perhaps even in revenge for a woman's rejection. Sometimes, too, it is possible to confuse deep attachment on the part of a father with a patriarchal wish for domination. Women, too, can be motivated by a wish to win out in a battle of the sexes, even if they are less likely to be prepared to use their children for that end. Tensions like these may be at least in part a consequence of what one feminist commentator, Sara

Ruddick, calls a 'thin' vision of fatherhood, itself part of a wider social analysis that is built on a defective understanding of male and female. This 'thin' vision is fatherhood defined in terms of just two main functions, provision and protection, possibly augmented by a third, which Ruddick describes as 'a complex exercise of paternal authority, paternal legitimation, discipline, and the right to punish'.[32] Ruddick sees this conceptualizing of fatherhood as part of a philosophical tradition that assigns reason to men, defines rationality partly by contrast with emotion, particular attachment, and practicality, then assigns these traits to women and to lower-class, less 'developed' men.[33]

It may well be resentment at this 'thin' vision of fatherhood that has led to the strong emergence of advocacy groups pressing the case for fathers' rights. David Blankenhorn, a strong defender of fathers' role in the family, is equally critical of a view that sees fathers as no more than possibly distant providers: 'From the child's perspective, child support payments, even if fully paid, do not replace a father's economic provision. More fundamentally, they do not replace a father.'[34]

In face of challenges like these to stereotyped interpretations of male and female roles, there has been a move towards adjusting power relations between men and women on a more egalitarian basis. This in turn has led to a shift in the social organization of parenting in which men share more of the traditional maternal role and have greater participation in their children's lives. The arguments of feminists like Susan Moller Okin have received a sympathetic hearing, in particular her view that 'any just and fair solution to the urgent problem of women's and children's vulnerability must encourage and facilitate the equal sharing by men and women of paid and unpaid work, of productive and reproductive labor'.[35]

But, while it is right to reject crude stereotyping, it is possible to take the gender-neutral ideal of parenthood too far. In particular, Ruddick herself is reluctant to sacrifice to the principle of the gender-neutral parent the unique importance of giving birth. She explains: 'In my own work I have increasingly felt the need to talk about mothering, not as male-inclusive but as a work in which women engage.'[36] Part of the reason for her hesitation may be a suspicion that, while the conjunction of the 'new father' ideal and the fathers' rights movement may be good for fathers, it could carry unintended costs for women. Indeed, the idea of shared parenting has been described by another feminist commentator, Carol Smart, as an aspect of the politics of gender that has moved from being a progressive ideal in the early days of the women's movement to becoming a Trojan horse in the context of child-custody disputes. She writes: 'Mothers who have encouraged shared parenting might now worry that they have conceded legal powers in a context in which they are socially and economically disadvantaged in comparison with their male partners.'[37] Ruddick's own observation on this is:

It remains very tempting to adopt the safe-speak of 'parenting'. Perhaps my final, odd, reason for wanting to acknowledge sexual difference is that it is so difficult to do so. It is a challenge to relish female and male procreativity, mothers and fathers, without suffering under the illusion that one's own sex, one's own sexuality, one's own procreative act, one's own way of living is the only thing there is or should be. It is an effort to create a nonimperialist ethics of sexual difference, in the midst and in respect of the poignant complexities of sexual lives.[38]

So, while the gender-neutral 'parent' is rapidly taking the place of mothers and fathers in the statute books, in schools, and in political parlance, there is still room for serious reflection on the richer and more distinctive aspects of being a mother or being a father. As far as motherhood is concerned, it is not only in relation to giving birth that sexual difference shows itself. There are other ways in which women are the keepers of the hearth. While it is, on the whole, men who influence the public domain with its ceremonial recording of battles, revolutions, and the anniversaries of living and dead leaders, women are the keepers of the intimate anniversaries, the individual birthdays, dates of first meetings or marriage. Where couples remain together, these are complementary differences that can add to the richness of a child's view of the world. When they separate, they add to the complex backcloth involving both justice and gender relations against which custody debates are played out.

Judgements of Solomon: The custody issue

Often a child can become a mere cipher in conflicts over custody. Finding the right balance between the claims of two separating partners is not easy. Judges have more commonly been willing to award custody of young children to mothers on the 'tender-years' principle: the idea that, because of the strong natural bond between mother and child, if young children cannot be with both parents, they are better off with their mother. In the opinion of one Australian judge: 'young children are best off with both parents, but if the parents have separated, they are better off with their mother. The bond between a child and a good mother ... expresses itself in an unrelenting and self-sacrificing fondness which is greatly to the child's advantage. Fathers and stepmothers may seek to emulate it and on occasions do so with tolerable success. But the mother's attachment is biologically determined by deep genetic forces which can never apply to them.'[39] Three years later, however, the High Court rejected the 'mother principle' and the 'tender-years' doctrine, basing the change on the increased role of fathers in family care and the possibility that a mother may herself be working.[40]

So, while the case for women in the custody battle may be strong, it is increasingly recognized that men, too, have grievances to be addressed and that current law can disadvantage them in a number of ways.[41] In the vast majority of cases, custody of children on divorce is awarded to women, and contact orders, largely made to men, are often broken. There are particular cases where court decisions are likely to strike anyone as totally unfair—a non-working wife who ends a marriage because of another liaison may well be awarded children, house, and most of the couple's financial assets, notwithstanding her responsibility for the collapse of their joint family-building project and her lack of any financial input. She is free to introduce unofficially into the family structure another man to replace the natural father in the lives of her children. With the growth of these disadvantages has come the loss of many of the previous advantages of marriage for a man, as traditionally the best way of securing not only a steady sex life, but also status in the community, and a substantial and satisfactory personal project in which he could reasonably regard himself as a vital element.

Despite this decline in the relative influence of men, women's advocates see a risk that, rather than protecting the interests of children, any extension of fathers' rights could become an extension of men's power over women. Smart sums up this argument: 'The more men's interests and children's interests are seen to coincide, the more mothers are disempowered, not least because for women to argue against joint custody or generous access for fathers can now be interpreted as a sign of selfishness, of a lack of maturity, and hence as a sign that women are not fit parents.'[42]

Another writer, Julia Brophy, describes the possible effect of one suggested compromise—seeking to balance sole custody orders by forcing the custodial parent, usually the mother, to consult the other on all important matters—in this way: 'it may well return many mothers to the very power structures which they as mothers (as well as wives) experienced within marriage. This is a situation which can consist of substantial inequalities in the distribution of power and responsibilities between parents, whereby fathers retain the power to make final important decisions but continue to allocate to mothers major responsibility for children's daily care and needs.'[43]

Given these tensions, it is not difficult to see why the closing years of the twentieth century should have seen demands for a new approach to child custody, based on the principle that, even if divorce can end relationships between adults, it is important to maintain the child–parent relationship. The presumption is that a continuing relationship with both parents will enable both of them to offer physical, emotional, and financial support to their children. The practical goal, then, becomes a matter of seeking to ensure reasonable contact for both parties. But 'reasonable contact' is an imprecise concept, varying from contact on alternate weekends to a more extensive and rigid division of time mapped out in terms of days or even hours per year. So joint or shared custody, in the sense of children's time being relatively equally divided between parents, has become the arrangement of choice for some on the basis that it finally establishes the principle of equality and the equal legal standing of women and men. It may also be promoted from the child's point of view, as it is, for example, in parts of the USA, where co-parenting may be advocated as a matter of a child's rights—in this case, a right to live with either parent for some of the time.[44] But the burden such arrangements impose on children should not be underestimated.[45] It is often argued that disruption for children can be justified if it represents an escape from extremely difficult domestic situations. But, in general, the effects of divorce on children are poor and can be measured in terms of low educational achievement, difficult relationships with parents, especially fathers, and other emotional problems. Judith S. Wallerstein, the author of a longitudinal study spanning two generations, writes:

We have learned over many years of experience that divorce is not the brief circumscribed crisis in the life of adult and child that we anticipated. It is emphatically not a single event but a long-lasting process of radically changing family relationships that begins in the failing marriage, continues through the often chaotic period of the marital rupture and its immediate aftermath, and extends even further, often over many years of disequilibrium.[46]

Given these identifiable factors, it is worth thinking about the changes that the break-up of their original family may bring to children. A pattern of contact favoured in one American state, for example, means that children have to move midweek to their other parent's house. In another, devised to counter the disruption to the children that this causes, the children stay in the house and their parents move in and out in turn—an arrangement known as 'bird-nesting.'[47] In Britain, where, following the Children Act of 1989, the goal of 'shared' or 'co-parenting' following separation or divorce is also viewed favourably, the burden this can impose on both children and parents is mitigated by the recognition that, rigidly applied, it might be unsuitable for very young children, teenagers, or parents who live some distance from one another. But even the more usual fortnightly contact, unless those concerned live round the corner from each other, or at least in the same town, will mean children spending more time than is good for them in travel between locations and in the sole company of a parent rather than with their own friends and peers. But a ruling that keeps the custodial parent in the same town until the youngest child reaches the age of majority—a pattern obtaining in some North American states—may have a disastrous effect on both children and the custodial parent, preventing them from reconstructing their lives following the breakdown of the relationship. It may also leave little room for children's own choice and perspective. Because of their predictably interrupted availability, especially where travel is involved, children may be called upon to sacrifice the chance of taking part in sports teams, choirs, drama productions, and other children's birthday parties. A life like this would be intolerable to many adults. But, as a judge remarked in an Irish court judgment: 'The main need of children, if they are to be happy, is the sense of security which comes from a feeling of being loved, for their own sake. They are not pieces of furniture to be moved around from house to house.'[48]

All this leaves unanswered the fundamental question of who *should* care for the child when a couple splits up. This is often described as a judgement of Solomon—a description that may mean little more than that it is a very difficult question with strong claims on both sides. There is, though, more to the story of Solomon's judgement than this. Faced with the equal balance of the two rival claims, Solomon intends, or at least pretends to intend, to take a sword and split the child in two. The false claimant is ready to accept this. But the true mother calls for an end to the legal battle and its dire outcome, saying that she is ready for the sake of her child to allow it to go to the other claimant. Solomon gives the child to her for, by her willingness to sacrifice her own interest, she has unintentionally demonstrated the truth of her claim.

In many ways, equal joint custody resembles the solution proposed by King Solomon—the child must live a split life between two homes, with little time or opportunity to create a place for itself in either, and much of its potential time with peers taken up by outings with a displaced parent. In these circumstances, it may be that some parents will express their love for the child by relinquishing maximum rights, asking only reasonable and modest access, in order to give the child a life of its own.

Current 'equity' considerations have had the effect of turning custody into a political issue. But, however it is presented, the 'equal-shares' case is more likely to be pressed by advocates of rights for fathers, who may be reluctant to accept that there are *any* circumstances in which contact should be denied or minimized.[49] This creates a particular problem in a situation in which the constant use of 'best-case' scenarios lulls decision-makers into a false sense of security. But the possibility of 'worst-case' scenarios involving violence is far from negligible, and those who legislate for enforced contact whatever the circumstances take on a frightening responsibility.[50] Where children do suffer some kind of ill-treatment at the hands of a violent parent, usually a father, it often takes place in the context of court-ordered contact meetings.[51] Of these, the ultimate and most dreaded examples are those cases in which a father uses a contact meeting to kill both his children and himself in a final act of extreme revenge.[52]

Cases involving extreme violence represent, of course, the outer limits of the way in which custody can serve the needs or preferences of parents and ignore the vulnerability of children. But, even where violence is not a factor, contact and residence rulings can be a way, deliberate or not, for one parent to exercise control over the other, making it impossible for the other parent to gather up the threads and start again, free from harassment and disruption. There are no easy answers to post-separation arrangements looked at from the point of view of the children themselves. It would be better if parents could recognize this and acknowledge that their own decision to split up means that, as far as their children are concerned, their security, home life and frame of reference for living their lives has been unpicked. If it is difficult to secure fairness for both parents, it is even more difficult to provide an outcome that fits what their children want and need. The custody issue, then, is a central dilemma. However, it is not the only consequence of parental break-up that can affect children's lives.

Reconstituted families

In practice, separations often bring into already complex situations new people, both adults and children, who have their own needs and perspectives. For, while the initial situation may be focused on the problem of how two individuals are to share their children's lives between them, in practice one or both partners may bring someone else into the picture, posing a challenge of adjustment both for the adults and for their children. As far as the adults are concerned, it may be difficult to accept that their children are living with the person who has replaced them in their partner's life. It will be difficult if the new mother or father is not caring properly for the children, but in some ways just as difficult if they are doing so successfully. A mother, particularly if she is not responsible for the breach, may find it very hard to accept that the woman who *is* responsible for it has taken over her role and formed a bond with her children. The same applies to fathers. A man, too, may find it hard to accept the reality of his children living with the man who has taken over his own role. But, by the first decade of the twenty-first century, the step-family had become in many countries the fastest growing family type. In the United Kingdom, for example, more than a fifth of men in their thirties were stepfathers, and one in ten of the siblings of 6- to 8-year-olds were step-siblings or half-siblings.[53]

As for the children themselves, for some, living in a step- or reconstituted family will be a happy, or at least a satisfactory, situation. For others, things will not work out so well.[54] Relationships with step-siblings may be as difficult to adjust to as those with a step-parent or a parent's non-resident partner. The starkest findings relate to the most extreme cases. In a UK-based study, Robert Whelan reports on the basis of findings from the NSPCC (National Society for the Protection of Children) that children living with their natural mother and a father substitute were at more than eight times the risk of abuse than children living with their two natural parents.[55] Since current ways of collecting such data may fail to discriminate between biological and non-biological parents, the unwary may be left to believe that abuse is a family matter rather than what it is more likely to be—a *broken* family matter.[56] So, while it is no doubt possible to over-interpret figures for ill-treatment by step-parents, there is no reason to disagree with the observation of the psychologists Martin Daly and Margo Wilson: 'Step-parents are primarily replacement mates, and only secondarily replacement parents.'[57]

In some cases, and not only the extreme ones involving physical ill-treatment, the problems will seem so insoluble that the child or young person will end up as a runaway from the new domestic set-up.[58] Young people in refuges for runaways are overwhelmingly from reconstituted families, and they frequently give abuse or ill-treatment as a reason for running away. According to the sociologist Patricia Morgan, a survey of seven major British cities and four inner-London boroughs in the 1990s found that in some areas 5 per cent of the 16–19 age group were classified as homeless.[59] So these accounts cannot be dismissed as unrealistically subjective. On the contrary, the problems can be quantified, and they cast a cautionary shadow over the reconstituted family.

Of course, no one would claim that all alternative arrangements are bad for children, and the world would be a darker place if it were never possible for children to find loving care in a family where those who care for them are not biologically related to them. Those who adopt, those who foster, and those who replace a parent in a child's life through their relationship to the other parent—in other words, a step-parent or *de facto* step-parent—can indeed, and often do, offer love, friendship, and care to a child. But the issue here is how the broader picture shapes out; it is also a matter of what is brought about by choice as opposed to necessity—a distinction that even a young child can appreciate.

While a consensus has developed in political life on both the left and some parts of the libertarian right that the traditional family has no place in a world of gender equality and the democratization of family relationships, it is impossible to ignore the very considerable body of empirical research that shows it to be the essential underpinning and best guarantor of child security. Another more positive way to put this is that the safest environment in which a child can grow up is a home with its own natural father and mother. This recognition, honestly thought through, should set limits to the right of adults to enjoy a Sartrean form of quasi-existentialist freedom, making and remaking their own relationships to suit the immediate goals of the moment.

What children really want

Children, then, have a perspective and a point of view on those post-divorce arrangements that face them with a need to adjust to new family relationships. Sometimes, they vote with their feet as runaways to distant towns where street-living, prostitution, and drug-dealing may be the only immediate opportunities of support on offer. To repeat, new parental arrangements are not, of course, always bad, or always disruptive. Nevertheless, children are conservative about their own lives. They would rather not be faced with the consequences of upheaval in their parents' relationships, and adults deceive themselves when they fail to recognize this.

What, then, would be the effect on adult decision-making of listening to the unheard voice of children? There is an increasing willingness to set up procedures for listening to young people in custody disputes, but, as the socio-legal scholar Adrian James, observes, 'the process revolves around disputes (both social and legal) between and constructed by adults—disputes that ultimately can only be resolved by the adults involved—children's ability to participate fully and effectively is heavily circumscribed.' James adds:

Based upon a set of adult-orientated and legally-endorsed assumptions that attempt to resolve the ambiguity inherent in the task of allowing the child's wishes and feelings to be heard, whilst also responding to parents' claims for justice, such constructions serve to drown out the sound of the child's voice in a system that struggles, but largely fails, to acknowledge the individual child as a competent actor with agency.[60]

But even a critic who recognizes, as James does, the inherent limitations of attempts to treat children as free agents—to listen to what a child wants—may feel obliged to take it for granted that the task in question is to help the child accept the reality of the parental situation.

This, realistically, may be the best that can be done in today's climate of opinion. But the aim of this chapter has been to raise the question of the child's voice in a different sense. It has been an invitation to the reader to step outside the circumstances of particular cases and to ask the broader question: what do children *really* want? It would be almost banal to say that, presented with the options, a child's primary preference would be for security, continuity, and a long-term home base. Children are effectively disenfranchised in a vote on this. The liberty of their parents trumps their claims. But there is a difference between respecting the liberty of others and actively assisting them in their projects—between preventing someone from doing something and refusing to help them do it. Many of the legal innovations introduced to ease the arrangements people choose to make in their personal family lives, especially those involving children and relationships, can be construed as helping rather than merely permitting. They can make it possible for people to enter into arrangements that, without this help, they might otherwise have chosen to avoid. Often the difficulties or counter-considerations are financial, and the liberal requirement to be non-judgemental is extended, usually in the name of child support, to include assisting with the financial arrangements, first legally, then by providing a second home and child-care costs, when the first family is left unsupported. In this way, something that only a rich few could contemplate in the past—setting up a second family following divorce or separation—becomes an easy option for the many.

There is a widely accepted view that divorce or separation can be good for children if the atmosphere between their parents is difficult. Jeffrey Blustein sums up this view: 'Unhappy marriages of parents have empirically a very demoralizing effect on the growth of the child's character, and it is in the interests of children that the interests of their parents as individual persons be respected by marriage. Indeed, it could be argued that precisely on account of the children the parents' unhappy marriage should be dissolved rather than forcibly maintained.'[61] Not surprisingly, he links this to a rejection of the importance of the family structure as something that involves both parents and children: 'We have to explore alternatives to our traditional practice of linking the parental and the conjugal relationships in the nuclear family.'[62]

However, contrary to this commonly held view, there is in fact empirical evidence that, short of abuse or violence, quarrelling parents are less damaging for children than family break-up. Children are in fact better able to accept their parents' separation when the level of parental conflict is high because then they can see the reasons for it. However, evidence suggests that most divorces do not involve high levels of conflict, and that children whose parents divorce from low-conflict marriages are particularly likely to suffer long-term psychological and emotional distress, and to have fewer ties with kin and friends. In a ground-breaking longitudinal study of a large sample of American families over a period of fifteen years between 1980 and 1992, the sociologists Paul Amato and Alan Booth found that the vast majority of divorces—about 70 per cent—represent the termination of low-conflict marriages whose continuation would have been better in the long run for the children involved than the break-up of the family.[63] Short of extreme situations such as those mentioned earlier, children are resilient in the way they cope with less than ideal parental relationships. The impact of a parental split, on the other hand, can have a much greater impact on their lives. It is unlikely to leave them in secure possession of the most important elements of their lives: home, school, friendships, and community ties and activities.

So is the regulation of custody and contact an inevitably doomed attempt by the state to interfere in family life by repairing its rifts and rectifying their necessary sequel? It is not surprising that one legal scholar has concluded: 'the existing state of custody law satisfies no one. Feminists declare that women are losing the custody wars ... fathers' rights groups insist that mothers are blocking fathers' access to their children ... Custody law is riddled by irony but also by an increasing coherence. A single source supplies both: the insistence that the law recognizes the continuing ties of parents and children without a corresponding insistence that parents stay together.'[64] Custody and access are, of course, intended to protect parents' relationships with their children and also to secure the best interests of those children. But these are difficult goals to reconcile. Even in the best of cases, children do not like to be asked to choose between their parents. Listening to the child's voice is a worthwhile step, but no one should be deceived into thinking that that is a universal panacea. Like the apocryphal traveller whose request for advice evokes the response 'I would not start from here', in most cases the child does not want the split in the first place. What children most need and most want is what normal family life provides: a chance to build their own lives and relationships with their peers, with their parents in the background for support and comfort, and preferably not as judicially ordered companions for parent and child outings.

What children want, sadly they will not always get, and sometimes society itself will pay the price. But it is worth adults at least being clear about what they are doing and not deluding themselves with anodyne suggestions that their children will be happier, or at least benefit, when their aspirations for simple childhood constants are shattered and exchanged for a new life that includes mobility, fluctuating relationships, new 'siblings' to negotiate with, and new parental whims to accommodate. The old mantra 'I am only staying with you for the sake of the children' may often have been the simple truth in the past and in many cases could have been the better choice. From the child's point of view, it may still be so. For, on the whole, children *like* families—the family is a child-friendly institution and only secondarily there to keep adults happy.

8

Law, policy-making, and the contemporary family

In the previous chapter, family structure, marriage, and divorce were looked at in terms of the question, what do children want? Even apart from this question, however, policy-makers take seriously the effects changes in these areas may have on children, and so it would be useful to keep in mind a distinction that emerged in earlier chapters between two functions of marriage: the first, individual—two people's emotional desire or need for each other—the second social—raising children who will later form the nucleus of society. People can, in the end, only determine for themselves how they will behave in relation to the first, and, in a free society, they must be allowed to do so. But where the second is concerned, a huge body of evidence suggests that a purely temporary partnership between parents is, in the vast majority of cases, inadequate and that the involvement of both parents in a child's life is, in almost all cases, an indisputable good.

This places the issue of the family in a much broader political and social frame, which includes many aspects of public policy, from tax structure and welfare provision to the laws governing marriage and divorce. While sexual relationships, marriage, and family are often viewed as matters belonging to the private realm on which the state should take a neutral view, the opposite is in fact the case. Not only *should* it not take a neutral view; in fact it cannot do so. It is a truism that private actions can have public consequences—less commonly recognized that public action can have private consequences. Increasingly, however, evidence is accumulating in this area that it is policies themselves that have driven forward some of the remarkable social changes of the late twentieth and early twenty-first centuries in the area of marriage and the family.[1]

To some extent, lawmakers do see themselves as simply responding to social change. This is, for example, how many see the introduction of civil unions for same-sex couples. But legal structures are not merely a reflection of social norms; they also influence them. Recognizing that marriage has a strong function of this sort is a development of what the American economist Gary Becker once described as the new institutionalism—an understanding of social change that explains the way institutions evolve as something that is ultimately determined by the rational responses of individuals to the changed conditions in which they find themselves.[2] Becker was a pioneer in applying this thesis to the economic aspects of the family. The underlying assumption that the rational behaviour of a human being is necessarily self-seeking is open to criticism, but for policy purposes there is no need to make that assumption: it is sufficient to accept that it would be unwise to rely entirely on human altruism in framing political and social policy. Others have dismissed Becker's application of the theory to family issues, however, for a rather different reason. Becker was writing in the 1950s, and part of his thesis was that a division of labour in the family between one partner working in the home, the other in the world of paid work, was economically advantageous to both of them. Feminists committed to equality in both the domestic and the workplace spheres objected to this at the time and have continued to see it as a reason for dismissing Becker's approach.[3] But, while the division of labour argument may no longer be viable, given women's greatly improved economic opportunities and involvement, the theory itself has a much broader relevance than this. Indeed, it forms the basis of a wider and much more far-reaching claim: that legal and fiscal changes in areas affecting the family have produced a number of effects, intended or otherwise, that form a pattern common to many Western countries: expanding rates of divorce and separation, increases in one-parent families, and an unprecedented shift from marriage to cohabitation. In addition, as argued in the previous chapter, the children who are caught up in the shifting sands of adult relationships often find themselves in situations in which new policies of co-parenting generate demands that can be both impractical and unfair to those involved.

While in Britain there are many who take a positive view of today's more flexible lifestyles, there is a strong body of opinion in the United States supporting the belief that the community as a whole benefits from successful family life. While it would be rash to overstate the role of US policymakers in this, there are claims that America has now seen some quantifiable and beneficial social changes. The authors of a paper from the Princeton-based Brookings Institution report that previously rising figures for teenage and unmarried pregnancies, single-parent households and divorce rates have either stabilized or dropped.[4]

As far as the British attitude is concerned, the American social philosopher Charles Murray sees it as the position of someone who, having run off the edge of a precipice at high speed, remains blissfully unaware for a time that he is suspended above an abyss. In contrast, he says: 'there is no longer an American scholarly debate about whether single parenthood has large social costs.'[5] Murray's warning against British complacency might be dismissed as that of an outsider, and one whose opinions are generally regarded as contentious. But the claim that children brought up by their two married parents are better off by most social measures—they have more school success and are less likely to be involved in criminal or disruptive behaviour—is supported by research from both sides of the Atlantic.[6] At every income level the demise of the two-parent family has been identified as an adverse factor, even in matters as prosaic as health. Indeed, these effects are likely to be long term. As the American social theorist Maggie Gallagher reports: 'The negative health effects of parental non-marriage and divorce linger long into their children's adult lives. This health gap cannot be explained entirely by lower incomes or reduced access to medical care.'[7] A revealing exception to this rule is the case of single status coming about through the death of one partner. This may well be because, while a loss of this sort is traumatic for both the surviving partner and any children, they can understand in this situation that they were not voluntarily abandoned, and memories of a loyal partner and a loving parent can be kept intact.

Just living together: The cohabitation option

The way in which family life has been developing since the mid-twentieth century reveals some remarkable transitions. The United

Kingdom provides a model of how life has changed in only a single generation. In 1979 data for England and Wales showed that 80 per cent of children under 16 were living with their two married parents. But by 1992 the figure had fallen to under 70 per cent.[8] Of the three in ten children who were not living with both of their natural parents, two were living with only one parent, and the third was in a 'reconstituted' family. The majority of two-parent families were also two-earner families, but there was also a significant minority of these with no earner at all. And finally, in a situation in which two in five marriages were likely to end in divorce, the annual marrying rate was at its lowest since records had begun 160 years earlier.[9]

By the end of the twentieth century, then, not only in Britain but also in the United States and elsewhere, the traditional, two-parent, one-earner family, had become, in the view of many commentators, a dwindling phenomenon. One phenomenon that was not dwindling but expanding, however, was living together without marrying. The legal theorist Antony Dnes describes the move towards cohabitation common to many European countries and North America over the forty years from 1960 to 2000 as a hugely significant shift in social behaviour.[10] This picture is not peculiar to the United Kingdom, although it does have one of the highest cohabitation rates in the EU, as well as the highest incidence of separation and divorce. The general trend, however, is typical of many parts of the developed world.

Not everyone regards the increase in cohabiting in entirely negative terms, however. Indeed, it can be seen as a positive aspect that having children outside marriage does not necessarily mean that mothers and children are living alone, or even that there is a lack of parental involvement on the part of the father. The authors of a US study of what were termed 'fragile families' described as one of their most striking findings the high rate of cohabitation among unmarried parents. They reported that, at the time of birth, half of unmarried mothers were living with the fathers of their children. Another third were romantically involved with the fathers, but living apart in what they called 'visiting relationships'. Of the remainder, some described their relationships as 'just friends' or said they had little or no contact.[11]

However, this is to take a fairly short-term view of such situations, and it offers no guarantee as to how the longer term might work out. While policymakers and opinion-leaders seem ineluctably drawn to using the term 'stable relationships' as a synonym for cohabitation, it is clear that there has been a change in what cohabitation actually means to couples. There have been historical periods when it would have been regarded as a prelude to marriage, and, within that pattern of expectations, the birth of a child would have led to the sealing of the relationship with marriage. But the pattern today is different: whether people choose to cohabit because they actually prefer more flexible relationships, or whether it is simply the case that marriage itself creates a more stable framework, the fact is that cohabiting couples are more likely to separate than those who marry.[12] As a result, a succession of short-term cohabitations is not unusual, and the birth of a child or children may well lead to the end of the relationship rather than its continuation in the form of marriage.[13]

Other things being equal, personal life is a matter for the individual. But, where social costs are incurred, other things are not equal, and this makes some aspects of personal life a legitimate matter of public concern. The trauma following divorce has been well documented; less so the effect of changing short-term cohabitations.[14] Why, then, do people choose to cohabit? One obvious answer is that they prefer the freedom it implies—the ability to move out or move on without legal hassle or interference. They may also choose to behave more like single people than married people in the way they live their individual lives. This means that some will interpret the terms of the relationship to exclude a commitment to fidelity as well as to long-term continuity. But these are very theoretical ways of construing choices about personal relationships, and not everyone makes such decisions on the basis of weighing up their lives in quite such explicit terms. By unspoken agreement, the stay-over lover becomes the live-in lover, the live-in lover the *de facto* partner. So, for those who do not think through their decisions quite so reflectively, it makes sense to look at the role, first of all, of government policies that affect people's well-being financially, and, secondly, of legal changes that determine important aspects of their personal lives.

Unsettling scenarios: The changing economics of family life

It is easy to assume that, if people do suffer adverse outcomes in their personal lives, either as never-married single parents, or following marital or relationship breakdown, this is because of the financial hardship often associated with single parenthood. It is natural, then, to look for a remedy in strategies for reducing poverty. Attempts by governments to do this by measures such as welfare provision, benefits, and tax changes, however, have usually turned out to be counter-productive. To understand this, it is worth looking back briefly at the steps by which change has come about. Once again, the United Kingdom's experience reflects a broader picture.

At the base of the welfare state, which was introduced in Britain at the end of the Second World War, the idea of the 'family wage' was taken as axiomatic. Before this, and also for some time afterwards, tax and benefit policy was based on a desire to support the family unit, in the sense of married parents and their children. Gradually, however, this principle was eroded, largely through a wish to recognize equality of need rather than equality of desert, and also because of an understandable aversion to the idea of penalizing women and children for reasons that might be tainted by moral censure or even hypocrisy. As a result, the last few decades of the twentieth century saw in Britain the end of the 'family wage' as the basis of tax policy. The married couple's tax allowance, once dismissed as 'an anomaly' by a Conservative Chancellor, Kenneth Clarke, was ended in Britain in 2000 and a male wage-earner's pay ceased to be significantly related to any assumption that he might be supporting a non-earning spouse caring for dependants. It remains the norm, though, under governments of diverse persuasion elsewhere in the world. Many other European countries still have joint taxation of married couples, and offer family allowances that benefit single-earner families in which the mother chooses to stay at home. A single-earner family in France, for example, keeps far more of its income than does a comparable family in Britain through the *quotient familial*, which gives proportionate tax allowances for both spouses and children. In Britain, by contrast, few couples any longer feel they can afford the luxury of a stay-at-home partner. Fiscal policy has not favoured the married couple, and welfare benefits based on need also tend to discriminate against marriage and in favour of lone parenthood, whether for the never-married or the divorced.

In these circumstances, it is hardly surprising that people ask themselves the question, does it pay to marry? A generous desire not to deprive people of support on moral grounds has shifted the balance of economic considerations so drastically that in many ways the traditional family unit is worse off than any other arrangement. While other European countries have been careful to avoid this effect, in the case of the United Kingdom it has been calculated that, if lower-income couples who are living together marry, this is likely significantly to increase their tax payments and lower their benefits. This makes it perhaps less surprising that the United Kingdom has a higher percentage of lone-parent families than any European country other than Sweden.[15]

Two centuries ago, the pioneer of rational choice theory, the economic philosopher Adam Smith, observed that people do, on the whole, respond rationally to the realities of their economic situation. Applying Smith's principle to the circumstances in which people make decisions about their personal lives today, if a couple is better off unmarried, then, other things being equal, they will choose to remain unmarried. And, if a young non-employed single mother has a more secure home and income without a male partner because the state will offer her a cast-iron, if modest, guarantee of support, this gives her a strong incentive to choose to keep any *de facto* partner at a distance. Smith believed that, on the whole, a 'hidden hand' ensured that rational economic choices, though selfish, work for the common good. But, whatever the truth of this in relation to trade and services, the same cannot be said for choices in the area of personal and family life.

In Britain, it seems that many policymakers have a peculiarly deterministic approach to these matters. They insist that the state is unable to affect people's choices in personal and family matters. And yet, in other areas, economic spurs are very commonly used to persuade people to behave in socially acceptable ways. For example, social opinion was surprisingly quickly persuaded to endorse governmental moves to stop smoking, a widespread and socially accepted practice, and heavy taxation of tobacco has long been used as a disincentive to smokers. And yet policymakers insist that choices in the area of relationships, sexuality, and reproduction must simply be accepted as unalterable trends. This may well be because they believe that, even if they *could* influence behaviour in this field, it would be wrong for them to try to do so.

However, as far as policymakers are concerned, since the enormous cost of family breakdown must in the end be met by the ordinary taxpayer, this means that it has indisputable economic aspects that are the legitimate business of government. Even excluding the psychological aspect—possible effects such as personal unhappiness, depression, and lack of motivation—there are more concrete harms to be considered, including, for example, pressures on housing and support services as the percentage of single-person households increases. There are also social security and healthcare costs as the network of family care disappears, not only for children but also for other relatives who become dependent through accident, age, or illness, leaving the deficit to be covered in hospitals, homes, or institutions by professional carers. And finally, because of the association between youth crime and the absence of family structure, it adds to criminal injury and justice costs.[16]

As far as this last point is concerned, it is often argued that one beneficial effect of marriage has been to transform youthful irresponsibility into more positive and socially worthwhile behaviour. But, whether or not marriage does make a difference to people's behaviour—and clearly it cannot do this in all cases—it may have other important public effects. One of these may be its usefulness as an indication to other people of the seriousness of purpose and likely stability of a couple's relationship. Economists explain this in terms of the technical notion of a signal, and it provides an additional economic argument for endorsing governmental strategies that are intended to assist the marriage-based household. Of course, in individual cases the signal may be misleading, but statistical probability is a useful guide for public authorities in deciding on such practical matters as tax and benefits policies. It should be a matter of concern for policymakers, then, if this useful function is currently being eroded. The Cambridge economist Robert Rowthorn, however, believes that this point has already been reached. He writes: 'In Western culture, marriage helps individuals to signal to each other and to the outside world, their desire for a sexually permanent union. However, modern legal and social trends have greatly reduced the credibility of this signal. As a result, marriage is no longer an effective signal of commitment.'[17] Rowthorn argues that the potential for marriage to continue to function as it did before should be recovered and retained; it is not unfair, he argues, to give special tax treatment to an institution that has benefits to society in terms of greater stability, better health, and lower criminality. On the contrary, it is right for the state to support an institution that is beneficial to the rest of society and reduces future claims on the public purse.

So does marriage pay? The answer from society's perspective is yes: there are immense economic advantages for society in general if legally recognized relationships are the norm for raising children.[18] It is perverse, then, if other factors, that are in principle controllable, have created a situation in which the answer to this question has been so drastically reversed for the central parties in that relationship. It would be hard to deny that this has indeed happened in the area of benefits and taxation, where many of the economic advantages of marriage have been removed. But marriage has also been undermined on a second front. This is the area of family law, where legal changes, particularly changes in the arrangements governing divorce and custody of children, can act as a deterrent for the rational from even embarking on the enterprise.

Enforced unfairness: Legal changes and their consequences

Legal reforms in the area of marriage and family have come about, at least in part, in response to a public feeling that the rigidity of marriage laws in times past fell short of the moral ideal of compassion. Indeed, the way the law used to operate could be said to have been in conflict with other basic moral sentiments as well, either justice in the form of human rights, or simply concern for the happiness of individuals. The original pressures for change, then, could claim a moral foundation, and, for those who believe that law is based upon and should reflect morality, this is a weighty consideration. What might not have been fully appreciated, though, is that law not only reflects standards, it also sets them. In other words, since most people are ready to accept what the law says as a guide to their own conduct, changing the law was bound, in the end, not only to right existing wrongs, but also to change the way people would behave in the future.[19] The risk, though, is that this may simply replace one set of wrongs with another.

Some will argue that the right to be morally self-determining is one of the most vital of human freedoms and that the best way to avoid this risk is to keep law and morality apart. As far as the family is concerned, the idea that law should not intervene in the choices people make about their personal life is often linked to Article 12 of the Universal Declaration of Human Rights (1948), which asserts that people have a right to privacy in home and family. But morality cannot simply be detached from its social setting, and the attempt to do this leaves a void as far as politics and society are concerned. Morality in the area of personal relationships and family life is based on broader ethical considerations that include trust, promise-keeping, loyalty, honesty, and a willingness to fulfil obligations to dependants.

Kindness and consideration, too, could and should play a role. Of course, it would hardly be possible to legislate for kindness, but it may be both possible and right to give legal support to voluntarily accepted commitments and obligations, or even to penalize serious deceptions that have life-affecting consequences.

The philosophical case for this can be made in terms of both Kantian and utilitarian ethics. First, law has a recognized role in upholding contracts, and marriage, even if it is not in law treated in its formation or its enforcement as a contract, is recognizably an agreement by the parties to create a legal relation between them.[20] And, secondly, it has a role in promoting the public good. This is an area in which many people's interests are involved, both directly and indirectly. Most obviously, the interests of children need to be protected, but also the interests of the wider community, since these are threatened by the power of family fragmentation to produce social instability. This means that it is a mistake to seek to exclude family matters from social or political decision-making on libertarian grounds, through fear of being 'judgemental'. And yet for lawmakers in some countries the fear of being moralistic or judgemental has become a driving force in policy-making. A British Home Secretary, chairing a policy group on the family, was not carving out unfamiliar ground when he is reported to have said: 'This government is committed to supporting families whatever form they take. This government will not preach about marriage.'[21]

If it is an aversion to moralizing that lies behind the economic measures that have made life hard for the 'traditional' family, it seems likely that it is this, too, that provides at least some of the motivation for recent changes in the laws governing marriage and divorce. Many key policy-makers do indeed believe that legal arrangements should be restructured so as to stand back from the choices people make about their private lives. This view is not peculiar to Britain. On the contrary, a widespread consensus amongst lawmakers and commentators in many European countries has interpreted the spirit of personal freedom in this area as a matter of embracing the idea of 'new families' of any diversity—a deconstruction and reconstruction of the family that seems to be an attempt to do all the moral work that is needed just by sponsoring a new dictionary definition. Others, looking to support the pluralistic ideal in more concrete ways, have translated it into proposals for alternative types of marriage contract: some, like civil partnerships, closely based on the marriage model, others more innovatory, such as flexible monogamy, three-year renewable agreements, or permanent and childless relationships.[22] Citing Herbert Marcuse as the inspiration for the idyll of eroticized relationships and universalized kinship, Alexander Comfort paints a picture of one sought-after model:

> a society in which pair relationships are still central, but initially less permanent, in which child-bearing is seen as a special responsibility involving a special life style, and in which settled couples engage openly in a wide range of sexual relations with friends, with other couples, and with third parties as an expression of social intimacy, without prejudice to the primacy of their own relationship, and with no more, and probably less, permanent interchange than we see in the society of serial polygamy with adultery that now exists.[23]

But this is not necessarily a consensus that is endorsed by the population as a whole. In spite of the message conveyed by many popular television soap operas, and whatever experts and educators in the field may claim, the media portrayal of sexual attitudes is a long way from the ideals people, if naively, secretly cherish for their own lives.[24] Even so, the shifts that have taken place in marriage law are generally regarded as a liberalization of law. The assumption is that they have placed more of the adult individual's life outside state interference. But this, as it turns out, has not been their real impact. For, paradoxically, as freedom is conceded to the individual to operate unilaterally in these core matters, the responsibilities traditionally associated with the family have to be assumed by the state, and, with the breakdown of the network of mutual obligations peculiar to families, care is increasingly institutionalized in the hands of paid professionals. But the more opportunities are provided for state intrusion into private life, the more the state encroaches on what were previously individual prerogatives. Briefly, as the intervention of the law decreases in sexual matters, so it increases in economic and child-related aspects, whether the relationships involved are formal or informal. In the end, then, freedom in one area may only be bought only at the cost of important freedoms elsewhere.

Economic strategies are unlikely in themselves to shake the family structure. Poverty and hardship, after all, have been a common experience of human beings. But, when legal interventions combine with these economic strategies, the tree begins to shake. The key principle that brings together the economic arguments with the legal ones is that it is not possible to secure the privacy and autonomy of the family by embracing forms of organization that are able to function only through a combination of massive public contributions and legal enforcement.

The second question, then, to be added to the economic debate is whether and how far recent legal changes have contributed to the process of structural disintegration. Two kinds of legal change are involved: first, those made from within the framework of the family as traditionally understood, especially those governing marriage and divorce, and, second, more drastic changes to the public understanding of the family that risk overturning that original framework altogether.

No-fault divorce

It is in the first context that the shifts that have taken place in family law in relation to divorce, and in particular the move to no-fault divorce, are relevant. Historically, divorce law in both the United States and England (divorce law in Scotland has long run its own distinctive course) is rooted in English common law, which, before 1857, had allowed divorce only in extraordinary circumstances and by a special Act of Parliament. Even up to the end of the 1960s, the notion of fault was central, and divorce by mutual consent was not allowed, nor was unilateral divorce without just cause. The moral responsibility of individuals for their own choices and actions was a key presumption. This meant that the status of husband or wife could not easily be set aside, and divorce was possible only if one of the parties had committed a fundamental breach of the marital contract, such as adultery, desertion, or cruelty. At the end of the 1960s, however, legal changes in both the United States and England replaced the notion of fault with that of marital breakdown. In 1970 California became the first US state to introduce no-fault divorce. In England, the Divorce Reform Act of 1969 included separation as evidence of marital breakdown—two years where there is mutual consent, five unilaterally. The old grounds are still allowed as 'unreasonable behaviour', but, rather than being seen as wrongs by one partner against the other, they are taken as signs of incompatibility or simply as something that has happened, not to them, but to their marriage, viewed as an abstract entity with an uncontrollable life of its own.[25]

Removing fault from divorce forms part of the community's increasing willingness to discount technical and formal requirements in these matters and to recognize what exists *de facto*. In practice, both the aim and the effect are to shift the focus of the legal process from moral to economic questions. In changes introduced in the United States, one influential view was that the idea that a husband must support his wife for life is anachronistic. With alimony 'drones' as the target, the Civil Code of California §4801 directed that 'the ability of the supported spouse to engage in gainful employment' should be a decisive consideration. But, although it was agreed that care should be taken not to treat older women who have been full-time mothers and homemakers unfairly, this was in practice the effect. For the ability of a woman who has been a full-time mother for twenty-five years to become self-supporting is quite disproportionately unequal to that of a man who has been in the labour market for his whole working-life. The Canadian economist Douglas W. Allen sums up the position in this way:

Though wives make many contributions to a marriage, a major one is pregnancy and the rearing of children. Though a mother may also work, the presence of more than one child causes major disruptions in workforce participation, and hence a reduction in her financial contribution to the household. Because this contribution takes place early in a marriage, the wife makes a sunk investment in the marriage and places herself in considerable jeopardy. The husband, on the other hand, makes no such investment. In fact, typical male incomes increase throughout his working life… Under these conditions it is easy to see why the inability to enter a binding contract with the husband is detrimental to wives.[26]

Leonora Weitzman makes a similar point: 'rules designed to treat men and women "equally" have in practice served to deprive divorced women (especially older homemakers and mothers of young children) of the legal and financial protections that the old law provided'.[27] She reports that her own research showed that divorced women and their children experience a substantial decline in their standard of living in the first year after divorce, while the economic position of their former husbands improves. In addition, if the family home has to be sold, a woman also suffers the possibly more important loss of her social context, friends, and neighbourhood links. On the other hand, court cases in which spouses have obtained enormous awards from wealthy husbands after only a few years of marriage have not helped the cause of other divorced women. In the case of industrialists and pop stars, sums in the millions have been awarded to former spouses. Breaking even newer ground, in a highly publicized case in Britain in 2004, Karen Parlour, the 33-year-old wife of the footballer Ray Parlour, was awarded, not only an annual income of £250,000 and a lump sum of the same amount, but also a share of his future earnings.

But, if continuing financial support after divorce is a contentious issue, the division of matrimonial assets is hardly uncontroversial, either. While the European Union has set itself the long-term goal of harmonizing family law across EU member states, the prevailing situation has significant variations. The Netherlands and Sweden divide assets on a 50–50 basis, but English law allows discretion on the part of judges that can result in one spouse receiving three-quarters or more of the existing assets. In contrast, in some jurisdictions, property owned before marriage remains the property of its original owner and only what is acquired after marriage is shared. And while there are countries that recognize prenuptial contracts that specify in advance what should happen to property if the relationship ends, others do not. One rather different approach is that of Belgium, where a last remnant of fault law still applies, meaning that, if adultery is proved, no award at all need be made.

Despite these practical differences, and apart from the Belgian example, there seems to be a common agreement across the liberal democracies that policy should be based on starting with the situation as it is without regard to how the situation was created and trying to do the best for the parties involved. Increasingly, however, the assumptions on which this strategy is based are being challenged. As already noted, economists see matters in hard-edged terms. Antony Dnes writes: 'Marriage is potentially a good mechanism for supporting long-term family investments, in which without marriage women may be vulnerable to opportunistic behavior, defined as "self seeking with guile".'[28] Robert Rowthorn, too, believes that, by weakening the notion of marriage and the security it offered in the past, no-fault divorce promotes opportunistic behaviour by men. But Rowthorn argues that legal reforms designed to improve the position of all divorced women independently of their role in the breakdown of the marriage may also encourage opportunism by women. His conclusion is that marriage as a trust-creating institution has been undermined—as things stand, the marriage contract has been diluted to the point that it is now much less binding than the average business deal—and that, if opportunism by either sex is to be avoided, fault must be reinstated and also seen as relevant to divorce settlements and decisions about the custody of children. He writes:

The fact that individuals can now exit easily, and unilaterally, from a relationship makes it difficult for couples to make credible commitments to each other. They can promise anything they want, but most of these promises are no longer legally enforceable, and many are undermined by social policies which reward those who break their promises. By eroding the ability of couples to make credible commitments to each other, modern reforms have deprived them of an important facility which, for all its defects, the old system provided.[29]

Criticism of no-fault divorce is not, however, confined to economics. There are also more purely philosophical and ethical considerations that centre on the notion of justice. The Australian philosopher Brian Trainor writes:

... in 'pure' no-fault divorce jurisdictions, such as Sweden and Australia, the courts are required by law *not* to take into account the terms of the marriage contract of the parties whose divorce and divorce settlement they are nevertheless to determine; what this means in effect is that contractual justice is denied and the possibility of achieving an equitable divorce settlement is negated. Marriage contracts may be breached with impunity for the law *requires* its courts to be silent and to ignore the plea for justice of the injured party. In brief, to even consider the claims of contractual justice is made illegal by the law itself.[30]

Trainor adds that, far from irretrievability of breakdown being a brute fact that hits a couple from outside like a meteor from the skies,

'if' the 'fact' of irretrievability is only a 'fact' mainly as a consequence of the unjust actions of one party towards the other and if it is clear that a breach of contractual obligations on the part of one party to a marriage has been mainly responsible for bringing the 'fact' of irretrievability into existence, then it seems positively strange to suggest that a court of law should be debarred from even considering the issues of justice raised in such cases.[31]

A tacit assumption behind the legal changes has been that people will go on behaving in the same way, whatever legal policy applies in the case of breakdown. But it is clearer now than it was at the start of the process of reform that a flexible divorce law that ignores fault can undermine the trust on which marriage and family life depends. If well-framed family law is law that provides incentives for a couple to honour their commitments, laws that do the reverse must be judged ill-conceived. However, this is a judgement that cannot depend simply on the facts of matter; the debate about no-fault divorce is more deeply ideological than this. As the legal scholar Michael Freeman observes: 'A fault-based divorce law was a reflection of a particular view of marriage. But of what is a no-fault divorce a reflection? What is left of the ideology of marriage? Is it a surprise that a new ideology had to be constructed to take its place, one which emphasized the responsibilities of parenthood?'[32]

The use of the past tense here suggests that, for some commentators, the debate about divorce already belongs to an earlier era. It finds its place in assumptions about marriage and family life that have been largely displaced by a new set of concerns. These new concerns are reflected in the title of a book by the American legal scholar June Carbone, *From Partners to Parents*. Carbone describes the shift as a legal revolution. Family law, she says, has long been situated on the boundary between public and private law. Now, however, she writes:

In the new era, courts and legislatures are busy disentangling (and weaving into different strands) the public and private dimension of family law. Sexual relationships are becoming more distinctly private, more a matter of personal preference and private bargaining, and at the same time more subject to the rules that govern other private relationships … Parent–child relationships in contrast are becoming more public, both in the sense that they are attaining greater visibility in their own right as the public importance of marriage fades, and in the sense that the state has become more willing to enforce public expectations of parents. Couples can renegotiate their relationship to each other, but the state continues to define their relation to their children.[33]

But while Carbone sees the new developments as a way of curing confusion, others see the current state of family law as adding to it. The Canadian ethical theorist Dan Cere locates the practical morass of often irresolvable claims concerning parenthood that it has generated in the changed view of the primary relationship:

The ongoing disputes in family law are centrally about competing visions of marriage. While at the far ends of a conceptual divide lie a bewildering variety of specific new proposals (same-sex marriage, covenant marriage, de facto parenting, cohabitation, constitutional amendments to define marriage, and more), these disputes begin with and are fueled by dramatically different concepts of marriage and of the role of the state in making family law.[34]

It may seem surprising that the legal recognition of different types of relationship can be viewed in two such diametrically opposed ways: either as a welcome elevation of private arrangements into formal and legal ones, or as socially damaging changes to a valuable existing institution. But the fact that there are such fundamental differences of opinion may well explain why it is that the momentum for change has taken different forms in different jurisdictions. The focus of debate has been three new types of partnership or union: civil partnerships that are available to both heterosexual and same-sex couples, civil partnerships that are only available for same-sex couples, and same-sex marriage.

Civil partnerships

Why are civil partnerships necessary? In a climate of opinion that is inclined to dismiss formal marriage as a mere 'piece of paper', this question forms an obvious starting point for discussion. But the answer to it must relate to who they might be thought necessary *for*. Civil partnerships that are open to both heterosexual and same-sex couples have been introduced in the Netherlands, Belgium, and some Canadian provinces. Elsewhere, as in the United Kingdom, they have been judged unnecessary for opposite-sex couples, since these already have the option of formal marriage; for a man and a woman, it is argued, a civil partnership would be needed only if it brought significantly different conditions from marriage.

But might it, perhaps, do this? Admittedly, marriage might offer a better chance of security for heterosexual couples than civil partnerships, but civil partnerships could offer *some* degree of security and stability both for heterosexual couples who don't want to marry and for those who cannot do so because marriage is not available to people of the same sex. In both cases, registering a partnership could bring measures to safeguard such fundamentals as residence and income by, for example, providing for both partners to share in the value of the home they have shared, or requiring that one support the other if their relationship breaks down. Pension rights earned by one might be transferable to the other, as in the case of married couples. Childcare and rights to custody and contact might also be specified to avoid contentious litigation if the relationship ends.

Some of these arrangements will seem fair and just in the case of couples who have lived together for a long time or if they have had children in the relationship, more questionable where the association has been brief or when any children involved are the natural children of only one of the partners. It is not surprising, then, that the question of cohabitants' rights was raised during the passage of the Civil Partnership Act 2004 by the UK Parliament, and that, as a result, the Law Commission was asked to consider cohabitation reform as a separate issue, focusing on the financial hardship suffered by cohabitants or their children on the termination of the relationship by breakdown or death. The American Law Institute, in a report entitled *Principles of the Law of Family Dissolution*, had already recommended that unmarried couples who break up after long relationships should be covered under traditional divorce, alimony, and child-support laws. However, it made it clear that this stemmed from its consideration of same-sex relationships and that the recommendation was intended to apply equally to same-sex and opposite-sex couples.[35]

It is, of course, possible that people of the same sex might be even more reluctant than people of the opposite sex to burden informal cohabitation with such extensive legal consequences as these. But, independently of take-up, the principle of equality might seem to require that, if a civil partnership, on whatever terms, is offered to same-sex couples, it should be offered to opposite-sex couples as well. The fact is, however, that it is unlikely that the case for civil partnerships for opposite-sex couples would have been seriously considered but for its link to the issue of partnerships for same-sex couples. A judgment in the Ontario Court of Appeal supports this assumption. It explicitly described what it saw as the need to redesign the law of marriage as being to meet the 'needs, capacities and circumstances of same-sex couples, not ... the needs, capacities and circumstances of opposite-sex couples'.[36]

This intriguing argument needs to be taken a little further back if it is to be properly understood. Its starting point can hardly be the same-sex *couple*, but rather homosexual people as individuals. There is, of course, a political and ethical debate about homosexuality that has taken on global dimensions, particularly given the religious divisions that exist on the subject. But this is not the place to look into that controversy. For present purposes, it is sufficient to accept that the civil partnership debate takes place in a social context in which homosexuality is largely understood and accepted within democratic communities that set much store by recognizing homosexual rights and securing them by law. The argument, then, can be put in these terms: that gay and lesbian men and women are discriminated against if they are barred from doing things that other people are allowed to do; that one of the things that heterosexual people can do and homosexual people cannot do is marry; that this cuts them off from the privileges and responsibilities that marriage brings and therefore that they are discriminated against in an important respect purely because of their sexual orientation.

If this analysis of the problem is accepted, several solutions seem possible: one would be to restore equal treatment by removing legal recognition of marriage and hence the privileges heterosexual people obtain by marrying.[37] Another would be to transfer some of the privileges and responsibilities of marriage to people of either sex, whatever their sexual orientation, in alternative kinds of partnerships—the civil-union option. A third would be to open up the possibility of marriage itself, together with its privileges, to gays and lesbians.

This last possibility must be considered separately, but first it is worth taking a closer look at the analysis itself. And here, the first thing to notice is that, in order to reach its conclusions, certain assumptions about the married state are embedded in the argument. The most important of these is that the link between marriage and parenting and family status is purely contingent and so is only artificially restricted to heterosexuals. But, despite the opportunities opened up by new reproductive technology, this claim goes beyond any common-sense understanding of the situation. At least some of the limitations involved, particularly those connected to parenting and procreation, are not discriminatory at all but natural consequences of the human condition. It is worth noting, too, that the idea of a civil union itself conceals an important ambiguity. Couples affected by these legal changes are commonly described as heterosexual, on the one hand, or homosexual, gay, or lesbian, on the other. This in turn is understood to mean people who are sexually attracted either to people of the opposite sex or to people of the same sex. But many legal pronouncements now more cautiously use the terms 'opposite sex' and 'same sex'. This suggests that, whereas the recognition of heterosexual marriage is explicitly related to heterosexuality and heterosexual behaviour—a marriage is consummated by a sexual act—legislators have drawn back from making this a condition for legal recognition of same-sex civil partnerships. While most people do assume that the relationship is a sexual one, the couple are not required to have a sexual relationship or to declare a particular sexual orientation.[38]

A second assumption is the re-emergence of the notion of an adult dependant. At a time when the idea of a wife as a dependant hardly survives in the case of normal marriage, it seems to have made an unexpected return in the case of same-sex relationships. A partner may, for example, want to pass on benefits to the other partner and to provide for the partner's future. But many of these wishes—for example, in relation to inheritance or the protection of a shared home—can be achieved by available legal means and do not have to involve the tax-payer. Others, such as transferred pension rights or special reduced rates on public transport, do, and the case remains to be made out for paying for these out of public funds.

To return to the question raised at the beginning, why should couples, especially same-sex couples, want civil partnerships? First, it is understandable that two people who have a long-term intimate association with each other may want to register this publicly, and the symbolic value of doing this may well be important to them. A second motive in practice, however, is to achieve parity with others in secur-ing the benefits that a legal tie brings. But, while few could object to the first aspiration, it must be questioned why so many legal and financial consequences must be linked to fulfilling this personal and emotional wish. Most of the financial advantages of formal marriage have their origin in older assumptions about the need to provide support for children and a home-based carer. It is reasonable to assume, in the case of same-sex couples, that they have not come together in the first place in order to have or to raise children—that their primary priority will be each other. This may not be the same in the case of those who press the case for marriage rather than a civil union. At least some of these may have a reverse priority: they may be looking for something that is indeed more like marriage and a traditional family structure.

Same-sex marriage

When the debate about same-sex marriage burst out of the shadows of academia into the public arena, it was called the social debate of the decade. But it has not been as widely adopted in its fully-fledged form as have civil unions. Canada became the first country in the western hemisphere—and the third country in the world—to adopt it when, after much controversy, the Canadian Civil Marriage Act, which legalized same-sex marriage in all the Canadian provinces, was finally signed into law on 20 July 2005. In contrast, in the United States, while same-sex marriage is available in Massachusetts, two nearby states, Vermont and Connecticut, offer only civil unions, and another, New Hampshire, allows neither. It has been suggested that these geographically neighbouring states are well positioned for a social experiment that would make it possible to judge the practical outcome of these different arrangements, particularly as they affect children. The suggestion is accompanied, however, by an important caveat: 'It is important to recognize that social science cannot settle the debate over same-sex marriage, even in principle ... social research will for the most part follow rather than lead the national debate.'[39]

The issue of children and their welfare and entitlements has already been discussed in Chapter 6 in relation to assisted reproduction and again in Chapter 7 in connection with related and unrelated parenting. The subject comes up independently, however, and yet more strongly, in the context of same-sex marriage. While some advocates of same-sex marriage are simply interested in achieving institutional equality, others, including especially lesbian couples, want their relationship to form the basis for a socially recognized unit that includes children. Campaigning groups have produced manifestos that set out remarkably similar objectives, given their wide geographical spread. A Paris-based association of gay and lesbian parents dedicated to promoting reform of family law in France asks for equal access to assisted reproduction, the institution of a model of parenthood based on social rather than purely biological links, and a document that would list all the participants in a child's genesis and care.[40] This would replace the traditional birth certificate, which gives the names of the child's two natural parents, and would also create the legal possibility of multiple 'parents'. They also ask for co-parent or second-parent adoption, a possibility already established by law in the Netherlands and in a number of North American states. The American Academy of Pediatrics outlines similar goals in a 2002 policy statement and recommends the protection of a second 'parent's custody rights if the first parent falls ill or dies, and the protection of the second 'parent's' rights to custody and access if the partners separate.[41]

The common approach amongst these groups contributes to a picture of a kind of *de facto* alliance to create a new ideology of marriage and the family across the Western democracies. The broader perspective supports this perception. In September 2001 a Commission on European Family Law (CEFL) was set up to add a specifically European voice to those of the American Law Institute (ALI) and the National Conference of Commissioners on Uniform Laws (NCCUSL). Its declared aim was to look into means for harmonizing family law across the European countries, linking this with parallel developments in other parts of the Western world. So what are being proposed are not, as many people imagine, a set of minor changes to conditions affecting only a small minority. On the contrary, it is an ambitious attempt to rewrite the concept of the family in its entirety. This perception was clearly expressed by a Canadian judge, Justice Robert Blair. Commenting on the issue of same-sex marriage, he said:

This is not an incremental change in the law. It is a profound change. Although there may be historical examples of the acceptance of same-sex unions, everyone acknowledges that the institution of marriage has been commonly understood and accepted for centuries as the union of a man and a woman. Deep-seated cultural, religious, and socio-political mores have evolved and shape society's views of family, child-rearing and protection, and 'couple-hood' based upon that heterosexual view of marriage. The apparent simplicity of linguistic change in the wording of a law does not necessarily equate with an incremental change in that law. To say that altering the common law meaning of marriage to include same-sex unions is an incremental change, in my view, is to strip the word 'incremental' of its meaning.[42]

These remarks are given substance by the social theorists David Blankenhorn and Elizabeth Marquardt in discussing the consequences of the 2003 decision to legalize same-sex marriage in Massachusetts. They report that, shortly after this decision was taken, officials in the State Department of Public Health recommended changing the wording of the standard marriage certificate, replacing 'husband' and 'wife' with the terms 'Party A' and 'Party B', and amending birth certificates for children in Massachusetts to read 'Parent A' and 'Parent B' rather than 'mother' and 'father'.[43] Similar developments have begun to take place in European countries as well. Following its legal recognition of same-sex marriage in 2006, the head of Spain's Civil Register reported that Spain is creating new birth certificates intended to avoid discriminating against gay couples with children. In the new birth certificates, the terms 'father' and 'mother' are replaced by 'Progenitor A' and 'Progenitor B'.[44] The idea that a child's birth certificate should report a child's actual biological parents is increasingly becoming a thing of the past. In the USA it is common for same-sex couples, adoptive parents, and people using donor gametes to petition to have one or both biological parents left off the birth certificate. Some, indeed, would like to see the same-sex partner of a woman who conceives with donor sperm given an automatic right to be listed as a birth parent on the child's birth certificate—without having to go through formal procedures to adopt the child—just as in some jurisdictions the husbands of women who use donor sperm are listed.

Led by a few special-interest campaigners and without adequate discussion of the implications, radical legal changes have gone ahead in many parts of the democratic West, not least this move to abolish the ancient presumption that there is something special about the relation between a child and its two natural parents. Redefining and re-gendering the couple dramatically redefines the parent in relation to offspring: as a consequence, parents must be recognized by law and society in purely legal and social terms: a parent is a person who has recognized a child, intended its existence, and accepted responsibility for it. Many have been won over by the original argument that a ban on same-sex marriage is public discrimination.[45] But the issues are at the same time wider and also deeper than they may have appreciated. To quote one of the strongest voices of dissent: 'Marriage is not primarily a way of expressing approval for an infinite variety of human affectional or sexual ties; it consists, by definition, of isolating and preferring certain types of unions over others. By socially defining and supporting a particular kind of sexual union, the society defines for its young what the preferred relationship is and what purposes it serves.'[46] While the same-sex marriage debate is governed by concern to promote equal rights for a minority, it cannot but have drastic implications for those of the majority. In the next chapter these will be looked at in a broader social and political perspective.

PART IV
Preserving identities:
A future for the family?

9

Family, identity, and community

In widening discussion to the broader social and political functions of the family, it is worth recalling where we began: with reflection on the position of individual human beings, each driven by a need to form a deep bond with another person, not only to escape the loneliness of the human condition, but also to become, together with another person, part of something that could transcend the ephemeral nature of individual existence. However, this picture would not be complete without recognition of the wider context in which this basic nucleus of human communities functions. Whatever the origins of today's human beings, there has undoubtedly been a dramatic increase from a small number of common forebears in the lost terrain of prehistory to the crowded contemporary world. Two centuries in particular saw a dramatic escalation of numbers. From one billion at the beginning of the nineteenth century, the human population had risen to more than six billion by the end of the twentieth. It is hard not to see this exponential increase as a matter of concern in a planet whose living space and resources are limited. But population growth and family are intimately connected. If the issue is population, then, there could be a duty not to add to it.

Fertility, demography, and population trends

As far as this possible duty to the family is concerned, some would argue that the very rationale of the family—contributing new members to the population—is damaging in today's world: it adds to world poverty, uses up scarce resources, and contributes to environmental deterioration, or at least makes the goal of remedying any of these problems a Sisyphean task. But opinion has shifted since the late 1960s when the biologist Paul Ehrlich alarmed the world with his book *The Population Bomb*, which warned of planetary catastrophe brought about by sheer human overload.[1] Future trends are notoriously prone to change, and future world numbers are still threatened by all the factors famously identified by Thomas Malthus in the eighteenth century: war, famine and disease.[2] Malthus had argued that population and territory needed to be in balance, and that, if a population exceeded the carrying capacity of its land, nature would restore the balance through these unwelcome mechanisms. But, while the forms they take may have changed, the world still faces these old enemies: war in new and more destructive forms; shortages of the basics of life, not least food and water; and intractable health issues, not only new diseases like HIV/AIDS and SARS, but other more familiar enemies such as TB or malaria as they become increasingly resistant to modern scientific remedies.[3] In warning of the population bomb, Erlich was one of many twentieth-century prophets of doom, but prophets can err, and only a few decades after his warning the growth in the world's population has slowed. The adverse impact of uncontrolled population growth has been taken seriously by some of the world's most populous nations, not least China, which, despite its historic respect for the family, has sought to impose on its population of over one billion a policy of just one child per couple.[4] The growth of urbanization, too, has slowed population growth. This is at least partly because, while children can be an asset in a rural context, they may become a burden and an expense in a town or city. For these and other reasons, world fertility has halved since the 1960s. Falls in fertility rates have been recorded for China, Indonesia, East Asia, Latin America, and parts of Africa, as well as for many of the countries of the developed world. The United Nations has predicted that by 2050 the global average number of children per woman will be less than two—a trend that could lead to a halving of the world's population. Previous projections of escalating populations, then, have been replaced in a few short decades with astonishing predictions of worldwide decline, and the mid-twentieth century's fear of an ever-expanding world population begins to look more like an optimistic than a pessimistic projection.

But, while this may be viewed as an overall good on a world scale—for there are indeed boundaries to the numbers of a single species that the planet can support—it may be less welcome when viewed on a smaller and more personal scale. While well-founded speculations about the probable future for the world's population as a whole are important, not least for resource-planning and for health and environmental policy, it may be of more direct concern to individuals to know whether the numbers of their own group—cultural, ethnic, or geographical—are increasing or decreasing. In a world of inter-group hostility and hatred, too, the *relative* increase or decrease of populations takes on political significance. Indeed, even without compounding factors of this sort, real fears have grown that European civilizations could gradually die out, as other groups defined by language and culture have done: the Aztecs, the Ancient Greeks, the Romans. At the end of the nineteenth century, the inhabitants of Western Europe made up about 14 per cent of the world's population. At the beginning of the twenty-first this had fallen to 6 per cent, with a further decline expected to only 4 per cent. The UN assessment is that the European population as a whole is likely to decline, even allowing for immigration, by almost one hundred million over the first fifty years of the twenty-first century—a fall at least as dramatic as that caused by the Black Death in the fourteenth century, when the population of Europe was reduced by about one-third.

In addition, while European populations are declining, they are also ageing, partly as a result of healthier life styles and longer life expectancy. But continuing increases in life expectancy, when combined with declining fertility, generate new social problems. In some European countries, within a few decades one-third of the population will be aged 65 or over, a situation that is bound to affect tax rates, pensions, and healthcare arrangements. Some experts see the Japanese experience as an accelerated version of what Europe may expect. Japan is the world's fastest-ageing industrialized society, and the prediction is that, by 2050, 15 per cent of Japanese people will be over 80 years old. Meanwhile, in both Western and East European countries, as in Japan, population growth has fallen well below replacement level. The key driver for this is the fertility rate—the number of children per woman. The rate needed simply to reproduce a population is a little over two. But it is now just over one in the developed world.[5]

Some see immigration as a way of solving the problems of the developed countries. As far as people in countries where living standards are lower are concerned, their individual interests would often seem to justify migration. For, attachment to place of birth apart, why should people remain in a setting that holds out only a prospect of life long poverty if they can secure admission to one of the privileged locations of the world? But from the point of view of the receiving countries the position is more complex. To try to solve the problems of labour shortages and ageing populations by immigration is to chase a moving target. Immigration cannot in the longer term supply enough people of working age to provide for the needs of children and old people, since immigrants themselves will have children and will age. So, while immigration might help the demographic problem for a time, it cannot do so in the long run.[6] Robert Rowthorn offers a striking analogy: 'A country seeking to retain its youth through immigration is like the sixteenth-century Princess Elizabeth of Transylvania, who sought to keep herself young by bathing in the blood of young maidens. Each bath appeared to restore her youth for a time, but the effect would soon wear off and she would then require another bath, and then another bath, and so on ad infinitum.'[7]

It is hardly surprising, then, if the populations affected by falling birth rates view their situation with concern and have begun to search for remedies. It may be better, however, to address the causes rather than to rely on unattainable solutions. As far as the United Kingdom is concerned, the birth rate has been below replacement level since it peaked briefly in the 1960s, stabilized in the 1980s, and decreased slightly in the 1990s.[8] It fell consistently every year from 1996 to 2002, and a socially unsatisfactory polarization has developed between, on the one hand, early births to single mothers often supported by welfare benefits, and, on the other, late births to more established self-supporting couples. It is a situation in which there are not enough births to maintain the population at its existing level, although the actual size of the population may in fact continue to grow for another generation because of extended life spans—there are more older people—and inward immigration. In these circumstances, were it not for the failure of government targets to curb teenage pregnancy, the fall in fertility rates might be more marked, and the British position would not be so different from that which has caused concern in other European countries.

For a culture and society that has pushed sex into the place Marx attributed to religion—it is the new 'opium of the people'—British society is surprisingly averse to procreation. People are less likely to marry, and when they do, they do so later in life.[9] The tendency for cohabitation to take the place of formal marriage and the increase in lone-parent and one-person households was referred to in the previous chapter. But these factors, together with divorce and multiple relationships, have a bearing on delayed and renewed child-bearing, as many women defer having children until it is too late to do this without medical intervention. In seeking for explanations, though, it would be a mistake to focus entirely on women. The role and position of men have been affected by changes in social and economic structures. In a number of European countries, a high proportion of men in their forties are unmarried, and, for many of these, the reason for remaining single is that jobs are insecure and poorly paid, placing houses—and hence the project of setting up an independent home—beyond their financial reach.[10] On the broader front, too, the role of the *paterfamilias*—the traditional breadwinner—is an element in fewer and fewer households, as social policy has ceased to give any recognition to the difference between working to support yourself, and working to support both yourself and a dependent spouse and children.

But, if public policy is a contributing cause of population decline, biological factors also play a part. Male sperm counts have been falling for many years, while the trend to later child-bearing and the increase in sexually transmitted diseases amongst both sexes have led to predictions of fertility problems for as many as one in three couples in the United Kingdom.[11] And, finally, as a result of 'second-time-around' marriages, usually involving an older man and younger woman, young men must now compete with their own fathers' generation for the young women of their own age who might have been their natural child-bearing partners.[12] Of course, there are also more positive reasons for declining birth rates: women have access to education and careers, and reliable, if limited, social provision means that people do not have to look to their direct progeny for care in their old age. At the same time, effective contraception offers them a choice about how many children they want to have, or whether to have children at all. The fact is, though, that the element of choice may be more illusory than real, at least from the community's perspective. Since there are too few women of child-bearing age to reverse the decline in the near future, Europe's population would continue to decline even if birth rates were to improve.

The United States presents a different picture, at least as far as the population taken in its entirety is concerned. To begin with, it is a younger country. The median age of the United States population will be 36 in 2050, as compared with the European Union where it is expected to be 53. The United States is the third most populous country in the world. In 1960 an average of 365 children were born to each 100 women of child-bearing age. This had dropped by 1976 to 174 per 100, but has gradually risen again to 208 and beyond. The rise has been mainly due to the increase in the Hispanic population, and 1971 remains the last year that Americans of non-Hispanic white ancestry reached replacement level in terms of births.[13] A rather similar explanation accounts for an expected increase in the United Kingdom's population, which its Office for National Statistics predicts will rise from 60 million to 67 million over the period up to 2050. It is an increase resulting from births to recent immigrants—that is, to parents not themselves born in the UK—rather than from births to the original population.[14]

There are some, however, who do look to natural increases in their existing population: the French predict that by 2050 their numbers will rise from sixty million to seventy-five million, mainly as a result of new policies to encourage people to have children. These include financial and employment incentives. For example, couples with children are allowed to split their income for tax purposes, and French workers pay less tax with each additional child. Three children enable a family to be classified as a *famille nombreuse* and so to qualify for travel discounts and other benefits. France spends more than any other EU country on policies to promote families, but Italy too, alarmed by its dramatically declining population, has experimented with generous direct payments on the birth of second children.

While many people are troubled by the threat of dwindling populations, there are others in Western countries who find the idea of a childfree lifestyle attractive or who are willing to recommend childlessness as a way of life. Economists often assess the individual judgement as to whether or not to have children in profit-and-loss terms, and, according to their calculations, children usually turn out to be an expensive commodity. They may also be judged to be so socially as well. But this may have more to do with social attitudes to children as much as to the children themselves. And, while the largely childfree gay consumer has for some time been recognized as a lucrative target for business, some commentators would like to see this target expanded to include child-free customers in general. Indeed, one American author and advocate of a childfree lifestyle sees provision for the childfree as potentially the fastest-growing segment of America's business sector.[15]

Costs and benefits, however, need to be viewed on a larger and more long-term scale than this, and, for advocates of freedom from children and childbearing, the history of a small American sect provides a salutary tale. In their heyday, the Shakers were a radical religious group, influential in the eighteenth and nineteenth centuries. Some of their social ideas carry echoes today. They held to the absolute equality of male and female, and women took on leadership roles in their society. Believing that the end of the world was near, they rejected sex and childbearing in favour of celibacy. At one time, they numbered about 6,000 members. Today there are no more than seven surviving members, and the simple and functional furniture that they made is their sole heritage. The story of the Shakers can be taken as a small but cautionary portrait of the link between personal and physical continuity and the long-term flourishing of a group. It is a reminder that culture and community can flourish in the long term only where there are new people to carry their spirit and ideas forward to future generations.

Cultural identity and the ethics of recognition

Fundamental to many people's sense of personal identity is another aspect of culture and community: the concept of recognition. A brief moral tale told to Russian children concerns a man who meets a stranger in a wood. The man's first reaction is fear: the stranger is immediately perceived as a threat, a potential enemy. But then there is recognition. This is a relative, a kinsman. Rightly or wrongly, the stranger is no longer feared; he is seen not as a threat but as a friend—someone to help, or to look to for help. But perhaps this is not so surprising. Many people see their kin relationships as part of their own identity, particularly as they themselves get older, even more when they become parents themselves. But for all but a few families—those with known illustrious antecedents—the historical map tends to run out or fade after grandparents and great-grandparents.

However, this may be more a matter of the lack of available records than real indifference to personal history and family origins. A remarkable discovery in an English town in the early years of the twenty-first century lends support to this hypothesis. A group of builders who were demolishing a house that had been used as a base for photographic work found some sealed drums in the basement. Instead of throwing them away with other rubbish, they pressed open the lids and discovered hundreds of reels of black and white moving film that had been made almost a hundred years before by the early photographic enthusiasts Sagar Mitchell and James Kenyon. These short films showed hundreds of ordinary people going about their everyday life in Edwardian

Britain—emerging from factories, taking a Sunday walk, enjoying a visit to the seaside. Some of those in the films could be identified, and their great-grandchildren, often living in the same town a century later, were able to view their forebears as living moving human beings, laughing and gesturing at the camera, dressed in the clothes of the period but often closely resembling them in looks and manner. These films made a forceful impact on those who were able, through them, to make a direct acquaintance with their own grandparent or great-grandparent. It was a sensation they found hard to describe, but perhaps the visual presentation of the link from generation to generation had thrown a new light on the way they viewed their own lives and their posterity—a concrete vindication of Edmund Burke's description of society as a compact between the dead, the living, and those not yet born.

But the family does not offer only a linear perspective, linking generations through time. It offers a horizontal one as well, providing a sense of role and mutual interdependence in contemporary as well as historical terms. The family is a unit within a larger unit—or, looked at the other way round, the nuclear family of parents and children opens out, first into the extended family and then into a broader group. Within Great Britain, for example, a look at a local telephone directory is enough to demonstrate this. English surnames, a well as Welsh, Irish, and Scottish surnames, are limited in number, but they are endlessly repeated, revealing a clan-like pattern of connectedness via the male line. The same is true of settled communities in other parts of Europe, and emigrants from those places have taken their names with them to other parts of the globe. At some point, though, just as in the historical encounter, the sense of 'we' dies out and the trail is lost in statistics and demographics. Many, however, including those African-Americans whose own names were lost in the era of the slave trade and who were obliged to take on the names of their owners, continue their search for their roots in genealogical records and through the new science of DNA analysis. The results of this analysis suggest that today's Europeans may be the descendants of seven female ancestors who lived between about 15,000 and 30,000 years ago—the originators of European 'clans' who inhabited particular areas of the European continent. Following the male line through surnames is equally fascinating. In the case of a boy, the male Y-chromosome is inherited directly from his father, his father's father, and so on. Both sexes, however, inherit some genetic characteristics from their mothers through their mitochondrial DNA—it is passed on by mothers to both daughters and sons. Genealogical speculation, aided by new genetic insights of this sort, paints a fascinating portrait of the past. However, it would be a mistake to read too much into these findings as a way of understanding personal identity. In the long run we are all related to each other, and, within fifteen generations, each human being living today has more than half a million direct ancestors.

So the search for 'we,' however expressed, takes us back to the question of identity in a way that science is able to answer only in part. For who *is* the 'we' that is the object of this search? In the past, national boundaries usually marked out the boundaries of a culture, and language was often, though not always, a defining feature. But identity is no more a purely geographical concept than a purely genetic one. Most Western societies would now describe themselves as multicultural, and it is commonplace to refer to, often to politicize, different identities within a common jurisdiction. But to describe some of these different identities as *cultural* groups can lead to confusion, both in the notion of a culture and also in the way 'multicultural' is to be understood. Societies contain, and always have contained, many differences, and different 'recognition' features may be important in different contexts. Depending on that social context, these features may be race, ethnicity, skin colour, language, religion, gender, (dis)ability, or even sexual orientation.

These multiple possibilities have little to do with the older, elite conception of culture, in which it means, in Matthew Arnold's words, 'the best that has been thought and known'.[16] Nor do they necessarily link directly to the popular conception of 'culture' in which the 'culture' of a group is to be found in the features that make up a common life—entertainment, food, lifestyles, and customs. These are indeed ways of recognizing minority groups, but not all group characteristics have political importance, while others that modern societies have chosen to recognize as important, in particular skin colour, gender, and sexual orientation, have little to do with cultural preferences or lifestyle. Indeed, many people would object to finding themselves singled out in these ways. As Anthony Appiah argues, the pressure to construct one's identity out of being gay or black may turn out to be a new kind of constraint. He writes: 'If I had to choose between the world of the closet and the world of gay liberation, or between the world of Uncle Tom's Cabin and Black Power, I would, of course, choose in each case the latter. But I would like not to have to choose. I would like other options.'[17] Similar observations apply where gender is concerned, for women, too, may prefer to claim a broader cultural identity than one

based on narrow gendered expectations. And, although groups identified in these ways are often referred to as communities, denominations
like these fail to pick out a *community* in any realistic sense. People do
not, on the whole, live in groups marked out by gender any more than
by sexual orientation, and, in practice, a community is often recognized simply by the fact that its members choose to live in the same
locality, or at least gather together in regular meetings and assemblies.

Religion and identity

But one of the features mentioned does have a stronger claim to recognition as a cultural marker. This is religion. The case for allowing it
this status is well founded, since a religion often seeks to determine
a whole way of life. In addition, religious and ethnic communities,
possibly marked out by a separate language, may live in distinguish-
able locations and they may also choose to raise their families separately
from mainstream groups. Differences, though, can be exaggerated, and
some faith groupings have more in common in their religious roots
than is widely recognized. Judaism, as represented by the Old Testa-
ment, has provided a cultural basis for Islam as well as for Christianity.
While events do not always take a predicted course, this should at least
mean that the potential for harmonious living in some of Europe's
newly multi-faith societies is there to be breathed into life. And, while
it is Christianity, with its Judaic roots, that has shaped and influenced
Europe's social practice, law, and politics over 2,000 years, inspiring its
literature and art, the European cultural heritage is not the exclusive
inheritance of believers; it is shared by its secular thinkers and is available also to members of other religions. If today the rise of militant
Islamist movements unsympathetic to Western values has intensified
some divisions—in particular that between a Western culture that is
broadly Christian and a strong Muslim culture whose roots lie south
and east of the Mediterranean—it has also given a stronger profile to
the notion of cultural identity based on religion—a notion that was
gradually dying away in increasingly secularized Western democracies.

It is in this setting that the link between family, culture, and religion can begin to be seen by the communities themselves from a
demographic perspective. Differential family size creates a potential
imbalance in populations—the forerunner of significant population
transformations.[18] Some argue that this process can already be seen

in part of the European continent and that, as a result, Western communities with their cultural roots in ancient Greece and Rome face a realistic possibility of becoming a numerical minority in regions in which the predominance of their cultural heritage was formerly unchallenged. This situation has already been reached in the great Dutch cities of Amsterdam and Rotterdam. These demographic differences in particular localities reflect a broader picture in which many Muslim countries—Egypt, Libya, Syria, Turkey—have birth rates that are at least twice the European Union average. Speculation about how these contrasts might develop in the future has led to apocalyptic pronouncements of a clash of civilizations in which fertility and family play a role in a dramatic confrontation between Islam and the West in a battle for religious and cultural supremacy.[19]

Meanwhile, Western countries either deny or seek to avoid this apocalyptic outcome by appealing to the principle of religious toleration within a multicultural ideal. For multiculturalism is not only a descriptive term. It is also a normative concept. Many respect it as a political position linked to the assertion of identity by neglected or marginalized groups, and as a demand for the recognition of that identity by others. Talk of the 'politics of equal recognition' suggests that there is some perspective from which all such judgements can be impartially surveyed and evaluated. However, those who have embraced a culture, or more particularly a religion, can hardly, without inconsistency, avoid giving it a position of privilege in their own lives. In these vital matters, impartiality is both practically difficult and logically incoherent.[20]

Partiality and preference

So can a preference for your 'own', whether your own group, your own culture, or even your own family, be ethically justified? Impartiality is often taken as the mark of morality, while the notion of partiality has a more disputed ethical status. Partiality has been defined as the claim that, everything else being equal, it is morally right to give a higher priority in your actions to the good of those to whom you stand in certain sorts of relationship than to others.[21] This is hard to reconcile with the moral requirement not to discriminate between people, other than for sound and relevant moral reasons. There is, though, a response to this challenge that is practical if paradoxical. The paradox lies in the fact that the idea of special obligations to family members places the principle of particularity *within* a universal morality. In other words, the duty to care especially for members of your own family is a moral requirement that applies equally to everyone; it is a universal duty. Indeed, as Lawrence Blum observes: 'Morally, the intuition that we have special ties to members of our family which we do not have to others is as secure a moral conviction as that every human being should be treated with dignity.'[22]

This is not a new ethical debate, even if the terms in which it is couched are new. A little over two centuries ago, in discussing the moral sentiments, Adam Smith wrote of the naturalness of partiality: 'Every man feels his own pleasures and his own pains more sensibly than those of other people ... After himself, the members of his own family, those who usually live in the same house with him, his parents, his children, his brothers and sisters, are naturally the objects of his warmest affections.'[23] In a more recent discussion of the classic confrontation between the personal and the impersonal, the British moral philosopher R. M. Hare defended the idea of norms that are *not* person specific in logico-technical terms, arguing that it is a distinctive feature of a moral judgement that it must be capable of being expressed in a form that involves no proper names.[24] Nevertheless, Hare later went on to modify his own universal prescriptivist position to include consequentialist considerations, and so, as Blum describes it, 'to craft a version of consequentialism that validates partialist phenomena'.[25] Hare recognized the paradoxical nature of mixing elements of Kantian ethics, which are based on a belief in universal moral principles, with utilitarianism—a moral theory that relates judgements of right and wrong, good and bad, to the consequences of actions—but he argued that even the impersonal ethics of Kant had to take account of the impact of our actions on the course of events in the world.[26] Whether or not Kant would have welcomed this chance to be reconciled with those whose views he so strongly opposed, a consequentialist (or a pragmatist) can achieve some reconciliation of the two viewpoints by arguing that there is a general public benefit, helpful to the community as a whole, when people give preferential attention to the needs of family and friends. And, if this is also supported by a strongly felt moral intuition, as Blum, like Smith, argues, the notion of partiality can be claimed to have the support of a broad spectrum of philosophic ethics.

It would be easy to see the partiality controversy as no more than a theoretical debate generated in the privacy of the academy. However, it cannot be confined to the academy, and, when it moves out into the public world, it acquires an important political dimension. Here it finds its expression in two competing political approaches: on the one hand, a rigorously individualistic approach that seems to neglect other people's needs; on the other, a rigid application of egalitarianism that would allow you to do for those you care for only what can be done for everyone.

Underlying this is an apparent opposition between an individualist political morality and a collectivist one. And when groups rather than individuals are the beneficiaries of partiality, a new gulf opens up that it may be even harder to bridge. For partisan claims for specific group rights are often seen as the province of the nationalist, the separatist, or religious adherent, and the liberal cosmopolitan is left to lay claim to the whole area of individual human rights. Recognizing this dilemma, Robert Rowthorn comments: 'there will always be a tension between universalism and particularism, between cosmopolitanism and nationalism. The problem is not to choose one or the other, but to hold these two poles in balance.'[27]

One way to approach this classic confrontation and to weaken the tension, at least at the level of family and community, would be to recognize that the familiar moral opposition between the personal and the impersonal is a distinction based on a false dichotomy. The 'rational contractors' posited in much political and economic theory are defined as people interested in maximising their *own* welfare. This leaves the 'view-from-nowhere' approach, according to which everybody's interests count equally, as the only counter to a selfish preoccupation with your own values and interests, of which your own family is just one. As Thomas Nagel puts this point: 'Each of us begins with a set of concerns, desires and interests of his own, and each of us can recognize that the same is true of others. We can then remove ourselves in thought from our particular position in the world and think simply of all those people, without singling out as *I* the one we happen to be.'[28] On the one hand, then, a universalist and impartialist position is commonly presented as altruistic and hence good, and, on the other, a partialist position is presented as essentially *egotistical* and hence bad. This may explain why liberal egalitarians object to partiality towards family members, particularly where important goods, such as health and education, are concerned—a perspective briefly summed up by Rawls in these words: 'The principle of fair opportunity can be only imperfectly carried out, at least as long as the institution of the family exists. The extent to which natural capacities develop and reach fruition is affected by all kinds of social conditions and class attitudes. Even the willingness to make an effort, to try, and so to be deserving in the ordinary sense is itself dependent upon happy family and social circumstances.'[29] This judgement finds a close echo in another comment by Nagel: 'So long as children grow up in families, they will inevitably benefit or suffer from the advantages or disadvantages of their parents.'[30]

It is unlikely that either of these authors intended to recommend the abolition of the family. Nevertheless, their remarks have enormous social implications. Pursued to its conclusion, the argument would seem to lead to nothing less than this in order to secure an egalitarian 'level playing field.' And, in the political and educational world of today, recognition of the way in which good parenting confers benefits on children often prompts not only a desire to remedy the disadvantages some children suffer, but also resentment that some should benefit from their parents' care and involvement. As a result, there are those who would like to remedy this inequality and nullify the effects of both good and bad parenting by transferring more control and responsibility for children to the state.

This is the inevitable consequence of a position that recognizes only two standpoints, the particular and the universal. For Nagel, the emphasis on these two standpoints is central. He writes: 'We see things *from here*, so to speak. But we are also able to think about the world in abstraction from our particular position in it—in abstraction from who we are.' But there is a third possibility—a midway position—that emphasizes neither detached impersonality of judgement nor a purely selfish concern with your own interests. For, while greater concern for your own child than for another is not impartial in the usual sense of that term—the 'view-from-nowhere' sense—it is not selfish either. What is missing from the position that recognizes only two possible standpoints is any recognition of empathy—of seeing the world from the self-focus of another individual and acting on that sensitivity. This could involve giving that person something he or she does not really deserve, or offering simply an act of kindness you would not extend to everyone, nor even think that other people should imitate as a matter of principle. Where it is your children who are the beneficiaries, there is a sense that these are children who in a sense belong to you, or at least with you. They are children with whom you have a special relationship, and it is this that generates your special obligations. An assumption of this sort is the essence of family affection, and even of some other relationships that generate less stringent obligations, such as good neighbourliness.

The difference that is significant in the context of interpersonal morality is that between wanting something 'for yourself' and wanting something for others, or even for one special person. This is not incompatible, of course, with sometimes acting on the more familiar ethical basis represented by the parable of the good Samaritan, of putting out a hand to help a stranger, although he is a stranger. Where nations are concerned, the sentiment of ownership or belonging is called patriotism—a word formed to encapsulate the idea that a citizen of whatever country has a duty to be loyal to that country and no other, so long, at least, as it respects the boundaries set by fundamental human rights. Applied to a culture rather than a nation, it is the claim that people may legitimately recognize a duty of loyalty to their own culture and seek to preserve it as their own heritage and way of life. Again, though, this is not incompatible with a broad compassion for need beyond those national or political frontiers, nor with an active desire to address issues of global poverty and inequality.

Philosophical discussion of the idea that special duties may be owed to particular others is not, of course new. It can be traced back in the Western tradition to discussions of friendship and filial duty in Plato and Aristotle. However, the debate has been taken in new directions in modern times, particularly by some of those who approach the issue from the point of view of feminist theory. It has been a distinctive claim of feminist writers that women often display a spontaneity of moral response that many philosophers, in particular Hegel and Kant, would say had no moral worth.[31] The idea, for example, that acts prompted by love are inferior to principled acts is a deep-rooted philosophical tradition as well as a central focus of plays and literature since classical times.

Much of the impetus for philosophical writing on this subject has been inspired by the work of Carol Gilligan, whose empirical work as a psychologist, described in Chapter 4, led her to recognize the pull of a valid ethical concern for particular others for whom one has a special responsibility.[32] Gilligan had noted that the research programme with which she was working asked women to consider the ethical choices of imaginary people divested of the details of their own situation, and lacking the history and psychology of their individual lives—something that the women involved tended to ask for, or to contribute out of their own imagination, in order to resolve the moral problem.

A similar point is made with equal effect by Robert Nozick in relation to Rawls's theory of justice. The device by which Rawls imagined his actors arriving at abstract principles of justice—the veil of ignorance—also strips the procedure of arriving at principles bare of all reference to the particular and concrete. The veil of ignorance is a device that ensures that principles will be chosen by people who know nothing of their position in society, their social status or class, their abilities, talents, or conceptions of the good.[33] Nozick argued that the very nature of Rawls's thought experiment guarantees the type of principles that will be chosen; that they will be impersonal and grounded in future-oriented principles of distribution, rather than being personal and grounded in current or past circumstances.[34]

While these commentators might not have sought to apply this analysis to the issue of partiality with any special reference to the family, it nevertheless offers a basis for the claim that the family has a distinctive ethical status: that it is right to care in a special way for your own—those with whom you share your identity, to whom you belong, and who belong, in a sense, to you. But, of course, in asserting this, you assert the same on behalf of other families and communities whose group or identity is different from your own. The challenge then is to find and respect principles for coexistence and a moral basis that can be held in common. When the dwindling populations of one culture come into potential conflict with the burgeoning population of another, the search for common values gains a critical urgency. It is this that creates the need, as well as the justification, for finding and occupying some moral ground between concern for all and concern only for self—between pursuing universal human rights and cultivating one's own interests as an individual. Another writer ably expresses this general position. Summing up what he describes as a form of indirect universalism, philosophically acceptable to both Kantians and utilitarians, Paul Gomberg writes: 'in order to realize universal principles (promoting well-being and respect for human rights) we need social norms that bind people together, and those norms create special relationships, with corresponding special duties. Hence universal principles can be realized only through relationships that require preferential treatment.'[35]

This challenge can best be met, not only by being aware of what all human beings as a matter of fact have in common and what, therefore, are their common needs, but also by recognizing that these needs will not be fully met by sustaining the life of a single generation. Survival and continuity are broad concepts that point towards the future. They are not confined to the present. In this, as the issues discussed in this chapter have illustrated, the role of the family is basic.

ℰ 10

Finding a way through the wood

As Western societies contemplate with increasing misgiving the decline of the family and a painful struggle for the realignment of gender roles, the issues that have been touched on here reveal that ideas about sexuality and reproduction are deeply embedded in broader political and philosophical ideologies. Despite the fact that it is usually thought to be the most intimate and personal of human relations, sex has almost always been the subject of social and legal regulation. But the widely held libertarian view that personal and sexual relationships between adults belong entirely in the area of individual choice needs some qualification. In particular, as I have argued in previous chapters, an emphasis on adults' choices too often disregards altogether the implications of those choices for the rights and future autonomy of children, as well as for their interests and future happiness. It may also overlook the more general question of the impact of these choices on society and community.

But freedom does matter, and, in general, other things being equal, less rather than more state interference and control are to be preferred. All things are not always equal, however, and where the family is concerned, it is necessary to look for a more consistent account of the practical implications of a commitment to the foundational principles of free societies. Such an account must begin by recognizing that it is the function of even the minimal state to protect the vulnerable against harm by the powerful, and that children, particularly at the inarticulate earliest stages of human existence, are vulnerable in relation to the adults surrounding them. For them, these adults represent absolute power. This is an area where, as the proverb says, 'freedom for the pike means death for the minnow'. And children are minnows in relation to the adult world. The stage of vulnerability begins even earlier than in the past, since the new technologies of reproduction have made it possible for a human being to sustain losses at the embryonic stage that may be experienced at the adult stage as deprivation of rights. Reflecting on this from a philosophical perspective, another commentator describes the creation of children who will be severed from all or part of their biological past as a vast social experiment. He adds: 'The experiment of creating these children is supported by a new ideology of the family.'[1]

The family and the left/right divide

To understand how this new ideology has emerged, it is necessary to see these developments in a wider context. Two philosophical positions in particular stand out. Seen on the broadest of spectrums, these are commonly presented in terms of a conflict between the political left and the political right. The French political scientist Jacques Donzelot describes the early evolution of this divide in relation to family policy in this way:

> the family constituted a clear dividing line between the defenders of the established order and those who contested it, between the capitalist camp and the socialist camp ... Who sided with the family? Mainly conservatives who favored the restoration of an established order centered around the family, a return to an idealized former regime; but also liberals who saw the family as the protector of private property, of the bourgeois ethic of accumulation, as well as the guarantor of a barrier against the encroachments of the state. Those who attacked the family, the scientific or utopian socialists, did so against those very functions ascribed to it by the ruling classes. Its disappearance was programmed for a dawning socialism, and its partial breakup, its crises, were considered so many signs heralding the latter's arrival.[2]

Today, however, both left and right represent a loose alliance of opposite tendencies. The first includes some who, reacting against rules about personal behaviour they see as a repressive attempt by one class to pursue its own interests at the expense of another, reject imposed boundaries in lifestyle and behaviour. But, it also includes others, often more politically influential, who are ready to endorse a controlling state centralism reaching into every aspect of personal life that can secure the mandate of health, safety, or other apparently ethically neutral goods.

The position of the right, on the other hand, is made up of an uneasy partnership between libertarianism and conservatism. This division may be more overt than that on the left, since many on the conservative right believe that liberty has drifted into licence. They find the source of many of the ills affecting today's liberal societies—crime, the drug culture, and sexual exploitativeness—in liberal individualism itself, which they have begun to see as fundamentally egotistical and socially damaging.[3] So some of those on the right who were previously enthusiastic supporters of *laissez-faire* policies in both economic and social life now believe that we are faced by a postliberal malaise in which unfettered individualism challenges the natural ties of family, neighbourhood and ethnic and national identity. Shocked by the crumbling of the social fabric in so many of the liberal democracies, they are beginning to look to more community-oriented strategies for remedies.[4] Some on the left accept this diagnosis too, but, where the conservative right looks to voluntary changes in private behaviour, so long as these are supported rather than undermined by the legal framework, those on the political left are more likely to turn to state intervention and social engineering as a solution.

The late twentieth and early twenty-first centuries, however, have added other ingredients to the original mix, first the feminist movement, and then the broader moves for gay and lesbian recognition. For some of these, the undoing of the patriarchal family will be completed only with the abandonment of basic presumptions about heterosexuality and biological and genetic relationships. As one contemporary writer puts it: 'Postmodern living arrangements are diverse, fluid, and unresolved, constantly chosen and rechosen and heterorelations are no longer as hegemonic as once they were.' Summing up this widely held view, she says: 'The heterosexual couple, and particularly the married, co-resident heterosexual couple with children, no longer occupies the centre-ground of western societies and cannot be taken for granted as the basic unit in society.'[5] This has become a widely accepted dogma of today's political and intellectual opinion-leaders, at least in the English-speaking world. Other voices are still to be heard from France, Germany, Austria, Italy, and some of the European countries that lived under communism. Africa, too, stands outside the consensus: overwhelmed by the threat of AIDS, some of its leaders favour secure monogamy as the best guarantee of personal and community health.

The 'postmodern' consensus, however, is influential. As described, it combines both an empirical and a normative claim: that the traditional family is in decline; and that it has now outlived its moral authority. In this book I have sought to disentangle these two elements and to explore the various arguments on which they stand. The normative aspect, however, may in the end turn out to be the more important of the two, for, while research findings are often contested, and social practices inevitably fluctuate over time, political and legal decisions can either propel change forward, arrest it altogether, or turn it in better-chosen directions. These are the alternatives now confronting many democratic countries in the West, and, if critical decisions are not to be left entirely to judges in courts of law or to small groups of experts in committee, it is not only the personal and practical issues involved that need to be more widely understood, but also their underlying philosophical and ethical assumptions.

The philosophical and ethical background

What, then, are these presuppositions? In gathering up the threads of this many-faceted discussion, it is possible to identify certain key ideas that form part of the new ideology of the family: the first of these must be the demotion of marriage as an institution through the weakening of its contractual aspect; the second, the separation of partnering from parenthood; the third, the rewriting of parenthood itself as no more than a legal or a social convention—the constructivist rejection of the belief that family relationships are, directly or indirectly, biological and natural. Some of the practical consequences of these ideas have been described in earlier chapters, as well as the role that family law has played in the process. But behind these legal and political decisions lie philosophical and ethical arguments of a more ideological nature.

The influence of two philosophers in particular has shaped social and political debate from the mid-nineteenth century. The contrast epitomised in the political philosophy of John Stuart Mill and Karl Marx is, in part, a matter of their view of human beings. Mill has a conception of society as made up of free individuals whose private lives should be free from interference by state and society; the Marxist analysis of society, on the other hand, sees it as a succession of power struggles between rival groups, in which individuals are no more than puppets pushed along in the sweeping tide of history. Feminists have added to these a critique of gender roles, whose influence may yet be more far-reaching. The political theorist Ferdinand Mount, in an account of the liberating function of the historical family, describes this last influence in more cautionary terms: 'The feminine variety of utopia has survived longer than other utopias because it started so much later and because it had such unanswerable evidence of male brutality and oppression to produce. In its exhilarating destructiveness, it encompasses the sweeping away not merely of class and poverty and cruelty and forced labour but of all distinctions of sex or age ... It is the ultimate utopia, unnerving and bewildering to most men, as it is meant to be.'[6]

These varied philosophical ideals, however, must be judged on their merits. The Marxist experiment may well have run its course as far as Western communities are concerned. But the libertarian philosophy of Mill and his modern-day successors deserves a longer probation, notwithstanding the views of those political opponents who condemn liberal individualism as the social face of a ruthless free-market economic approach and of religious leaders who charge that it has created a moral and cultural vacuum—a mass society of rootless privatized individuals. Such criticism seems to overlook the origins and history of the individualism of which Mill was only a late-stage exponent. Derived from principles that the seventeenth-century British philosopher John Locke set out in terms of a limited set of negative rights against repressive or despotic rulers, it provided a foundation for the American and French constitutions and later for the important international agreements on human rights painfully carved out in the aftermath of the bloody wars of the twentieth century. These ideas represented seminal and foundational goods in the long evolution of Western civilization. It would be wrong, then, to paint the libertarian tradition as a selfish and immoral doctrine and wise to recognize that its shortcomings may be due more to people failing to live up to their own ideals than because the original inspiration is faulty. There continue to be good reasons for holding on to these ideals. As far as the present day is concerned, the failure to cherish the individual—in Kant's terminology, to respect the human person—has made possible public acceptance of government intervention in personal and family life on an unprecedented scale. It has exposed democratic societies to the risk of infiltration by a creeping totalitarianism in which the child, from fertilized ovum to secondary-school student, is seen as the property of the state or even, in the area of reproductive medicine, as a saleable commodity.

But the early architects of the political philosophy of individualism did not, on the whole, see the individual in isolation. On the contrary, they understood, and expected their readers to understand, that individuals were part of wider family structures. But, because they also saw the family as a hierarchy generally headed by a male person, the individualism of social-contract theory is often identified with this patriarchal aspect and denounced by both Marxists and feminists for this reason.[7] Viewed in the context of its own period in history, however, classical individualism was a progressive notion. Underlying it was the assumption that the family is a natural unit and that the artificial structures of political society should respect and accommodate it, invading its private space only for compelling reasons.

Liberal individualism is not, on the other hand, the enemy of what are often called conservative family values. It is itself a rich tradition rooted in substantial moral values, central amongst which is a commitment to reason and to the protection of individuals in the pursuit of their legitimate ends. These ends cannot be protected without the security a state can provide. Even the minimal state, then, has to be understood as having two important positive obligations: to protect its citizens against dangers within the community and threats from without, and to enable them to enter into reliable mutual agreements. As regards the dangers within, it has become a truism to say that many of the ills of Western societies centre on the decline of the family, but less common for people to notice that this in turn is bound in with the breakdown of the contractual elements in human relationships. I have argued here that ill-judged interference in family life and misplaced social and legal remedies for problems that individuals could often deal with better themselves have also contributed to the disintegration of families on an unprecedented scale. While this claim is subject to the test of experience and may be open to debate, it is harder to dispute the fact that over-flexible and accommodating divorce laws have created insecurity in a central relationship that needs to be rock solid if it is to provide a viable base for a project—the raising of children—that may take two decades or more.

But a minimal state in which the implications of its dual obligation to enforce contracts and protect the weak from harm by stronger parties has been properly interpreted and applied provides a philosophical basis that is not, after all, incompatible with some of the political positions with which it is usually contrasted. These include the social values and traditions that are advocated by political conservatives. But there are also currents of thought on the left that should strike a sympathetic chord with those who advocate personal independence from unnecessary social interference: ethical socialism, for example, was a grass-roots working-class movement built on a strong moral foundation, and on a belief in voluntary cooperation for social projects and for risk-sharing against the hazards of life. In sum, it rested on the loyalty and solidarity of working-class family life. The social theory of the Scottish philosopher John MacMurray (1891–1976) and the Danish philosopher Knud Ejler Løgstrup (1905–81) could be said to belong in this tradition, for both these philosophers combined a belief in egalitarianism and opposition to class privilege with a deep interest in interpersonal relationships.[8] Contemporary communitarians, such as Amitai Etzioni, who see the institutions of family and relatedness as the building-blocks of a convivial community, are the natural heirs and successors of this philosophical tradition.

Protecting the vulnerable

While I have argued that the protection of the family as historically understood follows from a state's general obligation to protect its citizens from harm and provide them with a framework in which to make enduring commitments, it is clear that communities face hazards and problems that individuals as such can do little about—not only internal problems, but also environmental and economic problems of global proportions: potentially pandemic health threats, diminishing energy resources, war and terrorism, and the instability caused by the vast disparity in wealth of North and South.

Many will be vulnerable to the multiple effects of these background causes. This means that state involvement may have to expand to fill the vacuum left by individuals, for genuine dependency must be covered one way or another in a modern society. However, the nature of most of these problems is that the vulnerability of some impinges on the lives and safety of others, particularly if the social consequences of vulnerability include such social ills as crime, homelessness, and sexual exploitation. It follows, then, that the principle of the minimal state can be extended to include action to protect vulnerable categories of people, not only for their own sake directly, but also for the sake of others.

This help, however, has to be set within the parameters set by the arguments about the limits of state help and intervention that were discussed earlier. Financial arrangements are important for both individuals and families, but, while it is exceptional for a man to be able to support two families from his own earnings, generous and indiscriminate welfare provision makes this 'privilege' of the rich accessible to everyone. It is only to be expected, then, that more people will take up the opportunity offered. Similar considerations apply to routine mandatory provision of independent accommodation and support for single parents.[9] These factors have a tendency to nullify what might be called the 'market' aspect of setting up a family—the idea that, under free-market conditions, saving and sacrifice on the part of a couple is essential to provide, first of all, a roof and then reliable financial support throughout the process of child-bearing and child-raising. In other words, the risk is that the state may, by making one parent financially secure, encourage that parent to dispense with a partner.

If this is a risk to be avoided, the question remains, how *are* the vulnerable to be protected? It has been a central concern of this book to stress the special vulnerability of the young. I have argued, nevertheless, that in all normal circumstances the most effective way to protect the interests of children is for the state to uphold the commitment entered into by their parents. This need not mean returning to a situation in which divorce was an impossibility and law could do nothing to mitigate even the most dire of circumstances. But it is to draw back from endorsing a situation in which, as the writer James Q. Wilson notes, it is 'easier to renounce a marriage than a mortgage'.[10] So it is worth remembering that, while the family has recently become a matter of political contention, the idea of 'family' is rooted in the older and simpler idea of household, and that the function of families is to meet a range of practical needs, most of which depend upon secure long-term arrangements if they are to be met.

If so, at least some of the ground lost by recent legislation could be better and more effectively retrieved by less painful strategies than leaving women and children to languish without support, or pursuing reluctant 'absent parents' to the courts, by establishing a firmer contractual base between individuals for such ventures as marriage and parenthood. And, as Western democracies survey with concern their declining and ageing populations, the need to do this becomes more pressing. For the future of these populations must in the end depend on there being young people who are willing to find each other early in life and then to commit themselves to the long-term project of creating a secure setting in which to raise their young. But if young people are to do this, they need confidence that the law will help rather than hinder them in their project. It is only when people are given the protection from the actions of others that the original notion of a social contract requires that the personal ties of family, and the naturally evolving ties of neighbourhood, can be relied upon to assert themselves. And, in the end, the question of whether we have got our social and legal structures right is something that will be determined by the litmus test of children's lives.

Covenant marriage: An alternative conception?

I have argued that some of the apparently competing principles and political philosophies whether of left or right could in principle be brought together under a common theoretical structure that values individual freedom, personal independence, and autonomy. In considering what this implies in practical terms, both philosophical argument and empirical evidence point in one direction: the state must cease to undermine marriage, and with it the traditional family. Writing of the American experience, Maggie Gallagher puts this point strongly: 'Marriage is an institution in crisis ... The majority of children, at current estimates, will experience a fatherless or motherless household. Making substantial progress in reversing the trend toward family fragmentation will require law and society to reject the deepest presuppositions driving the postmodern family as an ideological and legal construct.'[11]

One of the deepest of these presuppositions is that the marriage contract is voidable. It was pointed out in an earlier chapter that Kant, reflecting on the basic underpinning of morality—its logical and philosophical structure—had argued that to make a promise while at the same time intending to break it if that should turn out to be convenient was not merely bad morality; it was actually in the end impossible. It would be to negate the very institution in which it was based: the institution of promising. Paradoxically, perhaps, you must have the concept of an unbreakable promise in order to be able to make a promise to break. The crumbling of the institution of marriage bears out Kant's logic, for marriage is the paradigm case of a promise.

So it is not a question of whether divorce laws are compassionate, or helpful, or better than manufacturing proof of 'fault'. It is rather a matter of whether there is any longer a recognizable line between, on the one hand, marrying and, on the other, living together until one or other wants out. With 'no-fault' divorce without consent, there is not.

Instead a situation is created in which both partners are on probation for the duration of their relationship. This is itself enough to impose an intolerable strain on relationships. Even those radicals who in the 1920s and 1930s boldly proposed 'trial marriage' might be taken aback to find that, by the beginning of the twenty-first century, *non*-trial marriages had been abolished. And yet it is doubtful that mood and inclination alone can keep people together through what a song-writer of long ago called 'the trials of life'. Gallagher writes: 'if we lose the idea that marriage is, at some basic level, about the reproduction of children and society, if our law rejects the presumptions that children need mothers and fathers, and that marriage is the most practical way to get them for children, then we cannot expect private tastes and opinions alone to sustain the marriage idea.'[12] In an attempt to break this circle, the idea of offering couples the possibility of choosing between a more and less binding form of marriage—one of them a legally binding nuptial agreement—has been promoted in some American states. It is an idea that had already been mooted in various forms. The American philosopher Jeffrey Blustein recommended establishing a distinction between what he suggested calling 'parental marriage' and 'childless marriage'. He described the idea in this way:

We can imagine an arrangement in which the private and public concerns now confounded in the single institution of marriage would be addressed by two types of marriage. One would be available to individuals who could not have children or agreed in advance that there would be no offspring of their union, and who wished only to take advantage of a certain legal power in order to express, affirm, and cement their commitment to and affection for one another or perhaps to create something analogous to a business partnership. Marriage of this type would include the renewable trial marriage ... Marriage for children would not be short-term marriage.[13]

Blustein's proposal was itself, as he acknowledges, derived from a similar proposal by the anthropologist Margaret Mead, who had outlined a two-stage approach to marriage. In the first stage, the couple would have a form of marriage that carried no right to have children. The next step, and the second type of marriage, would take place only after they had demonstrated their ability to raise and support children, and it would be marked by a formal ceremony.[14]

   The idea of covenant marriage that eventually found legal expression in the state of Louisiana and has parallels in two other states, Arkansas and Arizona, differs from either of these proposals. It focuses on the terms on which dissolution of a marriage might be allowed. The family-law scholar Kathleen Shaw Spaht, who was herself involved in the drafting of Louisiana's law, describes the position in these terms:

> The first and foremost objective of the covenant marriage legislation is to strengthen the institution of marriage, an objective achieved by: 1. mandatory premarital counselling that stresses the seriousness of marriage and the expectation that the couple's marriage will be life-long; (2) a *legally* binding agreement in the declaration of intent that if difficulties arise during the marriage the spouses will take all reasonable steps to preserve the marriage, including marriage counselling; and (3) limited grounds for divorce making termination of the marriage depend on either misconduct by a spouse within the marital relationship that society collectively condemns, or a lengthy waiting period of two years living separately and apart.[15]

This means that in Louisiana couples are able to choose between two types of marriage: the conventional type, which allows relatively easy divorce, and covenant marriage, in which divorce requires either significant lapse of time or proof of fault. The special features of covenant marriage are the requirement to accept counselling both prior to marriage and later on if difficulties threaten the marriage—counselling that would not be neutral but would treat divorce as a last resort. The serious misconduct recognized as a ground for divorce might include, for example, adultery or physical abuse, or a serious criminal conviction, and, where this does lead to divorce, damages would be payable. The principle behind this is that marriage law should be like ordinary contract law in accepting the idea of personal responsibility. Spaht believes there would be no greater difficulty in establishing fault in divorce cases than in other situations where fault is at issue. The justification for this approach to marriage is that it restores the freedom of individuals to make voluntary long-term binding commitments—to make what an earlier chapter described as a Ulysses contract.[16] Its defect is that, in offering an alternative to marriage as it currently is, it risks postponing indefinitely reform of that institution.

Even apart from this remedy, however, marriage in the usual sense is more popular with young Americans than it is with their European contemporaries. Some are also willing to make an open pledge to wait to begin their sex life until they have found someone with whom they can make a permanent commitment. Undoubtedly, the experience of the last half century has prompted some rethinking of personal relationships, perhaps because for both men and women the 'new dawn' has proved to be a flawed experience. Popular writers frequently add detail to what has become a generalized malaise. One of these, the American author Wendy Shalit, believes that, far from having achieved greater equality and respect in their personal relationships over this period, women have found themselves subject to immediate pressures to turn any relationships into sexual ones. Even establishing a long-term relationship, or indeed a marriage, she observes, is not the end of the matter if, in order to preserve that relationship, women must project the fiction of eternal youth, striving to maintain the immature figure of their teens by the extreme measures of surgery and semi-starvation.[17] Living with this Sisyphean struggle, both women and men may have reason to look back with a degree of regret to a different ideal: the family as a unit within which the lone individual, woman, man, or child, can find support in different ways and at different stages in the changing transitions of life.

Echoes from antiquity

But this is a fast-vanishing ideal, rapidly being overtaken by the new ideology of the family: the belief that the nuclear family is a fading vision, and that contemporary reality has expunged for ever the familiar triad of man, woman, and child. The steps by which we have arrived at this watershed were summarized earlier: the trivializing of marriage, the detachment of marriage from parenthood, and the rewriting of parenthood itself to separate it from the notion of biological connection. But, set out in these stark terms, this résumé evokes a striking sense of déjà vu, for a model with these features existed at the dawn of the Western intellectual, moral, and political tradition—the philosophical flourishing of fifth-century Athens. This was the brief vision sketched out in Plato's *Republic*, in which mating was random, and children were raised by strangers. Neither mothers nor fathers could claim their biological offspring as their own, nor could they raise their children for themselves. Men and women came together briefly, then separated. Fathers fathered children by many mothers. Mothers bore children by different men. Today finds Plato triumphant, as, with the aid of science and law, the Western world has in a few brief decades allowed the evolution of a situation in which it is possible to recognize the basic elements of the Platonic blueprint.

However, another influence from the literature, rather than the philosophy, of ancient Greece brings a counter-message—a possible antidote—in the story of Oedipus.[18] The tragedy of Oedipus, whether played out on a stage in ancient Greece two and a half thousand years ago or in a modern theatre, gains its whole meaning from the audience's belief in the priority of biological parenthood—that social or conventional family roles represent a different, albeit not always unfriendly, reality. Oedipus' guilt arose from the fact that, wholly unintentionally, he had killed his natural father and married his natural mother. This story would have had no meaning, and carried no horror, if the fact that by law and convention the first was indeed a stranger, the second a legitimate wife and mother of his own children, had been able to outweigh the reality of the biological relationship.

The attack on biology: Diminishing the blood tie

The attack on biology, however, is the most recent and most damaging development in the story of the family and it cannot be left to play itself out in the realm of theory, for its conclusions are necessarily deployed in practice, determining the shape of people's lives, sometimes for ever. This is reflected in the words of Marie-Thérèse Meulders, President of the International Society of Family Law: 'One of the main contemporary issues is the choice between the biological or the sociological truth as the legal basis of parenthood, and this is true not only for children born from assisted procreation, but also for adoption, fostering, step-parentage, and so on.'[19]

As these remarks imply, interest in the new reproductive technologies is one of the factors that have given a sense of urgency to the debate about the claims of natural ties. It has also brought anthropology and kinship studies back into fashion, but kinship as newly construed by many engaged in this field in terms of convention. It is no longer seen as rooted in the natural facts of procreation. In place of the old understanding of the primary relationships are accounts that replace the biological or genetic connection with psychological criteria—for example, the emotional attachment between child and adult.[20] But it is a short step from the psychoanalytic view that strong attachments between child and carer are the central component of a child's well-being to the conclusion that they should take priority over the child's relationship with its biological parents.[21] The same applies to some other criteria that have been proposed, such as intention—a criterion that can be advanced in resolving disputes in surrogacy cases, or where donated gametes are involved. In these cases, the question of who set out to have a child may be judged to outweigh that of who was physically instrumental in achieving it.

But some commentators are willing to take a more cautious approach to the issue and give *some* weight to biology. The British philosopher David Archard puts this in the form of a concession: 'There may be nothing wrong with a State permitting natural parents in the first instance to bring up their own children as they choose and within specified limits. What the State should not do is presume that natural parents have a right to rear which derives simply from biological parenthood.'[22] Archard's own account draws a distinction between biological and *moral* parenthood. He writes: 'Moral parenthood is the giving to a child of continuous care, concern and affection with the purpose of helping to secure for it the best possible upbringing. "Parent" should only be understood as meaning one of several adult caregivers. Thus moral parenthood is not restricted to any particular familial form.'[23]

Archard's remarks open the door to a much more wide-ranging welcoming of diversity in family structures. And the issue of diversity, when combined with the possibilities offered by the new reproductive technologies, and with claims on behalf of same-sex relationships, takes the debate about biological parenthood and its rights and obligations to a new plane. The legal scholar William Eskridge, a persuasive advocate of same-sex marriage, which he prefers to what he sees as the 'half-way house' of domestic partnerships or civil unions, acknowledges in unambiguous terms that the campaign for same-sex marriage necessarily involves 'the reconfiguration of family—de-emphasizing blood, gender, and kinship ties and emphasizing the value of interpersonal commitment'. He adds: 'Gay experience with "families we choose" delinks family from gender, blood, and kinship.'[24]

The case Eskridge argues has been well received in practice. The direction of legal thinking in Canada and the USA is summed up by the family-law theorist Daniel Cere as combining a family diversity model of the family with the 'close relationships' theory of conjugality.[25] As noted earlier, following the legalisation of same-sex marriage in some jurisdictions, including Canada and Spain, the wording of marriage certificates has been changed to replace 'husband' and 'wife' with neutered terms such as 'Party A' and 'Party B', and birth certificates redesigned to remove the gendered terms 'mother' and 'father'. That is to say, for the presumed interest of a tiny minority of adults and children in non-standard households, at least some influential bodies believe that understandings of parenthood for *all* children must be changed. Nor is it only a matter of changing language. In the Canadian province of Quebec, when a woman in a same-sex civil union gives birth, her female partner is presumed to be the father and can be registered as such on the birth certificate.[26] Canada moved quickly in embodying these perspectives in law. The view that prevailed there is that the privileging of biological parenting is a heterosexual constraint and it sought to remedy this in a new Civil Marriage Act by degendering marriage relationships and decoupling biology and parenthood.[27] A Report of the Law Commission of Canada also held out for consideration a new conception of parent-child relationships as 'intergenerational relationships that involve the rearing of children'.[28]

Of course, these moves are made in order to avoid a serious wrong. They are intended to guard against discrimination and prejudice. But, as Maggie Gallagher notes in reference to Vermont's debate about same-sex marriage:

Marriage as a universal human idea does not require the ruthless or puritanical suppression of alternatives. It is consistent with a variety of attitudes towards alternate forms of sexual expression, from stigma to acceptance. But it is not consistent with an understanding of marriage law such as that suggested by the Vermont court: that there is no rational relation between the law of marriage and children, fatherhood, or procreation ... if we lose the idea that marriage is, at some basic level, about the reproduction of children and society, if our law rejects the presumptions that children need mothers and fathers, and that marriage is the most practical way to get them for children, then we cannot expect private tastes and opinions alone to sustain the marriage idea.[29]

If these ideas are to be protected and preserved, the pressure to declare the genetic relationship something of little or at least negligible consequence has to be resisted. The genetic relationship—the blood tie—is deeply bound in with some fundamental aspects of human existence: conception, birth, nurturance, sex, death, and generational replacement. These constitute the necessary truths about humans in their embodiment. In the end, and whatever other attributes we may claim, we are another animal species, and, as such, the world of genetics has opened our eyes to the incredible intricacy and power of biological connection. The mere fact that a long-dead ancestor or a contemporary sibling or half-sibling can be identified from a microscopic scraping taken from the human body gives 'family' a new and extraordinary meaning.

On the more intimate day-to-day level of family life, too, biological or kin relationships matter. But is this enough to claim back the mother–father–child triad as the paradigmatic family form? Or is this a misplaced attempt to reclaim something that never really existed—a sentimental hankering after an illusory past? The Hull philosopher Paul Gilbert describes the alternatives in terms of two pictures of human relationships:

> One is a *nostalgic* picture, of relationships having once been more as they ought to be, when familial roles were accepted unquestioningly and close family bonds were forged by unreflective feeling. Modern *mores* distort and corrupt social lives that would otherwise be well spent. The other is a *Utopian* picture, of relationships as they have never been but ought to be, in which familial roles are redefined and our attachments and sympathies to others are determined by a rational assessment of our respective needs.[30]

Gilbert's view is that these two pictures are based on competing views about the plasticity of human relationships. But, while relationships can be moulded and shaped to some extent at least by choice, nature and consanguinity are not so malleable. As Dan Cere argues: 'In the plastic world of "intimate relationships", firm distinctions begin to dissipate. Severed from its link to the biology of heterosexual reproduction, conjugality begins to inflate and morph.'[31] Part of the explanation for this is that natural bonds are independent of individual preferences: they have a past and a future beyond our control. At the same time, they provide a stake in the future that is beyond individuality: the future they offer is a *shared* future.

Futures

Part at least of what it is for human beings to flourish, whether or not they are parents themselves, is for there to be continuity in human existence. It could be said, then, that the well-being of our descendants is part of our *own* flourishing—a thought that goes beyond Aristotle's dictum: 'Call no man happy till he is dead.' For would our own projects—cultural, political, or personal—have any worth if they, as well as ourselves, had no future? As human beings, it seems, we cannot help but hope for the long-term well-being of the human race. And, as biologists have noted, only societies that reproduce survive.

It is hard, then, to understand the hatred for the family that some intellectuals feel. The psychiatrist David Cooper seems to have spoken for many of these when he wrote: 'Nothing is to be left to the Family. Mothers, fathers, brothers, sisters, sons and daughters, husbands and wives have all predeceased us. They are not there as people to be left with anything of oneself or left anywhere in oneself... The age of relatives is over because the relative invades the absolute centre of ourselves.'[32]

Where such views prevail, even if the term 'family' remains in use, its meaning is changed beyond recognition. Not surprisingly, then, current non-procreative approaches to the family are part of a culture that now seems to value children less. And, as abortion has lost its negative connotation, many possible children have failed to find their waiting lives. We may not be willing to return to the forced choices of the pre-abortion era, and indeed simple means of terminating pregnancies that are hardly initiated mean that procreation has become and will remain voluntary in most circumstances. Nevertheless, we could become more honest about the matter, more willing to recognize what abortion means, and more serious in trying to avoid applying laws that were designed to offer a remedy in special and tragic circumstances to routine situations.

Shallow-thinking but influential intellectuals continue to promote the message that traditional family structures have no place in a world of gender equality. Some see the family as 'a peculiarly preliberal anomaly in a modern society'.[33] But the basis on which this view is put forward can often be shaky in the extreme. Giddens, for example, writes: 'If ever I am tempted to think that the traditional family might be best after all, I remember what my great aunt once said to me. She must have had one of the longest marriages of anyone, having been with her husband for over 60 years. She once confided that she had been deeply unhappy with him the whole of that time. In her day there was no escape.'[34]

This sample of one provides shaky ground for the enormous edifice of political reform it is intended to support. The case for the opposition—for lifelong marriage—would never stand on a similar base. But supposing that we did, in any case, want to follow Giddens in appealing to a few purely personal examples there is another potent source now available—the final phone calls of the 9/11 victims that provided an unintended testimony to their deeper 'real' values. Citizens of a country whose entertainment industry and whose public figures project a picture of a dysfunctional world of family failure and scepticism about relationships turned in those moments that really mattered to those who shaped their personal world—in the tritest of words, loved ones and family members. No sham was available here, no mockery, cynicism or doubt. And yet, for very many, with only minutes available, it was these to whom people sought to send those final words.

So, while opinion-leaders regard alternative lifestyles and new modes of family formation as matters of popular demand, there is as much evidence as it is reasonable to ask for that what matters to the overwhelming majority of people is the security of family relationships. This is not a newly validated social fact, although it is often presented as such. On the contrary, the dismissal of marriage as an archaic relic is aptly described by the philosopher David Selbourne as the product of a cynicism that dwells in moral darkness, and deepens it.[35] Others see the destruction that has been caused by freedom-loving adults to children whose lives are shattered because the people who came together to create them don't stay together to bring them up.

Sex and family are not, of course, the only powerful magnets in human affairs, and some would say time would be better spent attending to the 'big' questions of the day, rather than dwelling on the smaller world of domestic and personal life. But perhaps they should reflect on Adam Smith's warning, as timely for the present day as it was when he made it two centuries ago:

The administration of the great system of the universe … is the business of God and not of man. To man is allotted a much humbler department, but one much more suitable to the weakness of his powers, and to the narrowness of his comprehension; the care of his own happiness, of that of his family, his friends, his country: that he is occupied in contemplating the more sublime, can never be an excuse for his neglecting the more humble department; and he must not expose himself to the charge … that while he employed himself in philosophical speculations, and contemplated the prosperity of the universe, he neglected that of the Roman empire.[36]

The great affairs of politics, national and international, should, of course, not be neglected, but it is the more intimate and closer bonds that have the most natural and immediate force and may, for present times, be the more pressing. Libertarians in particular should think carefully before rejecting the distinctive claims of the natural family. Given the human tendency to construct hierarchies of power, and given pressures for conformity, institutions that cut across political, economic, and social hierarchies have a unique value. Of these institutions, the family as a biological and natural network is one of the most important.

This point has not passed unnoticed by totalitarian philosophers and political despots and ideologues through the long march of human history. From Plato's *Republic* to China under the Red Guards, *via* Soviet Russia and Nazi Germany, the family has been regarded as a source of subversion. The invisible bonds it creates between its members generate loyalties capable of resisting tyrannical political structures. This is what makes the family, in the end, not simply a conserving but also a progressive institution. Where religion and politics are carried along in the flux of opinion and interpretation, and ideological movements flow with the tide of popularity, personal attachment and family love can, at their best, provide an anchor for individuals in a storm-tossed world. While they sometimes fail and are sometimes distorted by cruelty and indifference, love and attachment are cultural and moral universals.

Stability in relationships is, for most people, a central need, and the family is one, perhaps the only one, of the means humans have available to them to break down the solitude and loneliness, the pure atomicity, of an individual life. People can find their lives disrupted either by their own choices or by the decisions of other people whom they trusted, or by natural intrusions such as illness or death. This exposes them to many quantifiable risks or breakdown resulting from the loss of secure relationships. But the quintessential network of bonding is the family; and at the heart of that system, the nuclear family, lies a central relationship between two people. Unlike all other family relations, this is not based on a biological or blood tie—it is not natural but has been created by the will of the two people themselves.

This book has been an attempt to build a philosophy of the family, to assemble the fragments of argument from various sources, from philosophy itself, from social research, from economic analysis and legal judgment, from feminism, science, and bioethics. I have tried to avoid arguments that depend on religious views, not to disparage or dismiss them, but in order to avoid the contention that resort to religion often brings. I have preferred instead to confine my appeal to reason and morality. Some of the writers whose views have been cited here speak of the 'postmodern' family, but in this appeal to reason and morality I have deliberately returned to what might be called a *pre*-postmodern strategy—to start at the beginning of the debate about the family, and to follow the argument where it leads.

In doing this, I have been obliged to challenge some of the cherished 'idols' or dogmas of our day: the belief that, whatever the personal evidence of shattered lives, divorce or parting doesn't hurt; that deep attachments can be unilaterally shattered; that what adults in their personal lives do cannot seriously harm their children; that not making a commitment in the first place can solve the problem; that cohabiting is better than, or at least as good as, marrying; that genetic relationships don't matter; that genetic ancestry is available for sale or transfer; that populations and cultures in decline can ultimately survive; that 'family' can mean whatever we want it to mean.

These, it seems to me, count as the serious mistakes of the last half century. In seeking to counter them, I have tried to view the family holistically, to gather the threads of argument from many diverse sources into a single perspective. That attempt needs a justification. Simply put, it is this: that a fractured and fragmented family will give us a fractured and fragmented world.

Notes

Introduction

1. G. K. Chesterton, *Brave New Family* (San Francisco: St Ignatius Press, 1990), 224.
2. American Law Institute, *Principles of the Law of Family Dissolution: Analysis and Recommendations* (Philadelphia: American Law Institute, 2002).
3. Law Commission of Canada, *Beyond Conjugality: Recognizing and Supporting Close Personal Adult Relationships* (Ottawa: Law Commission of Canada, 2001).
4. Dan Cere, *The Future of Family Law: Law and the Marriage Crisis in North America* (New York: Institute for American Values, 2005), 16.
5. Canada, Civil Marriage Act, 1st sess., 38th Parliament (2005), 'Consequential Amendments'.
6. The issue of partiality towards family members is discussed in Ch. 9.

Chapter 1

1. M. Johnson, 'A Biomedical Perspective on Parenthood', in Andrew Bainham, S. D. Schlates, and M. Richards (eds.), *What is a Parent? A Socio-Legal Analysis* (Oxford: Hart Publishing, 1999), 47–72, at 58. See also J. Eekelaar and P. Sarcevic (eds.), *Parenthood in Modern Society: Legal and Social Issues for the Twenty-First Century* (Dordrecht: Kluwer, 1993).
2. E. Westermark's three-volume history of human marriage sought to chronicle these developments. See E. Westermark, *The History of Human Marriage*, 3 vols. (London: Macmillan, 1901; New York: Allerton, 1922).
3. Aristotle, *Politics*, bk.1, ch. 2, 1252^{b}14.
4. Lawrence, Stone, *The Family, Sex and Marriage in England, 1500–1800*, (New York: Harper Row, 1977). For a geographically and historically broader modern history of the family, see Gary S. Becker, *A Treatise on the Family*, (2nd edn., Cambridge, Mass.: Harvard University Press, 1991).
5. The distinction between 'family' and 'household' conceived in rather broader terms is basic to much historical research on the family. See, e.g., P. Laslett, and R. Wall, in *Household and Family in Past Time* (Cambridge: Cambridge University Press, 1972).
6. Igor Primoratz, *Ethics and Sex* (London: Routledge, 1999), 173.
7. P. Singer, *Practical Ethics* (2nd edn., Cambridge: Cambridge University Press, 1993), 2.

8. Sophocles, *Antigone*, ll.452–60, in *The Theban Plays*, trans. George Young (Everyman; London: Dent, 1947).

9. Aristotle, *Ethics*, bk. 5, 1134^b24.

10. Contemporary writers such as John Finnis and Germain Grisez have sought to derive a sexual ethic from reason and nature. However, some critics argue that, in seeking to prove the truth of modern Catholic teaching in this way, they have tried to do too much on the basis of reason. See Gareth Moore, 'Natural Sex: Germain Grisez, Sex, and Natural Law', in Nigel Biggar and Rufus Black (eds.), *The Revival of Natural Law: Philosophical, Theological and Ethical Responses to the Finnis-Grisez School* (Aldershot: Ashgate, 2000), 223–41.

11. See Chris Shaw, Government Actuary's Department, 'United Kingdom Population Trends in the 21st Century', *Population Trends*, 103 (London: The Stationary Office, 2001), 37–46.

12. A number of legal theorists have argued for the 'disestablishment' of marriage. See, e.g., M. A. Fineman, *The Neutered Mother, the Sexual Family and Other Twentieth-Century Tragedies* (New York: Routledge, 1995).

13. For a full discussion of these matters, see Chs. 7 and 8. The issues have, however, been widely considered, and the general statistical trends are confirmed in sources from both ends of the political spectrum. See, from an organization regarded as representing the political left, Commission on Social Justice, *Social Justice: Strategies for National Renewal: The Final Report of the Commission on Social Justice* (London: Vintage, 1994), and, from one viewed as a source on the political right, Patricia Morgan, *Cohabitation* (London: Institute for Economic Affairs, 2000). For some comparable US data, see Sara McLanahan and Gary Sandetur, *Growing up with a Single Parent* (Cambridge, Mass.: Harvard University Press, 1994), and W. J. Doherty et al., *Why Marriage Matters: Twenty-One Conclusions from the Social Sciences* (New York: Institute for American Values, 2002). A further useful collection is Alan Booth and Ann C. Crouter (eds.), *Just Living Together: Implications of Cohabitation for Children, Families and Public Policy* (Hillsdale, NJ: Lawrence Erlbaum Associates, 2002).

14. Marriage between people of the same sex became a legal reality in Massachusetts in 2004 but was opposed by people who wanted to amend the law by substituting civil unions for same-sex marriage.

15 Sir John Wolfenden, *Report of the Committee on Homosexual Offences and Prostitution*, Cmnd. 247 (London: HMSO, 1957).

16. For a full and systematic defence of the case for same-sex marriage covering all aspects of family life including procreation and bringing up children see W. N. Eskridge Jr., *The Case for Same-Sex Marriage: From Sexual Liberty to Civilized Commitment* (New York: Free Press, 1996).

17. See Ch. 10.

18. Anthony Giddens, *Runaway World: How Globalisation is Reshaping our Lives* (2nd edn., London: Profile Books, 2002), 65.

Chapter 2

1. See, e.g., P. Gregory, 'Against Couples', *Journal of Applied Philosophy*, 1 (1984), repr. in Brenda Almond and Donald Hill (eds.), *Applied Philosophy: Morals and Metaphysics in Contemporary Debate* (London: Routledge, 1991), 90–5.

2. Lord Penzance in *Hyde* v. *Hyde*, 1866 LRIP & D.

3. Epictetus, *Arrian's Discourses of Epictetus*, Bk. III. xxiv. 8–12 (free translation).

4. Epictetus, *Arrian's Discourses of Epictetus*, trans. W. A. Oldfather (1928; London: Heinemann, 1985), III. xxiv. 85–8.

5. These tensions are reflected in organizations that recognize and seek to help the parties involved on a separate basis: fathers' organizations defending rights to contact with their children after separation or divorce, organizations providing refuges for women seeking protection from male violence, and organizations that offer children an independent voice to seek help in their own right. For discussion of these issues, see Ch. 7.

6. June Carbone, *From Partners to Parents: The Second Revolution in Family Law* (Chichester, NY: Columbia University Press, 2000), p. xiii.

7. P. B. Shelley, 'Against Legal Marriage', in *Shelley on Love*, ed. Richard Holmes (London: Anvil Press Poetry, 1980), 45.

8. R. Scruton, 'Gay Reservations', in Michael Leahy and Dan Cohn-Sherbok (eds.), *The Liberation Debate: Rights at Issue* (London: Routledge, 1996), 108–24, 119.

9. Letter dated 14 Apr. 1950, in *The Autobiography of Bertrand Russell* (London: Allen & Unwin, 1971), iii. 49.

10. See Ch. 10 for discussion of civil unions and same-sex marriage.

11. Nena O'Neill and George O'Neill, *Open Marriage: A New Life-Style for Couples* (New York: M. Evans & Co., 1972).

12. J. Margolis and C. Margolis, 'The Separation of Marriage and Family', in M. Vetterling-Braggin, F. A. Elliston, and J. English (eds.), *Feminism and Philosophy* (Totowa, NJ: Littlefield, Adams, 1977), 297.

13. Anthony Giddens, *Runaway World: How Globalisation is Reshaping our Lives* (2nd edn., London: Profile Books, 2002), 59.

14. M. Maclean, and M. Richards, 'Parents and Divorce: Changing Patterns of Public Intervention', in Andrew Bainham, S. D. Schlater, and M. Richards (eds.), *What is a Parent? A Socio-Legal Analysis* (Oxford: Hart Publishing, 1999), 259–70, at 261.

15. David Archard, *Children, Rights and Childhood* (London: Routledge, 1993), 116–17.

16. See Erich Fromm, *The Fear of Freedom* (London: Routledge & Kegan Paul, 1960). Fromm argues that loneliness is an inescapable aspect of a modern urban society.

17. Jonathan Gathorne-Hardy, *Love, Sex, Marriage and Divorce* (London: Jonathan Cape, 1981), 164.

18. Cited by Margaret Tims, in *Mary Wollstonecraft: A Social Pioneer* (London: Millington, 1976), 292.

19. In *An Enquiry Concerning Political Justice* (1793), Godwin had written: 'The supposition that I must have a companion for life is the result of a complication of vices ... It is the dictate of cowardice, and not of fortitude. It flows from the desire of being loved and esteemed for something that is not desert' Bk VIII Ch. 6 p. 849.

20. W. Godwin, *Memoirs of the Author of the Vindication of the Rights of Women*, cited by Don Locke in *A Fantasy of Reason: The Life and Thought of William Godwin* (London: Routledge & Kegan Paul, 1980), 130–1.

21. John Taylor to Harriet Taylor, 3 Apr. 1848, in F.A. Hayek, *John Stuart Mill and Harriet Taylor: Their Friendship and Subsequent Marriage* (London: Routledge & Kegan Paul, 1951), 121.

22. Mill wrote on the theme in *The Subjection of Women* (1869).

23. Thomas Carlyle to Dr John Carlyle, 28 Oct. 1834, cited in Hayek, *John Stuart Mill and Harriet Taylor*, 82.

24. J. S. Mill, *On Liberty* (1859; Everyman; London: Dent, 1954), 72–3.

25. Harriet Taylor to John Taylor, 19 Dec. 1848, in Hayek, *John Stuart Mill and Harriet Taylor*, 130–1.

26. J. S. Mill, renouncing the privileges given him by the laws of England on his marriage to Harriet Taylor, 6 Mar. 1851, in R. Fletcher (ed.) *John Stuart Mill: A Logical Critique of Sociology* (London: Nelson, 1971), 45.

27. Harriet Taylor to John Stuart Mill, 1832, in Hayek, *John Stuart Mill and Harriet Taylor*, 78.

28. Mill's concern to defend individual freedom continued to influence public policy on sexual matters long after his death. Initiated by an attack on Mill's principles by the British judge James FitzJames Stephen, this remained little more than an academic debate until the publication of the Wolfenden Report in 1957, which made recommendations that led to changes in British laws on prostitution and homosexuality. The principles it adopted, particularly that the behaviour of consenting adults in private is not the business of the state, closely followed Mill in endorsing the idea of a private realm of morality.

29. See Simone de Beauvoir, *A Transatlantic Love Affair: Letters to Nelson Algren* (N.Y. The New Press, 1998). Much of the correspondence between Sartre and de Beauvoir is held in the Bibliothèque Nationale. For further background, see Hazel Rowley, *Tête-à-Tête: Simone de Beauvoir and Jean-Paul Sartre* (New York: Harper Collins, 2005).

30. Jean-Paul Sartre, *Existentialism and Humanism*, trans. Philip Mairet (London: Methuen, 1948), 50.

31. Ibid. 34.

32. For comment on 'right for me' by the present author, see Brenda Almond, 'An Ethical Paradox', in *Moral Concerns* (Atlantic Highlands, NJ: Humanities Press, (1987), 113–24, and 'Seven Moral Myths', *Philosophy*, 64 (Spring 1990), 1–8. See also David E. Cooper (ed.), *The Manson Murders: A Philosophical Inquiry* (Cambridge, Mass.: Schenkmann, 1974).

33. For a sociological perspective on this topic, see William J. Goode, 'The Theoretical Importance of Love', *American Sociological Review* (1969), 38–47, repr. in B. B. Ingoldsby, S. Smith, and J. E. Miller (eds.), *Exploring Family Theories* (Los Angeles: Roxbury Publishing Company, 2003), 17–28.

34. Aristotle, *Nicomachean Ethics*, II, 69^{b}18.

35. R. Gaita, *A Common Humanity: Thinking about Love and Truth and Justice* (New York: Routledge, 2000).

36. B. Williams, 'The Priority of Personal Interests', in H. LaFollette (ed.), *Ethics in Practice* (Oxford: Blackwell, 1997), 191–4 at 193.

37. G. Santayana, *The Life of Reason*, ii, *Reason in Society* (London, Constable, 1905), 16.

38. Ibid. 15.

39. I. Kant, *Lectures on Ethics*, trans. Louis Infield (London: Methuen, 1930; repr. New York: Harper & Row, 1963), 166–7.

40. Scruton, 'Gay Reservations', 121. For Scruton's full theory of sexuality, see R. Scruton, *Sexual Desire: A Philosophical Investigation* (London, Weidenfeld & Nicolson, 1986).

Chapter 3

1. A. Schopenhauer, *The World as Will and Idea*, 2nd edn., ed. Wolfgang von Loehneysen (Vienna: Darmstadt, 1974), ii., 714; also in Irwin Edman (ed.), *The Philosophy of Schopenhauer* (New York: Modern Library, 1928), 373.

2. A. Schopenhauer, *The World as Will and Idea*, ed. D. Berman, trans. J. Berman (Everyman; London: Dent, 1995), supplement to bk. 4, ch. XLIV, 'On the Metaphysics of Sexual Love', 265.

3. J. Finnis, 'The Good of Marriage and the Morality of Sexual Relations: Some Philosophical and Historical Observations', *American Journal of Jurisprudence*, 42 (1997), 97–134, at 131.

4. See in particular, Ch. 8, 'Law, Policy-Making and the Contemporary Family'.

5. Cited by Roderick Phillips in *Untying the Knot: A Short History of Divorce* (Cambridge: Cambridge University Press, 1991), 35.

6. D. Hume, *An Enquiry Concerning the Principles of Morals,* ed. L. A. Selby-Bigge (Oxford: Clarendon Press, 1955), 207–8.

7. J. Locke, *Two Treatises of Government: Second Treatise of Government* (1680–2; Everyman; London: Dent, 1986), ch. VII, p. 155, paras. 78–9.

8. Ibid., ch. XV, p.204, para. 170.

9. Ibid., ch. VII, p. 157, para. 82.

10. Brian T. Trainor, 'The State, Marriage and Divorce', *Journal of Applied Philosophy*, 9 (1992), 135–48, at 138.

11. Ibid.

12. The impact of the new reproductive technologies is discussed in Ch. 6.

13. I. Kant, *Lectures on Ethics*, trans. Louis Infield, (London: Methuen, 1930; repr. New York: Harper & Row, 1963), 169.

14. An attempt is being made in some US states to resolve this by introducing a form of covenant marriage as a legal solution to this dilemma. See Ch. 10.

15. Kant, *Lectures on Ethics*, 167.

16. G. W. F. Hegel, *The Philosophy of Right*, trans. T. M. Knox (Oxford: Clarendon Press, 1952), pt. III, para. 163, p. 112.

17. Ibid., Addition 103, Para. 161, P. 262.

18. Ibid., pt. III, para. 173, p. 117.

19. See, e.g. Luce Irigaray, *Ce sexe qui n'en est pas un* (Paris: Les Éditions de Minuit, 1977), and Patricia Mills, *Woman, Nature and Psyche* (New Haven: Yale University Press, 1987).

20. See, e.g., Heidi M. Ravven, 'Has Hegel Anything to Say to Feminists?', *Owl of Minerva*, 19/2 (Spring 1988), 149–68.

21. Hegel, *The Philosophy of Right*, Addition 103, para. 163, p. 263.

22. Ibid., para. 175.

23. Anthony Giddens, *Sociology: A Brief but Critical Introduction* (London: Macmillan, 1982), 159.

24. Anthony Giddens, *Runaway World: How Globalisation is Reshaping our Lives* (2nd edn.; London: Profile Books, 2002), 58.

25. R. Nozick, *Anarchy, State and Utopia* (Oxford: Blackwell, 1974).

26. For further discussion of this aspect of the debate, see Ch. 10.

27. Much of this research is summarized in a consensus document authored by over a dozen family scholars: W. J. Doherty et al., *Why Marriage Matters: Twenty-One Conclusions from the Social Sciences* (New York: Institute for American Values, 2002), available via www.americanvalues.org. British research has been summarized in a parallel publication by the London-based think-tank Civitas: R. O'Neill, *Does Marriage Matter?* (London: Civitas, 2004). These issues are discussed in more detail in Chs. 7 and 8.

28. P. Devlin, *The Enforcement of Morals* (Oxford: Oxford University Press, 1965), 78–9. Devlin also commented: 'In the regulation of marriage and divorce the secular law is bound more closely to the moral law than in any other subject. This is quite natural. The institution of marriage is the creation of morality. The moral law of a society is made up from the ideas which members of that society have in common about the right way to live' (Ibid. 61).

29. Ibid., 9.

Chapter 4

1. Mary Wollstonecraft, *A Vindication of The Rights of Woman* (1792; Everyman; London: Dent, 1929), 203.

2. See Ch. 2. Mary Wollstonecraft's marriage to Godwin was only a few months before she died, and he would not in any case have been in a position to support her.

3. See Ch. 2.

4. Wollstonecraft, *A Vindication*, 110.

5. F. Engels, *The Origins of the Family: Private Property and the State* (1884), trans. A. West (Harmondsworth: Penguin, 1985).

6. B. Russell, *Marriage and Morals* (1929) (London: Allen & Unwin, 1976), 9–10.

7. Ibid. 122.

8. Ibid. 136.

9. The dependency issue has been addressed in both the USA and the UK by welfare-to-work initiatives such as the USA's federally funded programmes known as TANF (Temporary Assistance for the Needy) and MOE (Maintenance of Effort).

10. N. Dennis, 'Beautiful Theories, Brutal Facts: The Welfare State and Sexual Liberation', in D. Smith (ed.), *Welfare, Work and Poverty: Lessons from Recent Reforms in the USA and the UK* (London: Institute for the Study of Civil Society, 2000), 45–80, at 78.

11. Ibid., 79.

12. There is a considerable body of research on this subject. See, e.g., L. J. Weitzman, *The Divorce Revolution: The Unexpected Social and Economic Consequences for Women and Children in America* (New York: Free Press, 1985) and L. J. Weitzman and M. Maclean (eds.), *Economic Consequences of Divorce: The International Perspective* (Oxford: Clarendon Press, Centre for Socio-Legal Studies, 1991). See, too, P. J. Smock et al., 'The Effect of Marriage and Divorce on Women's Economic Well-Being', *American Sociological Review,* 64 (1999), 794–812.

13. See Disabled Persons (Employment) Act 1944.

14. Antoinette M. Stafford, 'The Feminist Critique of Hegel on Women and the Family', *Animus*, 2 (1997), 1–18.

15. S. Thornham, 'Postmodernism and Feminism', in Stuart Simon (ed.), *The Icon Critical Dictionary of Postmodern Thought* (Cambridge: Icon Books, 1998), 41–52, at 41.

16. S. Firestone, *The Dialectic of Sex: The Case for Feminist Revolution* (London: Jonathan Cape, 1971). The role of reproductive technology in relation to the family is discussed here in Ch. 6.

17. Hilde Lindemann Nelson (ed.), *Feminism and Families* (London: Routledge, 1997), 4.

18. Diana Tietjens Meyers, 'The Family Romance: A Fin-de-Siècle Tragedy', in Ibid. 235–54, at 247.

19. B. Friedan, *The Second Stage* (New York: Summit Books, 1982), 229.

20. G. Greer, *The Female Eunuch* (London: McGibbon & Kee, 1970); *The Whole Woman* (New York: Anchor Books, 1999).

21. I am grateful to Professor Lisa Q. Wang of Qingdao University and to Professor Yuli Liu of the Department of Philosophy, the Central Party School of the CPC in Beijing, for their helpful advice on the development of Chinese thought on the role and position of women.

22. Early comment on this as an ethical and philosophical issue was provided by Mary Anne Warren in her book *Gendercide: The Implications of Sex Research* (Totowa, NJ: Rowman & Allanheld, 1985) and by Dharma Kumar in her article 'Should one be Free to Choose the Sex of one's Child?', *Journal of Applied Philosophy*, 2 (1985), 197–204.

23. A. Sen, 'More than 100 Million Women are Missing', *New York Review of Books*, 20 Dec. 1990.

24. Shirish Sheth, the co-author of a study published in the *Lancet* in 2006, estimated that, although the use of prenatal scans to determine the sex of a fetus is legally banned in India, more than ten million female fetuses have been aborted there following medically provided scans in the twenty years up to 2005. The problem in India is not, however, confined to followers of one religion. S. Sheth, *Lancet*, 9 Jan. 2006; report *The Times*, 10 Jan. 2006.

25. Ayaan Hirsi Ali, *The Son Factory* (De Zoontjesfabriek (2003)). Also by Ayaan Hirsi Ali is *The Cage of Virgins* (De Maagdenkooi (2004)).

26. See Margot Badran and Miriam Cooke (eds.), *Opening the Gates: A Century of Arab Feminist Writing* (Indiana: Indiana University Press, 1990).

27. Badran, Margot, 'Islamic Feminism: What's in a Name?', *Al-Ahram Weekly Online*, 569, 17–23 Jan. 2002.

28. Edna Healey gives a detailed account of Mary Livingstone's married life and that of three other wives of famous men in *Wives of Fame* (London: Sidgwick & Jackson, 1986).

29. Daisy Bates, *The Passing of the Aborigines* (London: John Murray, 1938; 2nd edn., Melbourne: Heinemann, 1966).

30. J. Carbone, and N. Cahn, 'Which Ties Bind? Redefining the Parent-Child Relationship in an Age of Genetic Certainty', *William and Mary Bill of Rights Journal*, 11, (2002–3), 1011–70, at 1035. Carbone and Cahn also cite the claim by Justice Burger in *Stanley* v. *Iliniois*, 405, S. 645 (1972) that 'centuries of human experience' show that the biological role of a mother in carrying and nursing an infant creates stronger bonds than those of the father between her and the child (ibid. 1048 n. 144). The literature on attachment as a biological or sociobiological phenomenon is discussed here in relation to custody disputes in Ch. 6.

31. Gilligan develops this theme by reference to her 'rights and responsibilities' study, described in 'Images of Relationship', ch. 2 of her book *In a Different Voice: Psychological Theory and Women's Development* (Cambridge, Mass.: Harvard University Press, 1982), 24–63.

32. Ibid. 106–27. It is interesting to contrast this report of women's reactions to the large literature on the ethics of abortion in philosophical publications where a key issue is the stage at which a fetus becomes a 'person' and should therefore receive the protection of the law.

33. Susan Moller Okin, *Justice, Gender and the Family* (New York: Basic Books, 1989), 171. This issue plays an important role in child-custody disputes and is discussed in that context in Ch. 7.

34. M. A. Fineman, *The Neutered Mother, the Sexual Family and Other Twentieth-Century Tragedies* (New York: Routledge, 1995), 165.

35. H. Eisenstein, *Contemporary Feminist Thought* (Boston: G. K. Hall & Co., 1983), 144–5.

36. Susan Moller Okin, 'Families and Feminist Theory: Some Past and Present Issues', in Nelson (ed.), *Feminism and Families*, 25.

Chapter 5

1. Elizabeth Anscombe, *Contraception and Chastity* (1975; London: Catholic Truth Society, 2003).

2. In the United Kingdom, the Health Protection Agency reported a surge in sexual infections from 1995 to 2003, which showed a trebling in the incidence of chlamydia, a doubling in cases of gonorrhoea, and an eleven-fold increase in syphilis. In response, the Department of Health announced that it was to sponsor a project to provide chlamydia screening in local pharmacies. *The Times*, 9 Feb. 2005, p. 30.

3. See Ch. 9.

4. This aspect was caught in a widely read book by Sylvia Ann Hewlett, *Baby Hunger: The New Battle for Motherhood* (New York: Atlantic Books, 2002).

5. C. Overall, *Human Reproduction: Principles, Practices, Policies* (Oxford: Oxford University Press, 1993).

6. *Roe* v. *Wade*, 410 US 113 1973. The initiator of this famous case has subsequently attempted to have it repealed—*US Supreme Court Casey* v. *Planned Parenthood*, 1992.

7. BPAS (the British Pregnancy Advisory Service) was criticised for defending a policy of helping women to have late abortions (after twenty-four weeks) by recommending to them clinics abroad when practical difficulties have delayed the decision to seek abortion.

8. This argument was presented in an influential article by Judith Jarvis Thomson, 'A Defense of Abortion', *Philosophy and Public Affairs*, 1 (1971), 47–66. The force of her argument was that anyone finding herself in the situation of becoming either unwillingly or inadvertently a physical life-support system for another human being would be entitled to free herself from that position. A contrary perspective is provided by Don Marquis in 'Why Abortion is Immoral', *Journal of Philosophy*, 86/4 (1989), 183–202.

9. Mary Anne Warren, *Gendercide: The Implications of Sex Research* (Totowa, NJ: Rowman & Allanheld, 1985); A. Sen, 'More than 100 Million Women are Missing', *New York Review of Books*, 20 Apr. 1990. See Ch. 4, p. 71–72. The general issue of sex selection of either fetuses or embryos for social reasons and the question of whether this applies differently in different societies is also considered in Ch. 6.

10. R. Dworkin, *Taking Rights Seriously* (London: Duckworth, 1977), 267.

11. R. Dworkin, *Life's Dominion: An Argument about Abortion and Euthanasia* (London: HarperCollins, 1995), 20. Abortion is discussed from an Aristotelian perspective by Rosalind Hursthouse in *Beginning Lives* (Oxford: Blackwell, 1987), from a utilitarian viewpoint by Peter Singer in *Practical Ethics* (2nd edn.; Cambridge: Cambridge University Press, 1993), and by Michael Tooley in *Abortion and Infanticide* (Oxford: Oxford University Press, 1983). For a comprehensive discussion of issues in this area, see Overall, *Human Reproduction*. See, too, J. Glover, *Causing Death and Saving Lives* (Harmondsworth: Penguin, 1977).

12. R. Edwards, in *Scientific American* (1966), quoted in J. Gunning, and V. English, *Human In Vitro Fertilization: A Case Study in the Regulation of Medical Innovation* (Brookfield, Vt: Dartmouth Publishing Company, 1993), 7.

13. For more information about Cryos, see p. 116.

14. T. Jordan, 'Ethical Issues in Adoption: The Moral Significance of Relationships', in Committee for the Sixth Annual Conference, *Separation, Reunion, Reconciliation: Proceedings from the Sixth Australian Conference on Adoption, Brisbane, 1997* (Brisbane, 1997), 294–305, at 296.

15. M. Strathern, *Reproducing the Future: Anthropology, Kinship and the New Reproductive Technologies* (Manchester: Manchester University Press, 1992), 34. Elsewhere, Strathern describes parenthood as an amorphous concept

with roots in biology that varies with time, culture, and the status of the observer. M. Strathern, 'A Question of Context', in J. Edwards et al. (eds.), *Technologies of Procreation* (Manchester: Manchester University Press, 1993), 9–28.

16. The meaning of kinship is discussed in detail by Arlene Skolnick, who points out that there are circumstances in which kin relations are uncontroversially non-biological. For example, roles and relationships may be socially assigned, as in some African tribes, or assigned by legal and quasi-legal relationships such as adoption and godparenting. A. Skolnick, *The Intimate Environment* (Harlow: Longman, 1995), 54.

Chapter 6

1. The European Convention for the Protection of Human Rights and Fundamental Freedoms, 1950, as amended by Protocol No. 11. 1998, Article 8, in Ian Brownlie and Guy S. Goodwin-Gill (eds.), *Basic Documents on Human Rights* (4th edn., Oxford: Oxford University Press, 2002), 402.

2. Universal Declaration of Human Rights, 1948, Article 16, in ibid. 21.

3. R. Dworkin, *Life's Dominion: An Argument about Abortion and Euthanasia* (London: HarperCollins, 1993), 160.

4. See, e.g., J. Harris, 'Rights and Reproductive Choice', in J. Harris and S. Holm (eds.), *The Future of Human Reproduction* (Oxford: Oxford University Press, 1998), 5–37.

5. J. A. Robertson, *Children of Choice: Freedom and the New Reproductive Technologies* (Princeton: Princeton University Press, 1994), 24.

6. Ibid. 145.

7. R. Dworkin, *Taking Rights Seriously* (London: Duckworth, 1977), p. xi.

8. 'The Regulation of Donor-Assisted Conception', London, HFEA Consultation Doc. 2004, p. 10. 'Treatment together' was held to be understood as a 'joint enterprise' to have a child in ReB (Parentage) [1996] 2 FLR 15 and in a number of subsequent court judgments in the UK, although there have been conflicting interpretations (e.g. Re Q (Parental Order) [1996] 1 FLR 369).

9. A. Maura Ryan, 'The Argument for Unlimited Procreative Liberty', *Hastings Center Report* (July/Aug. 1990), 6–12, at 7.

10. Harris, 'Rights and Reproductive Choice', 14.

11. Ibid.

12. J. Harris, 'The Welfare of the Child', *Health Care Analysis*, 8 (2000), 27–34, at 30.

13. A number of significant wrongful life cases are discussed by D. Heyd in *Genethics: Moral Issues in the Creation of People* (Berkeley and Los Angeles: University of Califonia Press, 1992), 26–38.

14. Susan Moller Okin, *Justice, Gender and the Family* (New York: Basic Books, 1989), 83.

15. The issue is discussed in Z. Szawarski, 'Talking about Embryos', in D. Evans (ed.), *Conceiving the Embryo* (Dordrecht: Kluwer Law International, 1996), 119–33. Szawarski argues that the two 'boundary' positions on the status of the embryo—thing or person—are irreconcilable and incapable of rational answer, since there is no common measure to settle the disagreement.

16. See M. Spriggs, 'Lesbian Couple Create a Child who is Deaf like Them', *Journal of Medical Ethics*, 28 (2002), 283–8. Also J. Savulescu, 'Deaf Lesbians, "Designer Disability", and the Future of Medicine', *British Medical Journal*, 325/7367 (Oct. 2002), 771–3.

17. The first widely reported case was that of Adam Nash in the United States. In the case of Adam Nash, the intention was—and it was subsequently successfully carried out—to use cells from Adam's cord blood to treat his sibling.

18. The first successful transplant of a kidney from a living donor occurred in 1957, when three minors served as kidney donors for their twin siblings. For a detailed discussion of the issue, see L. F. Ross, 'Justice for Children: The Child as Organ Donor', *Bioethics*, 8 (1994), 105–26. The author argues that parental consent should override even a 14-year-old's dissent, except in extreme circumstances where the child has to be physically restrained in the operating theatre or runs away from home.

19. Sometimes an imaginative work of fiction can be a substitute for that voice, and in *My Sister's Keeper* (London: Hodder, 2004) the American author Jodi Picoult paints a compelling portrait of the dilemmas that could be faced by a child conceived in this way. The child in the novel seeks out a lawyer to help her challenge her parents' right to make medical decisions on her behalf.

20. M. Charlesworth, *Bioethics in a Liberal Society* (Cambridge: Cambridge University Press, 1993), 69.

21. See, e.g., R. Robson, 'Resisting the Family: Repositioning Lesbians in Legal Theory', *Signs*, 19 (1994), 945–96, cited in C. Calhoun, 'Family's Outlaws: Rethinking the Connections between Feminism, Lesbianism, and the Family', in Hilde Lindenmann Nelson (ed.), *Feminism and Families* (London: Routledge, 1997), 131–50, at 133.

22. C. Calhoun, 'Family's Outlaws', 146. She explores the theme in *Feminism, the Family, and the Politics of the Closet: Lesbian and Gay Displacement* (Oxford: Oxford University Press, 2000).

23. Calhoun, 'Family's Outlaws', 147.

24. European Parliament, Committee on Citizens' Freedoms and Rights, Justice and Home Affairs, Joke Swiebel, rapporteur, 'Report on the Situation concerning Human Rights in the European Union', A5–0451/2002.

Earlier, in 1984, the European Parliament had adopted a Report on Equal Rights for Homosexuals and Lesbians in the European Union.

25. Re T, Scotland, 1995.

26. See William Meezan and Jonathan Rauch, 'Gay Marriage, Same-Sex Parenting, and America's Children', *Future of Children*, 15/2 (Autumn 2005), 97–114. Meezan and Rauch describe several studies that have found no adverse results in physical or emotional terms for children brought up by same-sex couples: studies by Golombok and others focusing on lesbian families in England, and two studies specifically involving assisted reproduction, one from California (Chan, Raboy, and Patterson, 1998) and a Brussels-based study (Brewaeys et al., 1997).

27. While there is a large body of social-science research comparing heterosexual cohabitation and marriage, and comparing both in relation to outcomes for children, the issue of same-sex cohabitation has received less attention. However, New Hampshire's Commission to study same-sex marriage and other partnerships gave some weight to this issue and concluded that, up to the date of its Report, evidence from countries offering same-sex marriage or partnerships was that these are 'unusually prone to dissolution' (Commission to Study all Aspects of Same Sex Civil Marriage and the Legal Equivalents Thereof, Whether Referred to as Civil Unions, Domestic Partinerships, or Otherwise, SB 427, ch. 100:2, Laws of 2004).

28. Report, London, *The Times*, 8 Apr. 2005.

29. J. A. Robertson, 'Procreative Liberty and the Control of Conception, Pregnancy and Childbirth', Virginia Law Review, 69 (1983), 405–62, at 424.

30. J. Glover et al., *Fertility and the Family: The Glover Report on Reproductive Technologies to the European Commission* (London: Fourth Estate, 1989).

31. RvHFEA *ex p Blood* [1996] 3 WLR 1176 (HC), [1887] 2 A11 ER 687 (CA). See Ian Kennedy and Andrew Grubb *Medical Law, Texts and Materials* (London: Butterworths, 2000), 1296–308. Also P. Braude and S. Muhammed, 'Assisted Conception and the Law in the United Kingdom', *British Medical Journal*, 327 (2003), 978–81.

32. Harlow tested the effects on young monkeys of varying degrees of deprivation of a caring relationship. Bowlby's work with children led him to believe that the continuity of the mother–child relationship is vital for a child's future ability to form satisfactory relationships with other people. See H. Harlow, 'The Nature of Love', *American Psychologist*, 13 (1958), 573–685, and J. Bowlby, *Child Care and the Growth of Love* (Harmondsworth: Pengin, 1953).

33. See Claire Hughes, 'Making and Breaking Relationships: Children and their Families', in Andrew Bainham et al. (eds.), *Children and their Families: Contact, Rights and Welfare* (Oxford: Hart Publishing, 2003), 33–46, at 41.

34. These cases have thrown light on the contrast between biological and social fatherhood, a topic discussed in detail in Sally Sheldon, 'Fragmenting Fatherhood: The Regulation of Reproductive Technologies', *Modern Law Review*, 68/4 (2005), 523−53.

35. *Rose v. Sec. of State for Health and the HFEA*, [2002] EWHC 1593.

36. See n. 26 above.

37. J. David Velleman, 'Family History', *Philosophical Papers*, 34/3, (Nov. 2005), 357−78. p. 360.

38. Article 21, *Convention on Human Rights and Biomedicine*, Oviedo 4.4.1997: 'The Human Body and its parts shall not, as such, give rise to financial gain.'

39. Australians may pay around $40,000 for fertilized eggs to implant and $170,000 for babies borne for them by American surrogates. At the same time, there are other Australian women who travel to the USA to sell their eggs for $20,000. In an unrelated development, protests were raised when it was suggested that Canadian medical students might be offered free holidays in Australia in return for sperm donations.

40. The website of the Egg Donor Program says it has produced 2,500 children worldwide by the sale of eggs. Another organization, based in Los Angeles, also supplies these services for gay men.

41. In the United Kingdom, payment for supplying gametes and embryos is prohibited, but reimbursement of donors' expenses is allowed, and, in egg-sharing arrangements, women can be offered free IVF treatment in exchange for donating eggs.

42. In Denmark the limit is 25, a number that is supposed to guard against accidental incest between siblings. Cryos claims a good track record. Its website reported in 2005 that, since the company had opened in 1987, its banked of sperm has led to 10,000 pregnancies around the world.

43. Andrew Bainham describes Article 7 of this Convention as a response to the Argentine experience: 'The child shall be registered immediately after birth and shall have the right from birth to a name, the right to acquire a nationality and, as far as possible, the right to know and be cared for by his or her parents' (Andrew Bainham, 'Parentage, Parenthood and Parental Responsibility', in Andrew Bainham, S. D. Schlater, and M. Richards (eds.), *What is a Parent? A Socio-Legal Analysis* (Oxford: Hart Publishing, 1999), 25−46 at 37). See also J. Fortin, *Children's Rights and the Developing Law* (London, Edinburgh and Dublin: Butterworths, 1998), and L. J. Le Blanc, *The Convention on the Rights of the Child* (Lincoln, Neb., and London: University of Nebraska Press, 1995).

44. Leon Kass, 'Making Babies Revisited', in S. Gorowitz, R. Macklin, A. L. Jameton, J. L. O'Connor, and S. Sherwood (eds.), *Moral Problems in Medicine* (2nd edn.; Engelwood Cliff, NJ: Prentice Hall, 1983), 344−55,

at 345; cited by David Lamb, *Down the Slippery Slope: Arguing in Applied Ethics* (London: Croom Helm, 1988), 108.

45. David Hume, *A Treatise of Human Nature (1739–40)*, ed. Ernest C. Mossner (Harmondsworth: Penguin, 1985), bk. II, 'Of the Passions', Sect. 4, p. 401.

Chapter 7

1. For a brief account of the background to this debate, see Brenda Almond, 'Rights', in P. Singer (ed.), *A Companion to Ethics* (Oxford: Blackwell, 1991), 259–69.

2. See J. Eekelaar, 'Parenthood, Social Engineering, and Rights', in D. Morgan and G. Douglas (eds.), *Constituting Families: A Study in Governance* (Stuttgart: Franz Steiner Verlag, 1994).

3. In a study of 1,200 children for London and Oxford Universities, the child-care experts Penelope Leach, Kathy Silva, and Alan Stein concluded that children who experienced the one-to-one care of an involved adult did better in development tests than those cared for in nurseries, by childminders, or relatives. This research and other findings on the harmful effects on the under-3 age group of even high-quality extended-hours group care is discussed by Stephen Biddulph in *Raising Babies: Should Under 3s Go to Nurseries?* (London: HarperCollins, 2006).

4. Article 12 of the UN Convention, 1990, asserts: 'States parties should assure to the child who is capable of forming his or her own views the right to express those views freely in all matters affecting the child, the view of the child being given due weight in accordance with the age and maturity of the child.'

5. J. S. Mill, *On Liberty* (1859; Everyman; London: Dent, 1954), 73.

6. See Annette Baier, 'Hume's Account of Social Artifice', *Ethics* (July 1988) 757–78. Baier says of Hume's account: 'One striking feature is not just the emphasis on maternal devotion but also the total absence of patriarchal authority from his account of the natural family' (p. 771).

7. F. Engels, *The Origins of the Family: Private Property and the State* (1884), trans. A. West (Harmondsworth, Penguin, 1985).

8. N. V. Lowe and G. Douglas, *Family Law* (9th edn.; London: Butterworth, 1998) 302 n. 20. The two House of Lords decisions in question were *Johnstone* v. *Beattie* (1843) 10 C1 & Fin and *Stuart* v. *Marquis of Bute* (1861) 9 HL Cas 440. Both cases, however, concerned guardians rather than parents.

9. Nan Berger, 'The Child, the Law, and the State', in Paul Adams et al. (eds.), *Children's Rights* (London: Panther Books, 1972) 163–91, at 173.

10. *Gillick* v. *West Norfolk and Wisbech Area Health Authority and the DHSS* (1984) A11 ER 365.

11. A. Bainham, 'Growing Up in Britain: Adolescence in the Post-Gillick Era', in J. Eekelaar and P. Sarcevic (eds.), *Parenthood in Modern Society: Legal and Social Issues for the Twenty-First Century* (Dordrecht; Kluwer, 1993), 501–18, at 513.

12. The United Kingdom's Office for National Statistics (ONS), supplying figures for England Wales for the year 2003, reported that there were 34,200 abortions among girls aged 16–18 (that is just over 26 in every thousand). The number of pregnancies amongst girls under 18 was 42,173 (42.3 per thousand). It is possible to speculate that, in some cases, targets to reduce teenage pregnancies are being addressed by encouraging schools to provide easy access to abortion.

13. One illustration of this is provided by the experience of a Teenage Pregnancy Strategy Unit set up under government auspices in Britain with a mandate to reduce pregnancies by making condoms and the morning-after pill more easily available. Studies appeared to show that teenage pregnancies went up fastest in areas the unit focused on, and sexual infections amongst 16–19 year-olds increased. (Report from the Royal College of Nursing Conference, London, *The Times,* 28 April 2005.)

14. UNESCO, '*Unwanted Pregnancy and Unsafe Abortion*', (Bangkok: UNESCO, Regional Clearing House on Population, Education and Communication (RCHPEC), 2002).

15. For a very clear rehearsal of the US arguments on this issue, see the Testimony of Professor Teresa Stanton to the US House of Representatives Committee on the Judiciary, Subcommittee on the Constitution, 3 March 2005, regarding H.R. 748 'Child Interstate Abortion Notification Act'. Her testimony includes evidence that teenage pregnancies had consistently declined in a number of states, including Texas, Minnesota, Indiana, after the passing of parental involvement laws.

16. F. Shoeman, 'Rights of Children, Rights of Parents, and the Moral Basis of the Family', *Ethics,* 91 (1980) 6–19, at 14.

17. See Hugh LaFollette, 'Circumscribed Autonomy: Children, Care and Custody', in U. Narayan and J. Bartkowiak (eds.), *Having and Raising Children: Unconventional Families, Hard Choices and the Social Good* (Pennsylvania: Pennsylvania State University Press, 1999), 137–54. For an alternative view, see Francis Schrag, 'Children: Their Rights and Needs', in W. Aiken and H. LaFollette (eds.), *Whose Child?: Children's Rights, Parental Authority, and State Power* (Totowa, NJ: Rowman & Allenheld, 1980) 246–7.

18. This may even be a rational choice made for normal and understandable reasons, according to some experts. See A. James, 'Squaring the Circle: The Social, Legal and Welfare Organization of Contact', in Andrew Bainham et al. (eds.), *Children and their Families* (Oxford: Hart Publishing, 2003), 133–54, at 146.

19. The case, brought by 14-year-old Patrick Holland, was due to be heard in a Massachusetts court on 26 July 2004 but was abandoned when his father voluntarily terminated his rights.

20. One early presentation of arguments on both sides of this issue is J. Holt, *Escape from Childhood* (Harmondsworth: Penguin, 1974).

21. *Gregory K* v. *Ralph K*, 1992.

22. Laura M. Purdy, 'Boundaries of Authority: Should Children be Able to Divorce their Parents?', in Narayan and Bartkowiak (eds.), *Having and Raising Children*, 153–62, at 160–2.

23. LaFollette, 'Circumscribed Autonomy', 141.

24. Lord Justice James in the Chancery Court, 1878, cited by Berger, 'The Child, the Law, and the State', 163.

25. *R* v. *De Manneville* (1804) 5 East 221, cited in Lowe and Douglas, *Family Law*, ch. 8 'Parents and Children', 301.

26. The Guardianship Act, 1973.

27. The international position, however, differs from that of the United Kingdom. Article 3(1) of the UN Convention on the Rights of the Child, 1989, to which the UK is a party, provides: 'In all actions concerning children, whether undertaken by public or private social welfare institutions, courts of law, administrative authorities or legislative bodies, the best interests of the child shall be a primary consideration.' It is clear that the notion that best interests should be a *primary* consideration is less strong than the position that awards it *paramount* consideration.

28. In some countries, contact with both parents is regarded as a mental-health requirement.

29. See, e.g., the Court of Appeal ruling in *S(BD)* v *S(DJ)* (Children; care and control) [1977] Fam 109, [1977] 1 A11 ER 656.

30. An American judge expressed this view, albeit in a dissenting opinion: '[T]he biological role of a mother in carrying and nursing an infant creates stronger bonds between her and the child than the bonds resulting from the male's often casual encounter' (*Stanley* v. *Illinois*, 405 US 645 (1972) Id. at 665–6 (Burger, C.J., dissenting)), cited in J. Carbone and N. Cahn, 'Which Ties Bind? Redefining the Parent–Child Relationship in an Age of Genetic Certainty', *William and Mary Bill of Rights Journal*, 11 (2002–3), 1011–70. at 1048–9 n. 145.

31. Elie Wiesel, *Night* (New York: Bantam Books, 1960).

32. S. Ruddick, 'The Idea of Fatherhood', in Hilde Lindeman Nelson (ed.), *Feminism and Families* (London: Routledge, 1997), 205–20, at 207.

33. Ibid. 211. This supports the account offered by Genevieve Lloyd in her book *The Man of Reason: 'Male' and 'Female' in Western Philosophy* (London: Methuen, 1984).

34. D. Blankenhorn, *Fatherless America*, New York: Basic Books, 1995), 127.

35. Susan Moller Okin, *Justice, Gender and the Family* (New York: Basic Books, 1989), 171.

36. Ruddick, 'The Idea of Fatherhood', 216. For Ruddick's earlier discussion of the maternal role, see S. Ruddick, *Maternal Thinking* (Boston, Mass: Beacon Press, 1989).

37. Carol Smart, 'Power and the Politics of Custody', in Carol Smart and Selma Sevenhuijsen (eds.), *Child Custody and the Politics of Gender* (New York: Routledge, 1989), 1–26, at 17. See, too, Joseph, Goldstein, 'In Whose Interests', in Jay Folberg (ed.), (2nd edn.; New York: Guilford Press, 1991). *Joint Custody and Shared Parenting.*

38. Ruddick, 'The Idea of Fatherhood', 218.

39. *Epperson* v. *Dampney*, 1976, p. 241, per Glass JA, cited by R. Graycar, 'Equal Rights versus Fathers' Rights: The Child Custody Debate in Australia', in Smart and Sevenhuijsen (eds.), *Child Custody and the Politics of Gender*, 158–89, at 163.

40. See, however, J. Goldstein, A. Freud, and A. Solnit, *Beyond the Best Interests of the Child* (New York: Free Press, 1973), who introduced the idea of the 'psychological parent', not necessarily but normally the mother, defined as the parent who performs the main caring functions.

41. For example, a man may not prevent his pregnant wife from having an abortion and has no legal right to be consulted or informed about it. On the other hand, if she is pregnant and has the child, he is liable for its maintenance whether or not they are married, and in whatever circumstances it was conceived, including the use of deliberate deception.

42. Smart, 'Power and the Politics of Custody', 8.

43. Julia Brophy, 'Custody and Inequality in Britain', in Smart and Sevenhuijsen (eds.), *Child Custody and the Politics of Gender*, 219.

44. In Florida, 'normal' contact specifies the timings of weekend visits—6 p.m. Friday to 6 p.m. Sunday, with a Christmas Day handover at 4 p.m.

45. See P. Morgan, *Family Matters: Family Breakdown and its Consequences* (Wellington: New Zealand Business Roundtable, 2004). Morgan summarizes: 'Children are likely to be exposed to many stresses, such as moving homes, changing schools, conflicts over post-divorce arrangements, and declining household income' (p. 145).

46. Judith S. Wallerstein, 'Children of Divorce: A Society in Search of Policy', in Mary Ann Mason, Arlene Skolnick and Stephen D. Sugarman (eds.), *All our Families: New Policies for a New Century* (1998; 2nd edn., Oxford: Oxford University Press, 2003), 66–95, at 75. For the major study mentioned, see Judith S. Wallerstein, Julia M. Lewis, and Sandra Blakeslee, *The Unexpected Legacy of Divorce: The 25 Year Landmark Study* (New York: Hyperion, 2000).

47. Report, *Sunday Times*, 28 Sept 2003. While it has many disadvantages, and is likely to break down when one of the parents finds a new partner,

it does give the parents a sample of the disruption shared custody will mean for their children.

48. Kenny J in *E.K.* v *M.K.*, cited by Delma MacDevitt, in 'The Custody of Children in the Republic of Ireland', in Smart and Sevenhuijsen (eds.), *Child Custody and the Politics of Gender*, 210.

49. Yuri Joikimidis, President of the Joint Parenting Association, argues this case in the organization's Policy Monograph *Back to the Best Interests of the Child*.

50. For some British-based research on this subject, see Robert Whelan, *Broken Homes and Battered Children: A Study of the Relationship between Child Abuse and Family Type* (London: Family Education Trust, 1994).

51. Sandra Horley, the Chief Executive of Refuge, a London-based organization campaigning against domestic violence, describes the case of a 7-year-old girl who was forced to watch while her father tied up her mother, beat her, and then shot her in the stomach. The child was nevertheless forced into further contact by the court in spite of her insistence that she never wanted to see her father again (www.refuge.org.uk).

52. Women's Aid, a UK charity that campaigns against domestic violence, published a report that highlighted some of these more extreme possibilities. The organization gave details of the cases of 29 children from 13 families who were killed by their fathers in a ten-year period up to 2004—cases that involved disputes about contact or residence. Hilary Saunders, *Twenty-Nine Child Homicides: Lessons still to be Learnt on Domestic Violence and Child Protection* (Bristol: Women's Aid Federation of England, 2004).

53. Report, 'The Seven Ages of Man and Woman' (London: Economic and Social Research Council, 2004). Reported in *The Times*, 21 June 2004.

54. See N. Zill, 'Behavior, Achievement, and Health Problems among Children in Stepfamilies: Findings from a National Survey of Child Health', in E. M. Hetherington and J. D. Arasteh (eds.), *Impact of Divorce, Single Parenting, and Stepparenting on Children* (Hillsdale, NJ: Embaum, 1998). See also Wallerstein, 'Children of Divorce'.

55. Robert Whelan, *Broken Homes and Battered Children: A Study of the Relationship between Child Abuse and Family Type* (London: Family Education Trust, 1994).

56. Writing from the point of view of evolutionary psychology, Martin Daly and Margo Wilson reported that the risk of children being killed by a step-parent was 50 to 100 times higher than the risk of being killed by a biological parent. They also found a higher risk of child abuse, reporting that the presence of a step-parent is the best epidemiological predictor of child abuse. M. Daly and M. Wilson, *The Truth about Cinderella: A Darwinian view of Parental Love* (New Haven: Yale University Press, 1999).

57. Ibid. 64.

58. For a general discussion of the issue of youth homelessness by a philosopher who worked for some years in a children's refuge in London, see M. Parker, 'Children who Run: Ethics and Homelessness', in B. Almond (ed.), *Introducing Applied Ethics* (Oxford: Blackwell, 1995), 58–70. See, too, R. Young, G. Matthews, and G. Adams, 'Runaways: A Review of Negative Consequences and Diminishing Choices', *Family Relations*, 32 (1983), 275–81.

59. P. Morgan, *Farewell to the Family: Public Policy and Family Breakdown in Britain and the USA* (London: Institute of Economics Affairs, Health and Welfare Unit, 1999) 163. Her claim is based on research by J. Smith, et al., *The Family Backgrounds of Homeless Young People* (London: Family Policy Studies Centre, 1998), and R. Strathdee, *No Way Back* (London: Centrepoint, 1992).

60. James, 'Squaring the Circle', 145.

61. J. Blustein, *Parents and Children: The Ethics of the Family* (Oxford: Oxford University Press, 1982).

62. Ibid. 231.

63. An authoritative study is Paul R. Amato, and Alan Booth, *A Generation at Risk: Growing Up in an Era of Family Upheaval* (Cambridge, Mass.: Harvard University Press, 1997).

64. June Carbone, *From Partners to Parents: The Second Revolution in Family Law* (New York: Chichester, NY: Columbia University Press, 2000), 191.

Chapter 8

1. This is a matter of debate amongst researchers, particularly as to the effects of liberal divorce laws. A number of articles in Anthony W. Dnes and Robert Rowthorn (eds.), *The Law and Economics of Marriage and Divorce* (Cambridge: Cambridge University Press, 2002), address this issue. See, in particular, Elizabeth S. Scott, 'Marital Commitment and the Legal Regulation of Divorce', pp. 35–56, D. W. Allen, 'The Impact of Legal Reforms on Marriage and Divorce', pp. 191–211, and Ian Smith, 'European Divorce Laws, Divorce Rates, and their Consequences', pp. 212–29.

2. See Gary Becker, *A Treatise on the Family* (2nd edn.: Mass.: Cambridge, Harvard University Press, 1991), in particular ch. 11.

3. See, e.g., June Carbone, *From Partners to Parents: The Second Revolution in Family Law* (Chichester, NY: Columbia University Press, 2000). Part 1 of this book juxtaposes and contrasts the views of Becker and of the feminist writer Susan Moller Okin.

4. Adam Thomas and Isabel Sawhill, 'For Love or Money: The Impact of Family Structure on Family Income', *The Future of Children* (Policy Brief; Washington: Brookings Institution, 15 Feb. 2005), 57–74, at 69.

5. Charles Murray, *Underclass: The Crisis Deepens* (London: Institute of Economic Affairs, 1994), 19. For an authoritative presentation of the relevant research in an American context, see W. J. Doherty et al., *Why Marriage Matters: Twenty-One Conclusions from the Social Sciences* (New York: Institute for American Values, 2002).

6. See Paul Amato and Alan Booth, *A Generation at Risk: Growing Up in an Era of Family Upheaval* (Cambridge, Mass.: Harvard University Press, 1997). For an authoritative essay on the subject, see Judith S. Wallerstein, 'Children of Divorce: A Society in Search of Policy', in Mary Ann Mason, Arlene Skolnick, and Stephen D. Sugarman (eds.), *All our Families New Policies for a New Century* (1998; 2nd edn., Oxford: Oxford University Press, 2003), 66–95. For research specific to Britain, see Monica Cockett and John Tripp, *The Exeter Family Study: Family Breakdown and its impact on Children* (Exeter: University of Exeter Press, 1994). See also Martin Richards, 'Divorcing Children: Roles for Parents and the State', in John Eekelaar and Mavis MacLean (eds.), *A Reader on Family Law* (Oxford: Oxford University Press, 1994).

7. Maggie Gallagher, 'What is Marriage For? The Public Purposes of Marriage Law', *Louisiana Law Review*, 62 (2002), 1–37, at 12. For a specific study of the relationship of health problems in children to parental divorce, see Jane Mauldon, 'The Effects of Marital Disruption on Children's Health', *Demography*, 27/3 (1990), 431–46.

8. N. Dennis, 'Beautiful Theories, Brutal Facts: The Welfare State and Sexual Liberation', in D. Smith (ed.), *Welfare, Work and Poverty: Lessons from Recent Reforms in the USA and the UK* (London: Institute for the Study of Civil Society, 2000), 45–80, at 74.

9. Report, *Guardian*, 27 Mar. 2000. By 2004 official figures for the United Kingdom revealed that 1 in 4 dependent children were living in lone-parent families (London: Office for National Statistics).

10. Antony W. Dnes, 'Cohabitation and Marriage' in Dnes and Rowthorn, *Law and Economics*, 118–31. Dnes reports that in England first marriages fell from approximately 70 per 1,000 to 30 per 1,000 of the male population, while the proportion of women aged between 20 and 50 who were cohabiting trebled (p. 119).

11. Sara McLanahan, Irwin Garfinkel, and Ronald B. Mincy, 'Fragile Families, Welfare Reform, and Marriage', *Welfare Reform and Beyond* (Policy Brief No. 10; Washington: Brookings Institution, Dec. 2001).

12. Office for National Statistics figures from 2004 for England and Wales showed that three-quarters of all family breakdowns affecting young children involved unmarried parents.

13. See P. Morgan, *Marriage-Lite: The Rise of Cohabitation and its Consequences* (London: Civitas, 2000). In a foreword to this book, Robert Whelan writes: 'Cohabiting relationships are always more likely to fracture than

marriages entered into at the same time, regardless of age and income. It is no longer true that people cohabit until children come along and then tie the knot. Cohabitations with children are more likely to fragment than childless ones (p. vii). For some American perspectives, see Alan Booth and Ann C. Crouter (eds.), *Just Living Together: Implications of Cohabitation for Children, Families, and Public Policy* (Hillsdale, NJ: Lawrence Erlbaum Associates, 2002).

14. See, however, Steven Nock, 'A Comparison of Marriages and Cohabiting Relationships', *Journal of Family Issues*, 16 (Jan. 1995), 53–76. Using data from the National Survey of Families and Households, Nock identified significant differences in the way people viewed their experience of cohabiting or married relationships.

15. A calculation made in 2005 was that an average couple in the United Kingdom (one earner on £24,000 p.a.) paid £5,000 more in tax than they would receive in benefits. If they were to separate, their income could rise by at least 35 per cent because of benefits. Their two households could receive £7,000 more in benefits than they paid in tax. Jill Kirby, *The Price of Parenthood* (London: Centre for Policy Studies, 2005), Report, *The Times*, 21 Jan. 2005.

16. See N. Dennis, *Rising Crime and the Dismembered Family: How Conformist Intellectuals have Campaigned against Common Sense* (London: Institute of Economic Affairs, 1993).

17. Anthony W. Dnes and Robert Rowthorn, Introduction, in Dnes and Rowthron (eds.), *Law and Economics*, 1–9, at 7. See also R. Rowthorn, 'Marriage as a Signal', in ibid. 132–56.

18. Research on the 'marriage premium' tends to converge on the view that the economic advantages of marriage outweigh those of either cohabitation or single parenting. See Thomas and Sawhill, 'For Love or Money'. See also Daniel Kermit, 'The Marriage Premium', in Mariano Tommassi and Kathryn Ierulli (eds.), *The New Economics of Human Behaviour* (Cambridge: Cambridge University Press, 1996), 307–19, at 111.

19. See Dnes and Rawthorn (eds.), *Law and Economics*.

20. For the case for seeing marriage in contractual terms, see Lloyd R. Cohen, 'Marriage: The Long-Term Contract', in Dnes and Rowthorn (eds.), *Law and Economics*, 10–25. Also 'Marriage as Contract', in P. Newman, (ed.), *The New Palgrave Dictionary of Economics and the Law* (London: Macmillan, 1998), and 'Marriage, Divorce and Quasi-Rents; or, "I Gave him the Best Years of my Life"', *Journal of Legal Studies*, 16 (1987), 267–303.

21. Jack Straw, quoted in *Guardian*, 27 Mar. 2000.

22. Some of these positions are defended by contributors to J. Eekelaar and S. N. Katz (eds.), *Marriage and Cohabitation in Contemporary Society* (Toronto: Butterworths, 1980).

23. A. Comfort, 'Sexuality in a Zero Growth Society', in Robert T. Francoeur and Anna K. Francoeur (eds.), *The Future of Sexual Relations* (Englewood Cliffs, NJ: Prentice Hall, 1975).

24. A 1994 research survey conducted for the Lord Chancellor's Department found that 72% of those surveyed believed that 'marriage should be forever' and only 14% disagreed with that (MORI, *Public Attitudes to Marriage, Divorce and Family Mediation*, Research Survey Conducted for the Lord Chancellor's Department, 1994); see R. Rowthorn, 'Marriage as a Signal', in Dnes and Rowthorn (eds.), *Law and Economics*, 132–56.

25. Part II of the Family Law Act 1996 had envisaged further changes in divorce law, including abolishing even the need to establish irretrievable breakdown so that either spouse would be able to obtain a divorce without needing to provide grounds. A delay of twelve months would have been all that was needed, and mediation would have played a central role. It was on this latter requirement that the proposal fell, and this part of the Act was abandoned.

26. D. W. Allen, 'The Impact of Legal Reforms on Marriage and Divorce', in Dnes and Rowthorn (eds.), *Law and Economics*, 191–211. at 196.

27. L. J. Weitzman, *The Divorce Revolution: The Unexpected Social and Economic Consequences for Women and Children in America* (New York: Free Press, p. xi).

28. Dnes, 'Cohabitation and Marriage', 119.

29. Robert, Rowthorn, 'Marriage and Trust: Some Lessons from Economics', *Cambridge Journal of Economics*, 23 (1999), 661–91, at 661.

30. Brian T. Trainor, 'The State, Marriage and Divorce', *Journal of Applied Philosophy*, 9 (1992), 135–48, at 143.

31. Ibid. 145.

32. M. Freeman (ed.), *Family, State and Law* (Dartmouth: Ashgate, 1999). Freeman points to two legislative initiatives in England based on this new principle: the Children Act 1989 and the Child Support Act 1991.

33. Carbone, *From Partners to Parents*, 131–2.

34. Dan Cere, *The Future of Family Law: Law and the Marriage Crisis in North America* (New York: Institute for American Values, 2005), 9.

35. American Law Institute, *Principles of the Law of Family Dissolution: Analysis and Recommendations* (Philadelhia: American Law Institute, 2002).

36. *Halpern* v. *Canada* (Attorney General), [2003] 225 DLR (4th) 529 (Can.) par. 91. Cited in Cere, *The Future of Family Law*, 45 n. 24.

37. See, e.g., Eric Clive, 'Marriage: An Unnecessary Legal Concept', in J. K. Eekelaar, and S. N. Katz (eds.), *Marriage and Cohabitation in Contemporary Societies* (Toronto: Butterworth, 1980).

38. The Anglican Church has found itself in difficulty over this point, having accepted that homosexuality itself will not be a bar to the priesthood, if it is

non-practising or 'celibate'. It had not, however, anticipated the difficulty of how to respond to two clerics wishing to have a civil partnership.

39. The researchers William Meezan and Jonathan Rauch are advocates of same-sex marriage and argue that, since marriage is held to be good for the children of heterosexual couples, the same should be expected in the case of same-sex couples. William Meezan and Jonathan Rauch, 'Gay marriage, Same-Sex Parenting, and America's Children', *Future of Children*, 15/2 (Autumn 2005), 97–114, at 110.

40. Association des Parents et Futurs Parents Gays et Lesbiens, *De 'la famille' au singulier aux familles plurielles* (Paris: 2000).

41. The American Academy of Pediatrics, Press Release, 2002.

42. Justice Robert Blair in *Halpern* v. *Canada*, 215 DLR. (4th) 223 (Can.) par. 97–99 (2003). Cited by Cere, *The Future of Family Law*, 48 n. 74.

43. Elizabeth Marquardt and David Blankenhorn, personal communication with reference to research by the Institute for American Values on parenthood. For details of publications on this subject by the Institute, see www.americanvalues.org.

44. Report, London, *Daily Telegraph*, 8 Mar. 2006.

45. See Andrew Sullivan, *Virtually Normal* (New York: A. Knopf, 1995). Sullivan writes as a classical liberal who believes the state should intervene to prevent discrimination but not otherwise interfere in private life. See, too, Andrew Sullivan, *Same-Sex Marriage, Pro and Con: A Reader* (New York: Vintage Books, 2004). Same-sex marriage is also defended by William N. Eskridge in *The Case for Same-Sex Marriage: From Sexual Liberty to Civilized Commitment* (New York: Free Press, 1996).

46. Maggie Gallagher, 'What is Marriage For? The Public Purposes of Marriage Law', *Louisiana Law Review*, 62 (2002), 1–18.

Chapter 9

1. P. Ehrlich, *The Population Bomb* (New York: Ballantyne Books, 1968; rev. edn., New York: Rivercity Books, 1975).

2. T. Malthus, *An Essay on the Principle of Population* (1798), (Cambridge: Cambridge University Press, 1992).

3. By 2050, deaths from AIDS alone are likely to have reached 278 million (comparable to the entire population of the United States), and, because of the impact of the disease on women of child-bearing age, many fewer babies will have been born. There is a particular question mark over population prospects in some African countries, for example, Botswana, where life expectancy is estimated to have fallen to between 29 and 39 years in the first decade of the 21st century because of HIV/AIDS.

4. See Ch. 4.

5. While the fertility figure for the United Kingdom was 1.74 children per woman in 2004, it was lower still in Germany (1.37), Spain (1.32) and Italy (1.33). Many women in Spain, and also in Italy, have only one child and the United Nations forecasts a drop of a third in the Italian population by 2050 if reproductive trends continue at the current level. Germany's population, too, is predicted to fall from 82 million in 2005 to 70 million by the mid-twenty-first century. (Figures from the UK-based Office for National Statistics, EUROSTAT and Germany's Federal Institute for Demographic Research.) Russia also confronts a situation of population decline: the fertility rate of Russian women dropped as low as 1.17 in 1986, and rose only to below 1.3 by 2004.

6. According to the United Nations, France would need ninety million newcomers to achieve a satisfactory budgetary ratio between those in and out of work (Report, *The Times*, 30 Nov. 2004).

7. Robert Rowthorn, 'Numbers and National Identity', in H. Disney (ed.), *Migration, Integration and the European Labour Market* (London: Civitas, 2003), 65–81, at 78. Rowthorn bases his assessment on the calculation of the demographer David Coleman that to prevent the average age of the population of the United Kingdom from rising would require the immigration of sixty million people over a fifty-year period. This would mean that, by 2050, nearly 60 per cent of the population would consist of people who had arrived in the country since 1995 and their descendants. See also UN, Population Division of the Department of Economic and Social Affairs, *Replacement Migration: Is it a Solution to Declining and Ageing Populations?* (New York: United Nations, 2000).

8. According to its Office of National Statistics, the total fertility rate in the United Kingdom in 2003 was 1.71 children per woman. This was a slight increase from a record low of 1.63 in 2001, with the rate in 2000 and 2002 being at similar levels. Statisticians predict that the figure will stabilize at around 1.74.

9. In 1999 the British Government Actuary estimated that by 2011 married people would be outnumbered by those who are unmarried for the first time since records began in 1801 (Report, *The Times*, 9 Jan. 1999).

10. A report by the ESHRE (European Society for Human Reproduction and Embryology), which compares the reduced income expectations of young males with that enjoyed by their parents, suggests that this leaves them less confident of their ability to support a family. The ESHRE Capri Workshop, 'Social Determinants of Human Reproduction', *Human Reproduction*, 16/7 (2001), 1518–26.

11. An estimate of this order was provided by Professor Bill Ledger of Sheffield University and Jessop Hospital at a meeting of the ESHRE (European Society for Human Reproduction and Embryology), Copenhagen, 20 June 2005.

12. See Ch. 5.

13. Reports, London, *The Times*, 2 and 23 Jan. 2006 based on US Census Bureau Report, 2005. Immigration figures provided by Centre for Immigration Studies, Dec. 2005.

14. Existing immigration practice and policy in the United Kingdom means that the British population will increase by just over five million by 2025 and continue to grow till 2040 (Office for National Statistics), most of the increase being due to migration of dependants and spouses of immigrants who have already settled there. Figures for families with three or more children in the UK are: Bangladeshi 60%, Pakistani 54%, Indian 30%, Chinese 24%, Caribbean 22%. The figure for the native population (officially described as 'white British' but including the English, Scots, and Welsh) is less than one in five.

15. E. Burkett, *The Baby Boon: How Family-Friendly America Cheats the Childless* (New York: Free Press, 2001).

16. M. Arnold, *Culture and Anarchy* (1869; Cambridge: Cambridge University Press, 1960), 70.

17. K. A. Appiah, 'Identity, Authenticity, Survival: Multicultural Societies and Social Reproduction', in C. Taylor et al. (eds.), *Multiculturalism: Examining the Politics of Recognition* (Princeton: Princeton University Press, 1994).

18. Robert Rowthorn cites the demographic background to the Kosovo conflict as an indication of the way in which relative variations in population can have political consequences. He reports that in 1950 there was a rough balance in Kosovo between births to Albanian Muslims and births to Orthodox Serbs, but that by 1996, when the ratio had shifted to 4:1 in favour of the Albanians, the Serbs were beginning to see themselves as an endangered minority. Rowthorn, 'Numbers and National Identity', 76.

19. The historian Niall Ferguson argues that time and the birth rate could bring a Muslim Europe within fifty years. For his views on shifting global movements, see N. Ferguson, *Empire: The Rise and Fall of British World Order and the Lessons for Global Power* (New York: Basic Books, 2003), and N. Ferguson, *Colossus: The Rise and Fall of the American Empire* (Harmondsworth: Penguin, 2004).

20. I defend this point of view in 'Against Irrationalism', in A. Bondolfi et al. (eds.), *Ethik, Vernunft und Rationalitaet/Ethics, Reason and Rationality* (Munster: Lit Verlag, 1997), 91–104.

21. L. Blum, 'Against Deriving Particularity' in B. Hooker, and Margaret Little (eds.), *Moral Particularism* (Oxford: Oxford University Press, 2000), 205–226, at 208.

22. Ibid. 206.

23. Adam Smith, *The Theory of the Moral Sentiments* (1759; Oxford: Oxford University Press, 1976), pt. VI, ch. III.

24. R. M. Hare, 'Universalisability', *Proceedings of the Aristotelian Society*, 55 (1954–5).

25. Blum, 'Against Deriving Particularly', 208. Hare describes his approach to the partiality issue in 'Utilitarianism and the Vicarious Affects', in *Essays in Ethical Theory* (Oxford: Clarendon Press, 1989), 23–44, *passim*. See particularly pp. 236–7.

26. See R. M. Hare, 'Could Kant have been a Utilitarian?', in R. M. Hare, *Sorting Out Ethics* (Oxford: Oxford University Press, 1997), 147–65, at 165. Hare also discusses the issue in 'Ethical Theory and Utilitarianism' (1976), in *Essays in Ethical Theory*. The partiality issue is discussed from a variety of different perspectives by contributors to a special issue of *Ethical Theory and Moral Practice*, ed. B. Musschenga and R. Heeger, 8 (2005).

27. Rowthorn, 'Numbers and National Identity', 73.

28. T. Nagel, *Equality and Partiality* (Oxford: Oxford University Press, 1991), 10.

29. J. Rawls, *A Theory of Justice* (Oxford: Oxford University Press, 1972), 74.

30. Nagel, *Equality and Partiality*, 102.

31. For a comprehensive review of the opposition to Hegel in this context, see Antoinette M. Stafford, 'The Feminist Critique of Hegel on Women and the Family', *Animus*: www.mun.ca/animus/1997vol2/staford1/htm. See also Carol McMillan, *Women, Reason and Nature* (Oxford: Blackwell, 1982).

32. C. Gilligan, *In a Different Voice: Psychological Theory and Women's Development* (Cambridge, Mass.: Harvard University Press, 1982). See also Ch. 4.

33. J. Rawls, *A Theory of Justice* (Oxford: Oxford University Press, 1972), pt. I, ch. 3, p. 137.

34. R. Nozick, *Anarchy, State and Utopia* (Oxford: Blackwell, 1974), pt. II, ch. 7.

35. P. Gomberg, 'Patriotism is like Racism', *Ethics*, 101 (1990), 144–50, at 150.

Chapter 10

1. J. David Velleman, 'Family History', *Philosophical Papers*, 34/3 (Nov. 2005). 357–78. p. 360.

2. Jacques Donzelot, *The Policing of Families*, trans. Robert Hurley (New York: Random House, 1979) (*La Police des familles*, Paris: Éditions de Minuit, 1977).

3. See A. MacIntyre, *After Virtue* (London: Duckworth, 1981), and *Whose Justice? Which Rationality?* (London: Duckworth, 1988). These critics see in it the rootless cosmopolitanism in which, as Alasdair MacIntyre puts it, those who aspire to be at home anywhere become citizens of nowhere.

But for MacIntyre, contemporary liberalism is a non-culture and the differences between modern conservatives and radicals is less important than their similarities.

4. For this viewpoint, see R. Beiner, *What's the Matter with Liberalism?* (Berkeley and Los Angeles: University of California Press, 1992). For a counter-view, see Brenda Almond, 'The Retreat from Liberty', *Critical Review*, 8 (1994), 235–46. See, too, John Gray, *Liberalism: Essays in Political Philosophy* (London, Routledge, 1989), in particular 'Postscript: After Liberalism'.

5. Sasha Roseneil, 'Living and Loving beyond the Boundaries of the Heteronorm: Personal Relationships in the 21st Century', in Linda McKie and Sarah Cunningham-Burley (eds.), *Families in Society: Boundaries and Relationships* (Bristol: Policy Press, 2005) 241–58, at 247.

6. Ferdinand Mount, *The Subversive Family: An Alternative History of Love and Marriage* (London: Jonathan Cape, 1982), 246.

7. See, e.g., Carole Pateman, who argues in her book *The Sexual Contract* (Stanford, Calif.: University of Stanford Press, 1988) that women's position in the sexual contract is analogous to that of slaves—a view that echoes Lenin's dictum: 'The home life of a woman is a daily sacrifice to a thousand unimportant trivialities. The old master right of the man still lives in secret.' For the story of the communist attempt to abolish the family and its later reinstatement, see H. Kent Geiger, 'The Fate of the Family in Soviet Russia: 1917–1944,', in Norman W. Bell and Ezra F. Vogel (eds.), *A Modern Introduction to the Family* (rev. edn.; New York: Free Press, 1968), 48–67.

8. See John MacMurray, *The Form of the Personal*, ii. *Persons in Relation* (London: Faber & Faber, 1961; repr. Atlantic Highlands, NJ: Humanities Press, 1991). The introduction to this edition was written by the British politician Tony Blair. See also Knud Ejler Løgstrup, author of *The Ethical Demand* (1956; Notre Dame, Ind.: University of Notre Dame Press, 1997) with an introduction by Hans Fink and Alasdair MacIntyre. In ch. 4 of *The Ethical Demand*, Løgstrup criticizes the view that economic inequality is an inevitable feature of human society and argues that competition cannot be fair when it is between privileged and unprivileged people. He writes: 'Competition presupposes equality but results in inequality. It presupposes the abolition of privilege but results in creating privileges' (p. 91).

9. In the United Kingdom, more than half of families headed by a single parent are wholly or mainly dependent on the state for support and the social-security budget accounts for one-third of public expenditure.The Centre for Policy Studies has provided the following figures for the UK: the average couple with two children costs the state over £80,000 over ten years if they split up. Enabling single parents to raise children alone costs

the state between £71,000 and £123,000 over the same period (Centre for Policy Studies, UK, 2005).

10. James Q. Wilson, *The Marriage Problem: How our Culture has Weakened Families* (New York: HarperCollins, 2002). See in particular ch. 7, 'Divorce'. Wilson notes the absence of public discussion surrounding these changes and comments that the divorce revolution was produced by a quiet group of lawyers, judges, and legislators who worked out together, without much controversy, what they took to be the implications of gender equality (p. 164).

11. Maggie Gallagher, 'What is Marriage for? The Public Purposes of Marriage Law', *Louisiana Law Review*, 62 (2002), 1–37, at 18.

12. Ibid.

13. J. Blustein, *Parents and Children: The Ethics of The Family* (Oxford: Oxford University Press, 1982), 239.

14. Margaret Mead, 'Marriage in Two Steps', in Herbert A. Otto (ed.), *The Family in Search of a Future* (New York: Appleton-Century-Crofts, 1970).

15. Kathleen Shaw Spaht, 'Louisiana Covenant Law: Recapturing the Meaning of Marriage for the sake of the Children', in Anthony W. Dnes and Robert Rowthorn (eds.), *The Law and Economics of Marriage and Divorce* (Cambridge: Cambridge University Press, 2002) 92–117 at 104.

16. See p. 55–6.

17. W. Shalit, *A Return to Modesty: Discovering the Lost Virtue* (New York: Simon & Schuster, 1999).

18. Sophocles' trilogy *Oedipus Rex* is available in many editions.

19. Marie-Thérèse Meulders, President of the International Society of Family Law, in her Introduction to J. Eekelaar and Petar Sarcevic, *Parenthood in Modern Society: Legal and Social Issues for the Twenty-First Century* (Dordrecht: Marinus Nijhoff, 1993), p. xii.

20. The landmark work on attachment theory, originally a three-volume trilogy, is Joseph Goldstein, Albert J. Solnit, Sonja Goldstein and the late Anna Freud, *The Best Interests of the Child: The Least Detrimental Alternative* (New York: Free Press, 1996).

21. See Arlene Skolnick, 'Solomon's Children: The New Biologism, Psychological Parenthood, Attachment Theory, and the Best Interests Standard', in Mary Ann Mason, Arlene Skolnick, and Stephen D. Sugarman (eds.), *All our Families: New Policies for a New Century* (1998; 2nd edn., Oxford: Oxford University Press, 2003).

22. David Archard, *Children, Rights and Childhood* (London: Routledge, 1993), 109.

23. Ibid.

24. William N. Eskridge, Jr., *Gaylaw: Challenging Apartheid in the Closet* (Cambridge, Mass.: Harvard University Press, 1999), 11.

25. D. Cere, *The Future of Family Law: Law and The Marriage Crisis in North America* (New York: Institute for American Values, 2005).

26. See Civil Code of Quebec, Articles 538 and 525.

27. Canada, Civil Marriage Act, 1st sess., 38th Parliament (2005), 'Consequential Amendments'.

28. Law Commission of Canada, *Beyond Conjugality: Recognizing and Supporting Close Personal Adult Relationships* (Ottawa: Law Commission of Canada, 2001), pp. xxiv–xxv.

29. Gallagher, 'What is Marriage For?', 17. The reference to Vermont is to the case of *Baker* v. *State of Vermont*, 744A.2d 864 (Vt. 1999).

30. P. Gilbert, *Human Relationships* (Oxford: Blackwell, 1991), 143.

31. Cere, *The Future of Family Law*, 32.

32. D. Cooper, *The Death of the Family* (London: Penguin, 1971), 151.

33. W. Kymlicka, 'Rethinking the Family', *Philosophy and Public Affairs* (Winter 1991), 77–97 at 88.

34. Anthony Giddens, *Runaway World: How Globalisation is Reshaping our Lives* (2nd edn.; London: Profile Books, 2002), 66.

35. D. Selbourne, Moral Evasion (London: Centre for Policy Studies, 1998).

36. Adam Smith, *The Theory of the Moral Sentiments* (1759; Oxford: Oxford University Press, 1976), pt. VI, ch. III.

Bibliography

Adams, P., et al., *Children's Rights* (London: Panther Books, 1972).

Aiken, W., and LaFollette, H., *Whose Child: Children's Rights, Parental Authority, and State Power* (Totowa, NJ: Rowman & Allenheld, 1980).

Ali, Ayaan Hirsi, *The Son Factory (De Zoontjesfabriek* (2003)).

—— *The Cage of Virgins (De Maagdenkoop* (2004)).

Allen, D. W., 'The Impact of Legal Reforms on Marriage and Divorce', in Anthony W. Dnes and Robert Rowthorn (eds.), *The Law and Economics of Marriage and Divorce* (Cambridge: Cambridge University Press, 2002), 191–211.

Almond, Brenda, 'An Ethical Paradox', in *Moral Concerns* (Atlantic Highlands, NJ: Humanities Press, 1987), 113–24.

—— 'Seven Moral Myths', *Philosophy*, 64 (1990), 1–8.

—— 'Rights', in P. Singer (ed.), *A Companion to Ethics* (Oxford: Blackwell, 1991), 259–69.

—— 'The Retreat from Liberty', *Critical Review*, 8 (1994), 235–46.

—— 'Against Irrationalism', in A. Bondolfi et al. (eds.), *Ethik, Vernunft und Rationalitaet/Ethics, Reason and Rationality* (Münster: Lit Verlag, 1997), 91–104.

—— and Hill, D., *Applied Philosophy: Morals and Metaphysics in Contemporary Debate* (London: Routledge, 1991).

Amato, Paul, and Booth, Alan, *A Generation at Risk: Growing Up in an Era of Family Upheaval* (Cambridge, Mass: Harvard University Press, 1997).

American Law Institute, *Principles of the Law of Family Dissolution: Analysis and Recommendations* (Philadelphia: American Law Institute, 2002).

Anscombe, Elizabeth, *Contraception and Chastity* (1975; London: Catholic Truth Society, 2003).

Appiah, K. A., 'Identity, Authenticity, Survival: Multicultural Societies and Social Reproduction', in C. Taylor et al. (eds.), *Multiculturalism: Examining the Politics of Recognition* (Princeton: Princeton University Press, 1994).

Aquinas, *Opera omnia* (2 vols.; Rome: Commissio Leonina, 1969).

Archard, David, *Children, Rights and Childhood* (London, Routledge, 1993).

Aristotle, *Ethics*, trans. J. A. K. Thomson, rev. edn. H. Tredennick (Harmondsworth: Penguin, 1981).

—— *Politics*, trans. T. A. Sinclair, rev. edn. T. J. Saunders (Harmondsworth: Penguin, 1981).

Arnold, M., *Culture and Anarchy* (1869; Cambridge: Cambridge University Press, 1960).

Association des Parents et Futurs Parents Gays et Lesbiens, *De 'la famille' au singulier aux familles plurielles* (Paris: 2000).

Badran, Margot, 'Islamic Feminism: What's in a Name?', *Al-Ahram Weekly Online*, 569, 17–23 January 2002.

_____ and Cooke, Miriam (eds.), *Opening the Gates: A Century of Arab Feminist Writing* (Indiana: Indiana University Press, 1990).

Baier, Annette, 'Hume's Account of Social Artifice', *Ethics* (July 1988), 757–78.

Bainham, Andrew, 'Growing Up in Britain: Adolescence in the Post-Gillick Era', in J. Eekelaar and P. Šarčević (eds.), *Parenthood in Modern Society: Legal and Social Issues for the Twenty-First Century* (Dordrecht: Kluwer, 1993), 501–18.

_____ 'Parentage, Parenthood and Parental Responsibility', in Andrew Bainham, S. D. Schlater, and M. Richards (eds.), *What is a Parent? A Socio-Legal Analysis* (Oxford: Hart Publishing, 1999), 25–46.

_____ Lindley, B., Richards, M., and Trinder, L. (eds.), *Children and their Families: Contact, Rights and Welfare* (Oxford: Hart Publishing, 2003).

Bates, Daisy, *The Passing of the Aborigines* (London: John Murray, 1938; 2nd edn., Melbourne: Heinemann, 1966).

Becker, Gary S., *A Treatise on the Family* (2nd edn.; Cambridge, Mass.: Harvard University Press, 1991).

Beiner, R., *What's the Matter with Liberalism?* (Berkeley and Los Angeles: University of California Press, 1992).

Bell, Norman W., and Vogel, Ezra F., *A Modern Introduction to the Family* (New York: Free Press, 1968).

Berger, Nan, 'The Child, the Law, and the State', in Paul Adams et al. (eds.), *Children's Rights* (London: Panther Books, 1972), 163–91.

Berkeley, G., *Passive Obedience, Or the Christian Doctrine of not Resisting the Supreme Power, Proved and Vindicated upon the Principles of the Law of Nature* (London and Dublin, 1712).

Biddulph, Stephen, *Raising Babies: Should under 3s Go to Nurseries?* (London: HarperCollins, 2006).

Biggar, N., and Black, Rufus (eds.), *The Revival of Natural Law: Philosophical, Theological and Ethical Responses to the Finnis-Grisez School* (Aldershot: Ashgate, 2000).

Blankenhorn, D., *Fatherless America* (New York: Basic Books, 1995).

Blum, L., 'Against Deriving Particularity', in B. Hooker and Margaret Little (eds.), *Moral Particularism* (Oxford: Oxford University Press, 2000), 205–26.

Blustein, J., *Parents and Children: The Ethics of the Family* (Oxford: Oxford University Press, 1982).

Booth, Alan, and Crouter, Ann C. (eds.), *Just Living Together: Implications of Cohabitation for Children, Families, and Public Policy* (Hillsdale, NJ: Lawrence Erlbaum Associates, 2002).

Bowlby, J., *Child Care and the Growth of Love* (Harmondsworth: Penguin, 1953).

Braude, P., and Muhammed, S., 'Assisted Conception and the Law in the United Kingdom', *British Medical Journal*, 327 (2003), 978–81.

Brophy, Julia, 'Custody and Inequality in Britain', in Carol Smart and Selma Sevenhuijsen (eds.), *Child Custody and the Politics of Gender* (New York: Routledge, 1989).

Brownlie, Ian, and Goodwin-Gill, Guy S. (eds.), *Basic Documents on Human Rights* (4th edn.; Oxford: Oxford University Press, 2002).

Burkett, E., *The Baby Boon: How Family-Friendly America Cheats the Childless* (New York: Free Press, 2001).

Calhoun, C., 'Family's Outlaws: Rethinking the Connections between Feminism, Lesbianism, and the Family', in Hilde Lindeman Nelson (ed.), *Feminism and Families* (London: Routledge, 1997), 131–50.

—— *Feminism, the Family, and the Politics of the Closet: Lesbian and Gay Displacement* (Oxford: Oxford University Press, 2000).

Carbone, June, *From Partners to Parents: The Second Revolution in Family Law* (Chichester, NY: Columbia University Press, 2000).

—— and Cahn, N. 'Which Ties Bind? Redefining the Parent–Child Relationship in an Age of Genetic Certainty', *William and Mary Bill of Rights Journal*, 11 (2002–3), 1011–70.

Cere, Dan, *The Future of Family Law: Law and the Marriage Crisis in North America* (New York: Institute for American Values, 2005).

Charlesworth, M., *Bioethics in a Liberal Society* (Cambridge: Cambridge University Press, 1993).

Chesterton, K., *Brave New Family* (San Francisco: St Ignatius Press, 1990).

Clive, Eric, 'Marriage: An Unnecessary Legal Concept', in J. K. Eekelaar and S. N. Katz, *Marriage and Cohabitation in Contemporary Societies* (Toronto: Butterworths, 1980).

Cockett, Monica, and Tripp, John, *The Exeter Family Study: Family Breakdown and its Impact on Children* (Exeter: University of Exeter Press, 1994).

Cohen, Lloyd R., 'Marriage, Divorce and Quasi-Rents; or, "I Gave him the Best Years of my Life"', *Journal of Legal Studies*, 16 (1987), 267–303.

—— 'Marriage as Contract', in P. Newman (ed.), *The New Palgrave Dictionary of Economics and the Law* (London: Macmillan, 1998).

—— 'Marriage: The Long-Term Contract', in Anthony W. Dnes and Robert Rowthorn (eds.), *The Law and Economics of Marriage and Divorce* (Cambridge: Cambridge University Press, 2002), 10–25.

Comfort, A., 'Sexuality in a Zero Growth Society', in Robert T. Francoeur and Anna K. Francoeur (eds.), *The Future of Sexual Relations* (Englewood Cliffs, NJ: Prentice Hall, 1975).

Commission on Social Justice, *Social Justice: Strategies for National Renewal: The Final Report of the Commission on Social Justice* (London: Vintage, 1994).

Cooper, D., *The Death of the Family* (London: Penguin, 1971).

Cooper, David E. (ed.), *The Manson Murders: A Philosophical Inquiry* (Cambridge, Mass.: Schenkmann, 1974).

Daly, M., and Wilson, M., *The Truth about Cinderella: A Darwinian View of Parental Love* (New Haven: Yale University Press, 1999).

Dennis, N., *Rising Crime and the Dismembered Family: How Conformist Intellectuals have Campaigned against Common Sense* (London: Institute of Economic Affairs, 1993).

—— 'Beautiful Theories, Brutal Facts: The Welfare State and Sexual Liberation', in D. Smith (ed.), *Welfare, Work and Poverty: Lessons from Recent Reforms in the USA and the UK* (London: Institute for the Study of Civil Society, 2000), 45–80.

Devlin, P., *The Enforcement of Morals* (Oxford: Oxford University Press, 1965).

Disney, H. (ed.), *Migration, Integration and the European Labour Market* (London: Civitas, 2003).

Dnes, Antony W., 'Cohabitation and Marriage', in Anthony W. Dnes and Robert Rowthorn (eds.), *The Law and Economics of Marriage and Divorce* (Cambridge: Cambridge University Press, 2002), 118–31.

—— and Rowthorn, Robert (eds.), *The Law and Economics of Marriage and Divorce* (Cambridge: Cambridge University Press, 2002).

—— 'Introduction', in Anthony W. Dnes and Robert Rowthorn (eds.), *The Law and Economics of Marriage and Divorce* (Cambridge: Cambridge University Press, 2002), 1–9.

Doherty, W. J., et al., *Why Marriage Matters: Twenty-One Conclusions from the Social Sciences* (New York: Center of the American Experiment, the Coalition for Marriage, Family and Couples Education, and the Institute for American Values, 2002).

Donzelot, Jacques, *The Policing of Families*, trans. Robert Hurley (New York: Random House, 1979) (*La Police des familles* (Paris: Éditions de Minuit, 1977)).

Dworkin, R., *Taking Rights Seriously* (London: Duckworth, 1977).

—— *Life's Dominion: An Argument about Abortion and Euthanasia* (London: HarperCollins, 1993).

Edman, Irwin (ed.), *The Philosophy of Schopenhauer* (New York: Modern Library, 1928).

Eekelaar, J., 'Parenthood, Social Engineering, and Rights', in D. Morgan and G. Douglas (eds.), *Constituting Families: A Study in Governance* (Stuttgart: Franz Steiner Verlag, 1994).

—— and Katz, S. N. (eds.), *Marriage and Cohabitation in Contemporary Societies* (Toronto: Butterworths, 1980).

Eekelaar, J., and MacLean, Mavis, *A Reader on Family Law* (Oxford: Oxford University Press, 1994).

―――and Petar Šarčević (eds.), *Parenthood in Modern Society: Legal and Social Issues for the Twenty-First Century* (Dordrecht: Marinus Nijhoff, 1993).

Ehrlich, P., *The Population Bomb* (New York: Ballantyne Books, 1969; rev. edn., New York: Rivercity Books, 1975).

Eisenstein, H., *Contemporary Feminist Thought* (Boston: G. K. Hall & Co., 1983).

Eliot, T. S. *The Family Reunion*, in T. S. Eliot, *Collected Plays* (London: Faber, 1962).

Engels, F., *The Origins of the Family: Private Property and the State* (1884), trans. A. West (Harmondsworth: Penguin, 1985).

Epictetus, *Arrian's Discourses of Epictetus*, trans. W. A. Oldfather (1928; London, Heinemann, 1985).

ESHRE (European Society for Human Reproduction and Embryology) Capri Workshop, 'Social Determinants of Human Reproduction', *Human Reproduction*, 16/7 (2001), 1518–26.

Eskridge, William N., Jr., *The Case for Same-Sex Marriage: From Sexual Liberty to Civilized Commitment* (New York: Free Press, 1996).

―――*Gaylaw: Challenging Apartheid in the Closet* (Cambridge, Mass.: Harvard University Press, 1999).

European Parliament Committee on Citizens' Freedoms and Rights, Justice and Home Affairs, 'Report on the Situation concerning Human Rights in the European Union', A5–0451/2002.

Evans, D. (ed.), *Conceiving the Embryo* (Netherlands: Kluwer Law International, 1996).

Ferguson, N., *Empire: The Rise and Fall of British World Order and the Lessons for Global Power* (New York: Basic Books, 2003).

―――*Colossus: The Rise and Fall of the American Empire* (Harmondsworth: Penguin, 2004).

Fineman, M. A., *The Neutered Mother, the Sexual Family and Other Twentieth-Century Tragedies* (New York: Routledge, 1995).

Finnis, J., 'The Good of Marriage and the Morality of Sexual Relations: Some Philosophical and Historical Observations', *American Journal of Jurisprudence*, 42 (1997), 97–134.

Firestone, S., *The Dialectic of Sex: The Case for Feminist Revolution* (London: Jonathan Cape, 1971).

Fletcher, R. (ed.), *John Stuart Mill: A Logical Critique of Sociology* (London: Nelson, 1971).

Folberg, Jay (ed.), *Joint Custody and Shared Parenting* (Washington: Bureau of National Affairs, 1984).

Fortin, J., *Children's Rights and the Developing Law* (London, Edinburgh and Dublin: Butterworths, 1998).

Freeman, M. (ed.), *Family, State and Law* (Dartmouth: Ashgate, 1999).

Friedan, B., *The Second Stage* (New York: Summit Books, 1981).

Fromm, Erich, *The Fear of Freedom* (London: Routledge & Kegan Paul, 1960).

Gaita, R., *A Common Humanity: Thinking about Love and Truth and Justice* (New York: Routledge, 2000).

Gallagher, Maggie, 'What is Marriage for? The Public Purposes of Marriage Law', *Louisiana Law Review*, 62 (2002), 1–37.

Gathorne-Hardy, Jonathan, *Love, Sex, Marriage and Divorce* (London: Jonathan Cape, 1981).

Giddens, Anthony, *Sociology: A Brief but Critical Introduction* (London: Macmillan, 1982).

——— *Runaway World: How Globalisation is Reshaping our Lives* (2nd edn., London: Profile Books, 2002).

Gilbert, P., *Human Relationships* (Oxford: Blackwell, 1991).

Gilligan, C., *In a Different Voice: Psychological Theory and Women's Development* (Cambridge, Mass.: Harvard University Press, 1982).

Glover, J., *Causing Death and Saving Lives* (Harmondsworth: Penguin, 1977).

——— et al., *Fertility and the Family: The Glover Report on Reproductive Technologies to the European Commission* (London: Fourth Estate, 1989).

Godwin, W., *An Enquiry Concerning Political Justice* (1793), ed. M. Philip (London: William Pickering, 1993).

Goldstein, Joseph, 'In Whose Interests', in Jay Folberg (ed.), *Joint Custody and Shared Parenting* (2nd edn.; New York: Guilford Press, 1991).

——— Freud, A., and Solnit, A., *Beyond the Best Interest of the Child* (New York: Free Press, 1973).

——— Solnit, Albert J., Sonja Goldstein, and the late Anna Freud, *The Best Interests of the Child: The Least Detrimental Alternative* (New York: Free Press, 1996).

Gomberg, P., 'Patriotism is like Racism', *Ethics*, 101 (1990), 144–50.

Goode, William J., 'The Theoretical Importance of Love', *American Sociological Review* (1969), 38–47; repr. in B. B. Ingoldsby, S. Smith, and J. E. Miller (eds.), *Exploring Family Theories* (Los Angeles: Roxbury Publishing Company, 2003), 17–28.

Gray, John, *Liberalism: Essays in Political Philosophy* (London: Routledge, 1989).

Graycar, R., 'Equal Rights versus Fathers' Rights: The Child Custody Debate in Australia', in Carol Smart and Selma Sevenhuijsen (eds.), *Child Custody and the Politics of Gender* (New York: Routledge, 1989), 158–89.

Greer, G., *The Female Eunuch* (London: McGibbon & Kee, 1970).

——— *The Whole Woman* (New York: Anchor Books, 1999).

Gregory, P., 'Against Couples', *Journal of Applied Philosophy*, 1 (1984); repr. in Brenda Almond and Donald Hill (eds.), *Applied Philosophy: Morals and Metaphysics in Contemporary Debate* (London: Routledge, 1991), 90–5.

Gunning, J., and English, V., *Human in Vitro Fertilization: A Case Study in the Regulation of Medical Innovation* (Brookfield, Vt.: Dartmouth Publishing Company, 1993).

Hare, R. M., 'Utilitarianism and the Vicarious Affects', in *Essays in Ethical Theory* (Oxford: Clarendon Press, 1989), 231–44.

——'Ethical Theory and Utilitarianism' (1976), in *Essays in Ethical Theory* (Oxford: Clarendon Press, 1989), 212–30.

——'Could Kant have been a Utilitarian?', in *Sorting Out Ethics* (Oxford: Oxford University Press, 1997), 147–65.

——'Universalisability', *Proceedings of the Aristotelian Society*, 55 (1954–5).

Harlow, H., 'The Nature of Love', *American Psychologist*, 13 (1958), 573–685.

Harris, J., 'Rights and Reproductive Choice', in J. Harris and S. Holm (eds.), *The Future of Human Reproduction* (Oxford: Oxford University Press, 1998), 5–37.

——'The Welfare of the Child', *Health Care Analysis*, 8 (2000), 27–34.

——and S. Holm, *The Future of Human Reproduction* (Oxford: Oxford University Press, 1998).

Hayek, F. A., *John Stuart Mill and Harriet Taylor: Their Friendship and Subsequent Marriage* (London: Routledge and Kegan Paul, 1951).

Healey, Edna, *Wives of Fame* (London: Sidgwick & Jackson, 1986).

Hegel, G. W. F., *The Philosophy of Right*, trans T. M. Knox (Oxford: Clarendon Press, 1952).

Hetherington, E. M., and Arasteh, J. D. (eds.), *Impact of Divorce, Single Parenting, and Stepparenting on Children* (Hillsdale, NJ.: Erlbaum, 1988, 1994).

Hewlett, Sylvia Ann, *Baby Hunger: The New Battle for Motherhood* (New York: Atlantic Books, 2002).

Heyd, D., *Genethics: Moral Issues in the Creation of People* (Berkeley and Los Angeles: University of California Press, 1992).

Holt, J., *Escape from Childhood* (Harmondsworth: Penguin, 1974).

Hughes, Claire, 'Making and Breaking Relationships: Children and their Families', in A. Bainham, B. Lindley, M. Richards and L. Trinder (eds.), *Children and their Families: Contact, Rights and Welfare* (Oxford: Hart Publishing, 2003), 33–46.

Hume, D., *An Enquiry Concerning the Principles of Morals* (1751), ed. L. A. Selby-Bigge (Oxford, Clarendon Press, 1955).

——*A Treatise of Human Nature* (1739–40), ed. Ernest C. Mossner (Harmondsworth: Penguin, 1985).

Hursthouse, Rosalind, *Beginning Lives* (Oxford: Blackwell, 1987).

Ingoldsby, B. B., Smith, S., and Miller, J. E. (eds.), *Exploring Family Theories* (Los Angeles: Roxbury Publishing Company, 2003).

Institute for American Values, *Why Marriage Matters: Twenty-One Conclusions from the Social Sciences* (New York: Institute for American Values, 2002).

Irigaray, Luce, *Ce sexe qui n'en est pas un* (Paris: Les Éditions de Minuit, 1977).

James, A., 'Squaring the Circle: The Social, Legal and Welfare Organisation of Contact', in Andrew Bainham, B. Lindley, M. Richards, and L. Trinder (eds.), *Children and their Families: Contact, Rights and Welfare* (Oxford: Hart Publishing, 2003), 133–54.

Johnson, M., 'A Biomedical Perspective on Parenthood', in Andrew Bainham, S. D. Schlater, and M. Richards (eds.), *What is a Parent? A Socio-Legal Analysis* (Oxford: Hart Publishing, 1999), 47–72.

Jordan, T. 'Ethical Issues in Adoption: The Moral Significance of Relationships', in Committee for the Sixth Annual Conference, *Separation, Reunion, Reconciliation: Proceedings from The Sixth Australian Conference on Adoption, Brisbane, 1996* (Brisbane, 1997), 294–305.

Kant, I., *Lectures on Ethics*, trans. Louis Infield (London: Methuen, 1930; repr. New York: Harper & Row, 1963).

Kass, Leon, 'Making Babies Revisited', in S. Gorowitz, R. Macklin, A. L. Jameton, J. L. O'Connor, and S. Sherwood (eds.), *Moral Problems in Medicine* (2nd edn.; Engelwood Cliffs, NJ: Prentice Hall, 1983), 344–55.

Kennedy, Ian, and Grubb, Andrew, *Medical Law, Texts and Materials* (London: Butterworths, 2000).

Kent Geiger, H., 'The Fate of the Family in Soviet Russia: 1917–1944', in Norman W. Bell and Ezra F. Vogel, *A Modern Introduction to the Family* (New York: Free Press, 1968), 48–67.

Kermit, Daniel, 'The Marriage Premium', in Mariano Tommassi and Kathryn Ierulli (eds.), *The New Economics of Human Behaviour* (Cambridge: Cambridge University Press, 1996), 307–19.

Kirby, Jill, *The Price of Parenthood* (London: Centre for Policy Studies, 2005).

Kumar, Dharma, 'Should one be Free to Choose the Sex of one's Child?', *Journal of Applied Philosophy*, 2 (1985), 197–204.

Kymlicka, W., 'Rethinking the Family', *Philosophy and Public Affairs* (Winter 1991), 77–97.

LaFollette, Hugh (ed.), *Ethics in Practice* (London: Blackwell, 1997).

_____ 'Circumscribed Autonomy: Children, Care and Custody', in U. Narayan and J. Bartkowiak (eds.), *Having and Raising Children: Unconventional Families, Hard Choices and the Social Good* (Pennsylvania: Pennsylvania State University Press, 1999), 137–54.

Lamb, David, *Down the Slippery Slope: Arguing in Applied Ethics* (London: Croom Helm, 1988).

Laslett, P., and Wall, R., *Household and Family in Past Time* (Cambridge: Cambridge University Press, 1972).

Law Commission of Canada, *Beyond Conjugality: Recognizing and Supporting Close Personal Adult Relationships* (Ottawa: Law Commission of Canada, 2001).

Le Blanc, L. J., *The Convention on the Rights of the Child* (Lincoln, Neb.: University of Nebraska Press, 1995).

Leahy, M., and Cohn-Sherbok, Dan (eds.), *The Liberation Debate: Rights at Issue* (London: Routledge, 1996).

Lloyd, Genevieve, *The Man of Reason: 'Male' and 'Female' in Western Philosophy* (London: Methuen, 1984).

Locke, Don, *A Fantasy of Reason: The Life and Thought of William Godwin* (London: Routledge and Kegan Paul, 1980).

Locke, J., *Two Treatises of Government: Second Treatise of Government* (1680–2; Everyman; London: Dent, 1986).

Løgstrup, Knud Ejler, *The Ethical Demand* (1956), with an introduction by Hans Fink and Alasdair MacIntyre (Notre Dame, Ind.: University of Notre Dame Press, 1997).

Lowe, N. V., and Douglas, G., *Family Law* (9th edn.; London: Butterworths, 1998).

MacDevitt, Delma, 'The Custody of Children in the Republic of Ireland', in Carol Smart and Selma Sevenhuijsen (eds.), *Child Custody and the Politics of Gender* (New York: Routledge, 1989), 190–212.

MacIntyre, A., *After Virtue* (London: Duckworth, 1981).

—— *Whose Justice? Which Rationality?* (London: Duckworth, 1988).

McKie, Linda, and Cunningham-Burley, Sarah (eds.), *Families in Society: Boundaries and Relationships* (Bristol: Policy Press, 2005).

McLanahan, Sara, and Sandetur, Gary, *Growing up with a Single Parent* (Cambridge, Mass.: Harvard University Press, 1994).

—— Garfinkel, Irwin, and Mincy, Ronald B., 'Fragile Families, Welfare Reform, and Marriage', *Welfare Reform and Beyond* (Policy Brief No. 10; Washington: Brookings Institution, Dec. 2001).

Maclean, M., and Richards, M., 'Parents and Divorce: Changing Patterns of Public Intervention', in Andrew Bainham, S. D. Schlater, and M. Richards (eds.), *What is a Parent? A Socio-Legal Analysis* (Oxford: Hart Publishing, 1999), 259–70.

McMillan, Carol, *Women, Reason and Nature* (Oxford: Blackwell, 1982).

MacMurray, John, *The Form of the Personal*, ii. *Persons in Relation* (London: Faber & Faber, 1961; repr. Atlantic Highlands, NJ: Humanities Press, 1991).

Malthus, T., *An Essay on the Principle of Population* (1798), (Cambridge: Cambridge University Press, 1992).

Margolis, J., and Margolis, C., 'The Separation of Marriage and Family', in M. Vetterling-Braggin, F. A. Elliston, and J. English (eds.), *Feminism and Philosophy* (Totowa, NJ: Littlefield, Adams, 1977).

Marquis, Don, 'Why Abortion is Immoral', *Journal of Philosophy*, 86/4 (1989), 183–202.

Mason, Mary Ann, Skolnick, Arlene, and Sugarman, Stephen D. (eds.), *All our Families: New Policies for a New Century* (1998; 2nd edn., Oxford: Oxford University Press, 2003).

Mauldon, Jane, 'The Effects of Marital Disruption on Children's Health', *Demography*, 27/3 (1990), 431–46.

Mead, Margaret, 'Marriage in Two Steps', in Herbert A. Otto (ed.), *The Family in Search of a Future* (New York: Appleton-Century-Crofts, 1970).

Meezan, William, and Rauch, Jonathan, 'Gay Marriage, Same-Sex Parenting, and America's Children', *Future of Children*, 15/2 (Autumn 2005), 97–114.

Meulders, Marie-Thérèse, 'Introduction', in John Eekelaar and Petar Šarčević, *Parenthood in Modern Society: Legal and Social Issues for the Twenty-First Century* (Dordrecht: Martinus Nijhoff, 1993).

Meyers, Diana Tietjens, 'The Family Romance: A Fin-de-siècle Tragedy', in Hilde Lindeman Nelson (ed.), *Feminism and Families* (London: Routledge, 1997), 235–54.

Mill, J. S., *On Liberty* (1859; Everyman; London: Dent, 1954).

——— *The Subjection of Women* (1869), in J. S. Mill, *Three Essays*, ed. R. Wollheim (Oxford, Oxford University Press, 1975).

Mills, Patricia, *Woman, Nature and Psyche* (New Haven: Yale University Press, 1987).

Moore, Gareth, 'Natural Sex: Germain Grisez, Sex, and Natural Law', in Nigel Biggar and Rufus Black (eds.), *The Revival of Natural Law: Philosophical, Theological and Ethical Responses to the Finnis-Grisez School* (Aldershot: Ashgate, 2000), 223–41.

Morgan, D., and Douglas, G. (eds.), *Constituting Families: A Study in Governance* (Stuttgart: Franz Steiner Verlag, 1994).

Morgan, P., *Farewell to the Family: Public Policy and Family Breakdown in Britain and the USA* (London: Institute of Economic Affairs, Health and Welfare Unit, 1999).

——— *Cohabitation* (London: Institute of Economic Affairs, 2000).

——— *Marriage-Lite: The Rise of Cohabitation and its Consequences* (London: Civitas, 2000).

——— *Family Matters: Family Breakdown and its Consequences* (Wellington: New Zealand Business Roundtable, 2004).

Mount, Ferdinand, *The Subversive Family: An Alternative History of Love and Marriage* (London: Jonathan Cape, 1982).

Murray, Charles, *Underclass: The Crisis Deepens* (London: Institute of Economic Affairs, 1994).

Nagel, T., *Equality and Partiality* (Oxford: Oxford University Press, 1991).

Narayan, Uma, and Bartkowiak, Julia J. (eds.), *Having and Raising Children: Unconventional Families, Hard Choices and the Social Good* (Pennsylvania: Pennsylvania State University Press, 1999).

Nelson, Hilde Lindeman (ed.), *Feminism and Families* (London: Routledge, 1997).

Newman, P. (ed.), *The New Palgrave Dictionary of Economics and the Law* (London: Macmillan, 1998).

Nietzsche, Friedrich, *On the Genealogy of Morals*, trans. Francis Golffing (New York: Doubleday, 1956).

Nock, Steven, 'A Comparison of Marriages and Cohabiting Relationships', *Journal of Family Issues*, 16 (Jan. 1995), 53–76.

Nozick, R., *Anarchy, State and Utopia* (Oxford: Blackwell, 1974).

O'Neill, George, and O'Neill, Nena, *Open Marriage: A New Life-Style for Couples* (New York: M. Evans & Co., 1972).

O'Neill, R., *Does Marriage Matter?* (London: Civitas, 2004).

Okin, Susan Moller, *Justice, Gender and the Family* (New York: Basic Books, 1989).

—— 'Families and Feminist Theory: Some Past and Present Issues', in Hilde Lindeman Nelson (ed.), *Feminism and Families* (London: Routledge, 1997), 13–26.

Otto, Herbert A. (ed.), *The Family in Search of a Future* (New York: Appleton-Century-Crofts, 1970).

Overall, C., *Human Reproduction: Principles, Practices, Policies* (Oxford: Oxford University Press, 1993).

Parker, M., 'Children who Run: Ethics and Homelessness', in B. Almond (ed.), *Introducing Applied Ethics* (Oxford: Blackwell, 1995), 58–70.

Pateman, C., *The Sexual Contract* (Stanford, Calif.: University of Stanford Press, 1988).

Phillips, Roderick, *Untying the Knot: A Short History of Divorce* (Cambridge: Cambridge University Press, 1991).

Picoult, Jodi, *My Sister's Keeper* (London: Hodder, 2004).

Primoratz, Igor, *Ethics and Sex* (London: Routledge, 1999).

Purdy, Laura M., 'Boundaries of Authority: Should Children be Able to Divorce their Parents?', in U. Narayan and J. Bartkowiak (eds.), *Having and Raising Children: Unconventional Families, Hard Choices and the Social Good* (Pennsylvania: Pennsylvania State University Press, 1999), 153–62.

Ravven, Heidi M., 'Has Hegel Anything to Say to Feminists?', *Owl of Minerva*, 19/2 (Spring 1988), 149–68.

Rawls, J., *A Theory of Justice* (Oxford: Oxford University Press, 1972).

Richards, Martin, 'Divorcing Children: Roles for Parents and the State', in John Eekelaar and Mavis MacLean, *A Reader on Family Law* (Oxford: Oxford University Press, 1994).

—— 'Children and Parents and Divorce', in J. Eekelaar and P. Šarčević (eds.), *Parenthood in Modern Society* (Dordrecht: Kluwer, 1993), 307–15.

Robertson, J. A., 'Procreative Liberty and the Control of Conception, Pregnancy and Childbirth', *Virginia Law Review*, 69 (1983), 405–62.

_____ *Children of Choice: Freedom and the New Reproductive Technologies* (Princeton: Princeton University Press, 1994).

Robson, R., 'Resisting the Family: Repositioning Lesbians in Legal Theory', *Signs*, 19 (1994), 945–96.

Roseneil, Sasha, 'Living and Loving beyond the Boundaries of the Heteronorm: Personal Relationships in the 21st Century', in Linda McKie and Sarah Cunningham-Burley (eds.), *Families in Society: Boundaries and Relationships* (Bristol: Policy Press, 2005), 241–58.

Ross, L. F. 'Justice for Children: The Child as Organ Donor', *Bioethics*, 8 (1994), 105–26.

Rowley, Hazel, *Tête-à-tête: Simone de Beauvoir and Jean-Paul Sartre* (New York: HarperCollins, 2005).

Rowthorn, Robert, 'Marriage and Trust: Some Lessons from Economics', *Cambridge Journal of Economics*, 23 (1999), 661–91

_____ 'Marriage as a Signal', in Anthony W. Dnes and Robert Rowthorn (eds.), *The Law and Economics of Marriage and Divorce* (Cambridge: Cambridge University Press, 2002), 132–56.

_____ 'Numbers and National Identity,' in H. Disney (ed.), *Migration, Integration and the European Labour Market* (London: Civitas, 2003), 65–81.

Ruddick, S., *Maternal Thinking* (Boston, Mass.: Beacon Press, 1989).

_____ 'The Idea of Fatherhood', in Hilde Lindeman Nelson (ed.), *Feminism and Families* (London: Routledge, 1997), 205–20.

Russell, B., *Marriage and Morals* (1929) (London: Allen & Unwin, 1976).

_____ *The Autobiography of Bertrand Russell* (London: Allen & Unwin, 1971), iii.

Ryan, Maura A., 'The Argument for Unlimited Procreative Liberty', *Hastings Center Report* (July/Aug. 1990), 6–12.

Santayana, G., *The Life of Reason*, ii, *Reason in Society* (London: Constable, 1905).

Sartre, Jean-Paul, *Existentialism and Humanism*, trans. Philip Mairet (London: Methuen, 1948); French edn., *L'Existentialisme est un humanisme* (Paris: Les Éditions Nagel, 1946).

Savulescu, J., 'Deaf Lesbians, "Designer Disability", and the Future of Medicine', *British Medical Journal*, 325/7367 (Oct. 2002), 771–3.

Saunders, Hilary, *Twenty-Nine Child Homicides: Lessons still to be Learnt on Domestic Violence and Child Protection* (Bristol: Women's Aid Federation of England, 2004).

Schopenhauer, A., *The World as Will and Idea*, 2nd edn., ed. Wolfgang von Loehneysen (Vienna: Darmstadt, 1974).

_____ *The World as Will and Idea*, ed. D. Berman, trans. J. Berman (Everyman; London: Dent, 1995).

Schrag, Francis, 'Children: Their Rights and Needs', in W. Aiken and H. LaFollette (eds.), *Whose Child: Children's Rights, Parental Authority, and State Power* (Totowa, NJ: Rowman & Allenheld, 1980), 246–7.

Scott, Elizabeth S., 'Marital Commitment and the Legal Regulation of Divorce', in Anthony W. Dnes and Robert Rowthorn (eds.), *The Law and Economics of Marriage and Divorce* (Cambridge: Cambridge University Press, 2002), 35–56.

Scruton, R., *Sexual Desire: A Philosophical Investigation* (London: Weidenfeld & Nicolson, 1986).

—— 'Gay Reservations', in Michael Leahy and Dan Cohn-Sherbok (eds.), *The Liberation Debate: Rights at Issue* (London: Routledge, 1996), 108–24.

Selbourne, D., *Moral Evasion* (London: Centre for Policy Studies, 1998).

Sen, A., 'More than 100 Million Women are Missing', *New York Review of Books*, 20 Dec. 1990.

Shalit, W., *A Return to Modesty: Discovering the Lost Virtue* (New York: Simon & Schuster, 1999).

Shaw, Chris, Government Actuary's Department, 'United Kingdom Population Trends in the 21st Century', *Population Trends*, 103 (London: The Stationery Office, 2001), 37–46.

Sheldon, Sally, 'Fragmenting Fatherhood: The Regulation of Reproductive Technologies', *Modern Law Review*, 68/4 (2005), 523–53.

Shelley, P. B., 'Against Legal Marriage', in *Shelley on Love*, ed. Richard Holmes (London: Anvil Press Poetry, 1980), 45.

Sheth, S., *Lancet,* 9 Jan. 2006; report, *The Times*, 10 Jan. 2006.

Shoeman, F., 'Rights of Children, Rights of Parents, and the Moral Basis of the Family', *Ethics*, 91 (1980), 6–19.

Simon, Stuart (ed.), *The Icon Critical Dictionary of Postmodern Thought* (Cambridge: Icon Books, 1998).

Singer, Peter (ed.), *A Companion to Ethics* (Oxford: Blackwell, 1991).

—— *Practical Ethics* (2nd edn.; Cambridge: Cambridge University Press, 1993).

Skolnick, Arlene, *The Intimate Environment* (Harlow: Longman, 1995).

—— 'Solomon's Children: The New Biologism, Psychological Parenthood, Attachment Theory, and the Best Interests Standard', in Mary Ann Mason, Arlene Skolnick, and Stephen D. Sugarman (eds.), *All our Families: New Policies for a New Century* (1998; 2nd edn., Oxford: Oxford University Press, 2003).

Smart, Carol, 'Power and the Politics of Custody', in Carol Smart and Selma Sevenhuijsen (eds.), *Child Custody and the Politics of Gender* (New York: Routledge, 1989), 1–26.

Smith, Adam, *The Theory of the Moral Sentiments* (1759; Oxford: Oxford University Press, 1976).

Smith, D. (ed.), *Welfare, Work and Poverty: Lessons from Recent Reforms in the USA and the UK* (London: Institute for the Study of Civil Society, 2000).

Smith, Ian, 'European Divorce Laws, Divorce Rates, and their Consequences', in Anthony W. Dnes and Robert Rowthorn (eds.), *The Law and Economics of Marriage and Divorce* (Cambridge: Cambridge University Press, 2002), 212–29.

Smith, J., et al., *The Family Backgrounds of Homeless Young People* (London: Family Policy Studies Centre, 1998).

Smock, P. J., et al., 'The Effect of Marriage and Divorce on Women's Economic Well-Being', *American Sociological Review*, 64 (1999), 794–812.

Sophocles, *Antigone*, in *Theban Plays*, trans. George Young (Everyman; London: Dent, 1947).

Spaht, Kathleen Shaw, 'Louisiana Covenant Law: Recapturing the Meaning of Marriage for the Sake of the Children', in Anthony W. Dnes and Robert Rowthorn (eds.), *The Law and Economics of Marriage and Divorce* (Cambridge: Cambridge University Press, 2002), 92–117.

Spriggs, M., 'Lesbian Couple Create a Child who is Deaf like them', *Journal of Medical Ethics*, 28 (2002), 283–8.

Stafford, Antoinette M., 'The Feminist Critique of Hegel on Women and the Family', *Animus*, 2 (1997), 1–18.

Stone, Lawrence, *The Family, Sex and Marriage in England, 1500–1800* (New York: Harper Row, 1977).

Strathdee, R., *No Way Back* (London: Centrepoint, 1992).

Strathern, M., *Reproducing the Future: Anthropology, Kinship and the New Reproductive Technologies* (Manchester: Manchester University Press, 1992).

____ 'A Question of Context', in J. Edwards et al. (eds.), *Technologies of Procreation* (Manchester: Manchester University Press, 1993).

Sullivan, Andrew, *Virtually Normal* (New York: A. Knopf, 1995).

____ *Same-Sex Marriage, Pro and Con: A Reader* (New York: Vintage Books, 2004).

Szawarski, Z., 'Talking about Embryos', in D. Evans (ed.), *Conceiving the Embryo* (Dordrecht: Kluwer Law International, 1996), 119–33.

Taylor, C., et al., *Multiculturalism: Examining the Politics of Recognition* (Princeton: Princeton University Press, 1994).

Thomas, Adam, and Sawhill, Isabel, 'For Love or Money: The Impact of Family Structure on Family Income', *The Future of Children* (Policy Brief; Washington: Brookings Institution, 15 Feb. 2005), 57–74.

Thomson, Judith Jarvis, 'A Defense of Abortion', *Philosophy and Public Affairs*, 1 (1971), 47–66.

Thornham, S., 'Postmodernism and Feminism', in Stuart Simon (ed.), *The Icon Critical Dictionary of Postmodern Thought* (Cambridge: Icon Books, 1998), 41–52.

Tims, Margaret, *Mary Wollstonecraft: A Social Pioneer* (London: Millington, 1976).

Tooley, Michael, *Abortion and Infanticide* (Oxford: Oxford University Press, 1983).

Trainor, Brian T., 'The State, Marriage and Divorce', *Journal of Applied Philosophy*, 9 (1992), 135–48.

UN, Population Division of the Department of Economic and Social Affairs, *Replacement Migration: Is it a Solution to Declining and Ageing Populations?* (New York: United Nations, 2000).

UNESCO, *Unwanted Pregnancy and Unsafe Abortion* (Bangkok: UNESCO, Regional Clearing House on Population, Education and Communication (RCHPEC), 2002).

Velleman, J. David, 'Family History', *Philosophical Papers*, 34/3 (Nov. 2005), 357–78.

Vetterling-Braggin, M., F. A. Elliston, and J. English (eds.), *Feminism and Philosophy* (Totowa, NJ: Littlefield, Adams, 1977).

Wallerstein, Judith S., 'Children of Divorce: A Society in Search of Policy', in Mary Ann Mason, Arlene Skolnick, and Stephen D. Sugarman (eds.), *All our Families: New Policies for a New Century* (1998; 2nd edn., Oxford: Oxford University Press, 2003), 66–95.

——Lewis, Julia M., and Blakeslee, Sandra, *The Unexpected Legacy of Divorce: The 25 Year Landmark Study* (New York: Hyperion, 2000).

Warren, Mary Anne, *Gendercide: The Implications of Sex Research* (Totowa, NJ: Rowman & Allanheld, 1985).

Weitzman, L. J., *The Divorce Revolution: The Unexpected Social and Economic Consequences for Women and Children in America* (New York: Free Press, 1985).

—— and Maclean, M. (eds.), *Economic Consequences of Divorce: The International Perspective* (Oxford: Clarendon Press, Centre for Socio-Legal Studies, 1991).

Westermark, E., *The History of Human Marriage*, 3 vols. (London: Macmillan, 1901; New York, Allerton, 1922).

Whelan, Robert, *Broken Homes and Battered Children: A Study of the Relationship between Child Abuse and Family Type* (London: Family Education Trust, 1993).

White, J. E., *Contemporary Moral Problems* (4th edn.; St Paul, MN: West Publishing Co., 1994).

Wiesel, Elie, *Night* (New York: Bantam Books, 1960).

Williams, B., 'The Priority of Personal Interests', in H. LaFollette (ed.), *Ethics in Practice* (Oxford: Blackwell, 1997), 191–4.

Wilson, James Q., *The Marriage Problem: How our Culture has Weakened Families* (New York: HarperCollins, 2002).

Wolfenden, Sir John, *Report of the Committee on Homosexual Offences and Prostitution* (London: HMSO, 1957).

Wollstonecraft, Mary, *A Vindication of The Rights of Woman* (1792; Everyman; London: Dent, 1929).

_____ and William Godwin, *A Short Residence in Sweden and Memoirs of the Author of 'The Vindication of the Rights of Woman'* (1796), ed. Richard Holmes (London: Penguin, 1987).

Young, R., Matthews, G., and Adams, G., 'Runaways: A Review of Negative Consequences and Diminishing Choices', *Family Relations*, 32 (1983), 275–81.

Zill, N., 'Behavior, Achievement, and Health Problems among Children in Stepfamilies: Findings from a National Survey of Child Health', in E. M. Hetherington and J. D. Arasteh (eds.), *Impact of Divorce, Single Parenting, and Stepparenting on Children* (Hillsdale, NJ: Erlbaum, 1998).

Index